# Business in the North West

Manchester Region History Review

Volume 21

2010

ISSN 0952–4320

ISBN 978–1–85936–209–9

© Manchester Centre for Regional History, 2010

All rights are reserved and no part of the publication can be reprinted without the permission of the editors and authors.

Typeset by Carnegie Book Production, Lancaster.
Printed and bound by Short Run Press, Exeter.

# Contents

| | |
|---|---|
| **Contributors' Notes** | vii |
| **Introduction** | xi |
|    John F. Wilson | |
| **Obituaries:** | |
|    Kevin Morgan on Ruth Frow (1922–2008) | xvii |
|    Alex J. Robertson on Yoshiteru Takei (1929–2009) | xix |
|    Yoshiteru Takei, 'In memory of Douglas Farnie' | xxii |

**Articles**

**D. M. Higgins and J. S. Toms**
Capital ownership, capital structure, and capital markets: financial constraints and the decline of the Lancashire cotton textile industry, c1880–c1965     1

**John Singleton**
Lancashire and the New Zealand market in the mid twentieth century: cotton, glass and locomotives     25

**David Martín López and John K. Walton**
Freemasonry and civic identity: municipal politics, business and the rise of Blackpool from the 1850s to the First World War     43

**Alistair Mutch**
Brewing in the North West, 1840–1914: sowing the seeds of service-sector management?     69

**Ken Brown**
'An absorbing epic'? The development of toy-manufacturing in the North West, c1851–1931     87

**Robin Pearson**
Working on the frontiers of risk: the insurance industry in north-west England since 1700     104

**Rosine Hart and Geoff Timmins**
Lancashire's highway men: the business community and road improvements during the industrial revolution     128

**Geoffrey Tweedale**
Straws in the wind: the local and regional roots of an
occupational disease epidemic                                                144

## Archives
**Gillian Lonergan**
'From the cradle to the grave': the National Co-operative
Archive                                                                      162

## Long Reviews
**Michael Rose on:**
J. F. Wilson, ed., *King Cotton: a tribute to Douglas A. Farnie*
(Crucible Books in association with the Chetham Society,
2009)                                                                        172

**Michael Nevell on:**
Ian Miller and Christine Wild, *A & G Murray and the cotton
mills of Ancoats* (Oxford Archaeology North, 2007)                           173

**David Walsh on:**
A. J. Randall, *Riotous assemblies: popular protest in Hanoverian
England* (Oxford University Press, 2006)                                     174

**Michael Howard on:**
Cécilia Lyon, *Adolphe Valette* (Phillimore, 2006)                           177

**Heather Norris Nicholson on:**
Hilary Fawcett, ed., *Made in Newcastle: visual culture*
(University of Northumbria Press, 2007)                                      178

**Dave Russell on:**
Gary James, *Manchester: a football history* (James Ward, 2008)  179

**Neville Kirk on:**
Robert G. Hall, *Voices of the people: democracy and Chartist
political identity, 1830–1870* (Merlin Press, 2007)                          180

**Dave Russell on:**
Robin Daniels, *Cardus: celebrant of beauty* (Palatine, 2009)                182

**Brian Maidment on:**
Brian Hollingworth, ed., *The diary of Edwin Waugh, 1847–1851*
(Carnegie Publishing, 2008)                                                  184

**Short Reviews**                                                            187

**Article Abstracts and Keywords**                                           195

**Editors**
Melanie Tebbutt
Craig Horner
John F. Wilson

**Editorial board**
Morris Garratt (Libraries)
Clare Hartwell
Karen Hunt
Alan Kidd
Neville Kirk
Brian Maidment
Chris Makepeace (Short Reviews)
Peter Maw
Paula Moorhouse
Heather Norris Nicholson
Catharine Rew (Museums)
Mike Rose
Bill Williams
Terry Wyke

**Book Reviews editor**
Craig Horner

**Corresponding members**
Robert Glen, University of New Haven, US
Kazuhiko Kondo, University of Tokyo, Japan

**Correspondence**
The Editors
Manchester Region History Review
Manchester Centre for Regional History
Manchester Metropolitan University
Geoffrey Manton Building
Rosamond Street West
Manchester M15 6LL
United Kingdom
http://www.mcrh.mmu.ac.uk

For full details of individual and institutional subscription rates for the UK and overseas, refer to:
http://www.mcrh.mmu.ac.uk/pubs/mrhr.htm

The editors would like to thank Alexandra Mitchell and the Manchester European Research Institute for their support in the preparation of this volume.

**Illustrations**
We are grateful to J. Gamble and Hersh Stern for permission in reproducing illustrations.
Every effort has been made to contact the copyright holders but if any have been inadvertently overlooked, the editors will be pleased to make the necessary arrangements at the first opportunity.

**Notes for contributors**
If you would like to contribute to this journal, please contact the editors before submitting copy. Authors should consult: http://www.mcrh.mmu.ac.uk/pubs/guidelines.doc
Conventional articles should not exceed 8,000 words including footnotes, although they can be much shorter. We encourage a variety of contributions and are willing to discuss ideas and draft articles at an early stage. Intending contributors to the Libraries, Museums and Societies sections should consult the editors in the first instance. Book reviews should be sent to the Book Reviews editor. All submitted work should be in Word format.

**Advertisements**
For details of advertising rates, please contact the editors.

**Indexing**
Articles appearing in this journal are abstracted and indexed in: HISTORICAL ABSTRACTS and AMERICA: HISTORY AND LIFE.

# Contributors' Notes

**Ken Brown** retired in September 2009 after spending forty years at Queen's University, Belfast, the last eight as Pro-Vice Chancellor. As Professor of Economic and Social History since 1988 he has published widely on various aspects of British and Japanese labour and industrial history, latterly with a particular interest in the development of the children's toy industry. His most recent book, *Factory of dreams* (2007), is a business history of Meccano Ltd, the Liverpool firm which gave to the world three iconic toys, Meccano construction sets, Dinky model vehicles, and Hornby trains.

**Rosine Hart** recently completed her PhD, which deals with financing industrial activity and infrastructural development in Lancashire during the industrial revolution period. Her first article arising from this research, entitled 'Weavers of profit: terminating building societies in Lancashire', appeared in *Financial History Review* (2009).

**David Higgins** is Reader in Economics at York Management School. He has written extensively about the Lancashire cotton industry, industrial welfare, and most recently trade marks. His publications have featured in all the leading journals, including *Business History*, *Economic History Review* and the *Journal of Industrial History*.

**Gillian Lonergan** is Head of Archive and Learning Resources at the Co-operative College and manages both the National Co-operative Archive and the Rochdale Pioneers Museum. She is a Chartered Librarian and Fellow of the Society of Indexers, a member of the Executive Committee of the Society for Co-operative Studies, Deputy Editor of the *Journal for Co-operative Studies* and a trustee of the Robert Owen Memorial Museum.

**David Martín López** is a member of the Departamento de Historia del Arte, Universidad de Granada, Spain. He is putting the finishing touches to a doctoral thesis, 'Masonic aesthetics, architecture and urban design from the eighteenth to the twentieth century', and also has an interest in British influences on the Canary Islands. He has published four articles on themes related to this work. He has been a visiting researcher at universities in Preston, Leeds and Paris.

**Alistair Mutch** is Professor of Information and Learning at Nottingham Trent University. His *The Liverpool pub: a cultural and business history* is published by the Bluecoat Press. He is currently working on the influence of church governance practices on the formation of modern management, with particular focus on Scottish Presbyterianism.

**Robin Pearson** is Professor of Economic History at the University of Hull. He has published extensively in business, industrial and insurance history, including *Insuring the industrial revolution: fire insurance in Great Britain 1700–1850* (Aldershot, 2004) and in a series of articles in top-class journals.

**John Singleton** is Reader in Economic History at the School of Economics and Finance, Victoria University of Wellington, New Zealand. He is author of *Lancashire on the scrapheap: the cotton industry, 1945–1970* (Oxford, 1991) and the principal author of *Innovation and independence: the Reserve Bank of New Zealand, 1973–2002* (Auckland, 2006). He has written extensively on the economic and business history of the UK, New Zealand, and the commonwealth.

**Geoff Timmins** is Professor in the School of Education and Social Sciences at the University of Central Lancashire. In addition to research into undergraduate history teaching, his recent publications have included 'Textile colonies and settlement growth in Lancashire, c1780–c1850' in J. F. Wilson, ed., *King Cotton: a tribute to Douglas A. Farnie*.

**Steven Toms** is the Head of York Management School and Professor of Accounting and Finance. Having won the Coleman Prize for the Best PhD at the Association of Business Historians conference in 1997, he has since led the field of studies in Lancashire cotton, as well as more general work on British business. He is now co-editor of *Business History*.

**Geoffrey Tweedale** is Reader in Business History at Manchester Metropolitan University Business School. His most recent books include: *Magic mineral to killer dust: Turner & Newall and the asbestos hazard* (Oxford; 2nd ed., 2001); and (with Jock McCulloch) *Defending the indefensible: the global asbestos industry and its fight for survival* (Oxford, 2008).

**John K. Walton** is IKERBASQUE Research Professor, Basque Foundation For Science, in the Departamento de Historia Contemporánea, Universidad del País Vasco UPV/ EHU, Vitoria/ Gasteiz, Spain. He was formerly Professor of Modern Social History at Lancaster University, and Professor of Social History at the University of Central Lancashire and at Leeds Metropolitan University. He is a historian of tourism, sport, popular culture and regional identities, with special reference to Britain and Spain. His doctoral thesis examined Blackpool before the First World War, and he has never been able to complete his escape. His books include *The Blackpool landlady: a social history* (Manchester, 1978); *Blackpool* (Edinburgh, 1998); (with Gary Cross) *The playful crowd: pleasure places in the twentieth century* (New York, 2005); and *Riding on rainbows: Blackpool pleasure beach and its place in British popular culture* (St Albans, 2007). He also edits the *Journal of Tourism History*.

**John F. Wilson** is Professor of Strategy at the University of Liverpool Management School. He has written leading textbooks on British business and management history, as well as monographs on Ferranti, Manchester Business School, Lyndall Urwick, and the north-west gas-supply industry. He is co-editor of *Business History* and sits on the editorial board of other leading journals.

# Introduction

Frequently referred to as 'the first modern industrial district', the north-west of England has a rich history of business activities. Dominated by Manchester and Liverpool, yet featuring a plethora of what until the 1960s were significant manufacturing centres dotted around Lancashire and Cheshire, few would dispute the importance of this region as a testing-ground for the development of effective business practices. Over time, of course, the nature of these practices has changed dramatically, with merchants and traders playing the key roles up to the early-nineteenth century, giving way to industrialists who built extensive firms that were often known across the world. By the late twentieth century, given the collapse of staple industries such as cotton textiles and heavy engineering, the consequent deindustrialization created an economy based on services and the rapidly expanding public sector as the principal engines of economic growth. At the same time, and irrespective of these changes, the North West has contained a wide variety of businesses, reflecting its early maturity and the highly conducive environment for entrepreneurs. This special issue has been specifically designed to reflect this diversity, providing insights into the business practices outside the staples of cotton textiles and engineering, while at the same time providing some coverage of these giants. Spatially, we have also attempted to move the focus away from Manchester and Liverpool, although inevitably these major agglomerations will feature in several of the articles.

While diversity is an overriding feature of this special issue, inevitably the role played by cotton textiles must be highlighted. After all, as Pollard outlined, it was in this industry that what we have come to regard as modern business practices emerged most forcefully as highly ambitious entrepreneurs drove the transition from mercantile to industrial capitalism.[1] While the former was characterized by the avoidance of management, the latter stimulated a much greater link between fixed investment and direct supervision, creating the first generation of organization builders. Running in parallel with this trend was the emergence of the multi-layered partnership system, employment of professional managers, and embryonic industrial relations, as both the scale and intensity of production increased.[2] As cotton textiles expanded rapidly from the 1770s, this also stimulated growth in vital support industries such as engineering, chemicals and coal,[3] significantly diversifying the region's economic base. In turn, the local business community was encouraged to initiate and fund significant transport innovations, for example, the Bridgewater Canal in the 1760s and the world's first commercial railway connecting Manchester and Liverpool by 1830, while banking, utility and distribution services also expanded in line with the region's demands.[4] By the 1830s, indeed, the North West was already evolving into a mature industrial region, with a business community that was heavily involved in global mercantile, financial and industrial activities that created the basis for the label applied to Britain as a whole by the mid century, 'The Workshop of the World'.

While space limitations forestall a full elaboration of this story,[5] it is clear that the North West business community provided a template for other regions experiencing similar forces. Moreover, the early phase of growth was sustained well into the twentieth century, with large-scale firms emerging in a number of industries, from cotton textiles and engineering to chemicals and metal processing. The late nineteenth century also witnessed significant diversification into the so-called 'new' industries of electrical engineering, automobiles and fast-moving consumer goods, while significant utility firms in railways, distribution and gas supply expanded rapidly.[6] One of the least researched businesses that emerged in the North West was the Co-operative Wholesale Society, created in 1863 in Manchester, building on the earlier achievements of the Rochdale Pioneers, which by 1907 employed almost 17,000 people across the UK. Other notable innovations were the world's first industrial estate, Trafford Park, built at the Manchester end of the equally ambitious Manchester Ship Canal during the 1880s, while the Mersey Docks and Harbour Board controlling the Liverpool port had expanded into a major business that in 1907 employed almost 35,000 in the UK.[7]

It is well recorded, of course, that alongside these innovatory success stories, the North West business community was not always responsive to new ideas, especially in terms of management techniques that were developed elsewhere. While this could well be regarded as a British, as opposed to a distinctly North West, phenomenon,[8] and the comparative advantage of other economies undermined the region's staple industries, it is nevertheless clear that during the first half of the twentieth century there was a resistance to change, in strategic, structural and managerial respects. For example, J. M. Keynes was extremely critical of the cotton industry's leadership, claiming that they were 'boneheads … who want to live the rest of their lives in peace'.[9] In spite of considerable government support, the cotton textile industry declined dramatically between its peak in 1919 and the 1970s, by which time its factories were either being taken over by electronics and distribution firms or left to decay. Another crucial trend was the decline in regional independence, in that while in 1907 forty-one of the North West's top fifty firms had their headquarters in this region, by 1993 this had halved.[10]

Having been the 'first modern industrial district', the North West could also be labelled the 'first deindustrialized society', given that the collapse of its staple industries by the 1970s was more than matched by the expansion of distribution, utility and other service-sector activities. Although significant manufacturing industries still existed in the late twentieth century – aerospace; petro-chemicals; automobiles; fast-moving consumer goods – the North West business community was increasingly dominated by the service and public sectors. An interesting illustration of this trend can be found in examining the occupancy of some of the region's most impressive houses. For example, on the outskirts of Preston is what today is called 'Greyfriars Hall', an impressive double-fronted house located in a 37-acre estate. 'Greyfriars' was built in 1849 by Joseph Clayton, Preston's most successful engineering entrepreneur who equipped many of the region's mills with steam engines and boilers. On his death in 1885, the house was acquired by Sir Frank Hollins, the head of the mighty Horrocks cotton textiles business. Using the impressive profits generated from this business, Hollins extended 'Greyfriars' and improved the grounds, even adding a cricket pitch. Having been built and expanded from the wealth generated by the North West's staple industries, however, throughout the twentieth century it has been owned by entrepreneurs from the service sector. Following Hollins's death in 1924, a property developer (George Yates Hazlett) bought 'Greyfriars', while from 1945 to 1965 it was owned by Ewart Bradshaw, a successful automobile retailer, to be followed by William Harrison, a successful building contractor. Most recently, 'Greyfriars' has been purchased and extensively refurbished by Owen McLaughlin, the co-owner of Enterprise plc, Britain's leading utility-servicing company.[11]

The 'Greyfriars' story is a microcosm of the North West's business history, in that while it demonstrates how significant entrepreneurial talent still exists in the region, this is being directed to different industries to those that helped to establish its economic foundations. The inexorable growth of the service sector has also been paralleled by a radical improvement in business practices, as the risk-averse first generations of industrialists gave way to more progressive counterparts in both new industries and the service sector. To reflect the importance of the North West, Manchester was chosen in 1965 as the base for one of Britain's first business schools.[12] Although university-based management education did not prove popular at that time, Manchester Business School pioneered a trend that by the 1990s was one of the foundations of British university expansion. Today, the North West boasts three members of the elite Russell Group of universities (Lancaster, Liverpool and Manchester), as well as vibrant newer institutions in Preston, Chester, Bolton, Liverpool and Manchester.

## The articles

Although the early industrialists that created the economy of the North West would barely recognize the region, given the transition that has occurred especially since the 1960s, they would be impressed by the diversity and continued innovation. This special issue will highlight the diversity by starting with the story of cotton textiles decline, related in fine detail by Higgins and Toms. This article reinterprets the decline of the Lancashire cotton textile industry by focusing more on governance issues which in turn affected attitudes towards investment in new technology. This business history approach demonstrates how by applying concepts derived from other social sciences we can produce highly original analyses of old problems. The overseas markets for this industry's output, of course, were extensive, a point well made in John Singleton's examination of New Zealand. Using three case-studies – cotton, glass and engineering – this perceptive article highlights the difficulties of exporting, contributing to the wider debate about the competitiveness of British firms.

Having outlined the reasons behind the demise of Lancashire's largest staple industry, attention moves to many other aspects of the North West business community. Martín López and John Walton initiate this with a highly original insight into the relationship between business and local government in the region's most popular tourist resort, Blackpool. In creating the world's first working-class seaside resort, it is apparent from their extensive research that freemasonry played a significant role in drawing the community together. Another major leisure-oriented activity is also analyzed by Alistair Mutch, who has researched the contours of brewing in the north-west of England between 1840 and 1914. This was another highly innovative industry that expanded substantially as a result of extensive urbanization and population growth. Mutch demonstrates that through the direct management of public houses, major brewers were able to grow impressively, although the heterogeneity of practice across the region limited expansion outside it.

Having examined the leisure-oriented activities, the special issue moves on to Ken Brown's incisive work on the toy industry of the North West. It is especially significant from Brown's research that far from emerging after the First World War, this was a long-standing industry that had been employing significant numbers for several generations. Another well established North West industry was insurance. Indeed, Robin Pearson authoritatively demonstrates how from the early seventeenth century a highly diverse insurance industry emerged in the North West, providing coverage for marine, fire, industrial and general activities. The property insurance firms that emerged in Liverpool during the middle of the nineteenth century were to become the largest multinational insurers in the world, confirming our earlier point that North West entrepreneurs were capable of building firms that would make a global impact.

Returning to more local themes, Hart and Timmins provide an original insight into how North West road-builders ensured that industrialists and merchants were able to move their goods both within and outside the region. Given that, for example, by the mid 1820s no fewer than 1,200 cotton-spinners were visiting Manchester on one or more of the three market days (Tuesday, Thursday and Saturday), it was clearly essential to create an efficient infrastructure that facilitated this industry's expansion. Hart and Timmins demonstrate clearly that it was the North West business community that funded the road-building activities, further confirming the work of other scholars who have made similar points about other utilities.

Finally, and looking at the downside of industrial expansion, Geoff Tweedale brings his extensive knowledge of occupational diseases to demonstrate graphically how asbestos killed many workers in that industry. It is especially tragic that in spite of mounting scientific evidence, as recently as the 1970s large numbers of workers were still being exposed to this highly dangerous substance in not only its production, but also the building industry.

**Conclusion**

Of course, while this special issue provides highly original insights into the diverse nature of business in the North West, it is by no means comprehensive. Much more research is required on a wide range of sectors before we can provide authoritative coverage of the totality. For example, we need to know much more about the links between orthodox business activities and the co-operative movement, as well as how the manufacturing sector stimulated considerable investment in a wide range of service industries that in the twentieth century would become major employers in their own right. Above all, this special issue demonstrates that business historians have contributed extensively to boosting our grasp of these processes, in terms of both the wide range of detailed case-studies generated, as well as the generalized overviews produced more recently, demonstrating the utility of investing more time to this kind of research.

John F. Wilson<br>
November 2009

**Notes**

1. S. Pollard, *The genesis of modern management* (London, 1965).
2. John F. Wilson, *British business history, 1720–1994* (Manchester, 1995), pp. 23–31.
3. For an overview of these trends, see A. E. Musson, *The growth of British industry* (London, 1978).
4. See John K. Walton, *Lancashire: a social history, 1558–1939* (Manchester, 1987); John F. Wilson and John Singleton, 'The Manchester industrial district, 1750–1939: clustering, networking and performance', in John F. Wilson and Andrew Popp, eds., *Industrial clusters and regional business networks in England, 1750–1970* (Aldershot, 2003).
5. A comprehensive coverage is provided in D. A. Farnie, T. Nakaoka, D. J. Jeremy, J. F. Wilson and T. Abe, eds., *Region and strategy in Britain and Japan: business in Lancashire and Kansai, 1890–1990* (London, 2000).
6. D. J. Jeremy, T. Abe and J. Sasaki, 'Comparisons between the development of big business in the north-west of England and in Osaka, 1900–1990s', in Farnie *et al*, eds., *Regions and strategy*, pp. 78–114.
7. Data derived from Jeremy *et al*, 'Comparisons'.
8. John F. Wilson and Andrew Thomson, *The making of modern management* (Oxford, 2006).
9. Quoted in Wilson and Singleton, 'Manchester industrial district'.
10. Jeremy et al, 'Comparisons', p. 81.
11. John F. Wilson and Carole Knight, *A history of Greyfriars Hall* (privately printed, 2009).
12. John F. Wilson, *The 'Manchester Experiment': a history of Manchester Business School, 1965–1990* (London, 1990).

# OBITUARIES
## Ruth Frow (1922–2008)

In the splendid Working Class Movement Library she founded with her husband Edmund, Ruth Frow, who has died aged 85, already has her lasting memorial. Originating in the Frows' shared love of labour history, by the 1980s the collection was bursting from every seam of their Manchester home. Fortunately, in 1987, neighbouring Salford council had the sense and public spirit to house the collection in the converted nursing home where it remains.

Run by an independent trust, the library today comprises tens of thousands of pamphlets, books and artefacts, dating from the days of Tom Paine and William Cobbett to more recent battles in which the Frows themselves played their part. It is one of the outstanding collections of its kind, in Britain and internationally.

Frow was born Ruth Engel, of partly Jewish, partly Irish extraction, and grew up between the wars in the north London suburb of Mill Hill. Her father had been a concert pianist who, due to rheumatism, had become an international commercial traveller. She was educated at Downhurst private high school in Hendon – receiving the grooming and education of a 'young lady' and later taking pleasure in recording its failure. The outbreak of war when she was seventeen introduced her to the altogether less restrictive environment of the WAAF. Enlisting under age in time for the Battle of Britain in 1940, she spent the war in Fighter Command on the Kent coast.

Having encountered left-wing politics, she campaigned for Labour in the 1945 general election, and on the advice of a Kent miner at Betteshanger colliery, joined the Communist Party at the same time. Her first husband, whom she had met in the RAF, joined with her. Returning to London after the war, Frow was one of many young party members whose appetite for social reform found an outlet in the emergency teacher-training programme. She was trained at Hampton, took her first teaching job in Mile End, east London, in 1949, and throughout the 1950s was active in CP-sponsored peace campaigns. She was secretary of Teachers for Peace and the Manchester Peace Committee, and co-founder and first chair of Manchester CND.

She had met Edmund Frow, a Manchester shop steward, at a Communist Party school in Sussex in 1953. Their first encounter was on the tennis court – Ruth was a former Middlesex junior county player – and they also discovered a common love of books. A memorable partnership was born. Eddie was a seasoned activist of impressive self-education, and Ruth never lost her admiration for his political understanding, though she did chip away at the male chauvinism she found in his shop-floor culture.

Their commitment to the CP was quickly tested. Eddie, too, had been previously married and the party was wary of any scandal that might affect its political activities. The couple were therefore directed to live apart and, for a year, Ruth worked in Liverpool while Eddie visited at weekends. This was the rule the party had pronounced – and, she later recalled, 'we were nitwits enough to stick to it'. Theirs was a steadfast commitment, and one of the shocks of Ruth's later years was her expulsion from the CP during the bitter factional rivalries of the 1980s. Though under no illusions as to the extent of its decline, she remained convinced of better days to come. From the overnight collapse of Europe's communist regimes, she took at least one positive lesson, that history had not yet done with great political changes.

This conviction underlay all the couple's activities. For the Frows, as they readily admitted, book-collecting was not just a pastime but a disease. Educators and proselytizers for the cause they believed in, they saw in the knowledge of working people's history both an argument for socialism and a precondition for its achievement. Academics were always welcome to their library, and their friends included many eminent historians. Nevertheless, they took special pride in the union and community activists who visited the library, and it was to them that their own publications were chiefly addressed. Titles on Robert Owen, Karl Marx, William Morris and Citizen Guillotine give a flavour of their enthusiasms. Their important collection on political women shows Ruth tilting the balance of a largely male socialist pantheon.

When the library moved to Salford, the Frows moved in with it. Although the constant round of visitors eventually proved too much for them, Ruth remained a regular presence, even after Eddie's death in 1997. Two days before she died, she was there as usual, attending the library committee. Her warmth, generosity and unflappable common sense will be missed. But she died with the satisfaction of having left not just a memorial, but a resource with which to take on future challenges.

*Kevin Morgan*
This article first appeared in the *Guardian*, 1 February 2008
© Guardian News & Media, 2008

# Yoshiteru Takei (1929–2009)

Yoshiteru Takei was a noted economic historian in his native Japan, and a well known figure to the members of the Department of Economic History in the University of Manchester from the time of his first visit in 1965 until his last in 2006. Indeed, almost every summer, certainly from the mid 1980s, he was to be found in the John Rylands University Library, the Manchester Central Library or any one of a variety of libraries and record offices in Macclesfield, Oldham, Stoke-on-Trent and other places, pursuing his research into the cotton, silk or pottery industries in the eighteenth and nineteenth centuries. As well as publishing a number of books on these matters in Japan, he was also a close observer of the modern British social scene and produced several books and articles based on his observations.

Prof Takei was born in 1929 in the Manchurian port of Dairen (now Dalian), which was then part of a kind of linear Japanese colony traced by the South Manchuria Railway (SMR) Company's extensive network in what was at least nominally Chinese sovereign territory at that time, though after 1931 the whole of Manchuria passed under Japan's imperial control. As a middle-school student during the Second World War, he was conscripted to work in the SMR's locomotive works in Harbin, and remained very proud of the fact that he was one of the few academics licensed to drive steam locomotives, as he told me on a visit to the National Railway Museum in York.

With the Russian invasion of Manchukuo in August 1945 and the territory's return to Chinese sovereignty, many of the Japanese residents were obliged to stay there for several years, and it was not until 1949 that Prof Takei and his family were permitted to return to Japan. He was then able to enrol as a student of economics in the University of Nagoya, where he took his doctorate. He proceeded to make his career as an economic historian in the prestigious National (i.e., central government) university sector of Japan's extensive higher education system, becoming Professor of Economic History in Shizuoka National University. Throughout his academic career, his interest centred on the economy and society of Britain, a focus he explained in a recent Economic History Society publication[1] in the following terms. Japanese economic historians in the immediate post-war period were divided into two essentially Marxist but nevertheless mutually hostile schools. One, known as *Koza-ha*, regarded the Meiji Restoration of 1867 as merely a reform of Japan's traditional feudal society, whereas the other (*Rono-ha*) saw it as a complete and revolutionary break with the feudal past which ushered in a mature capitalist economy and society. Both schools of thought, the young Dr Takei noticed, regarded the development of capitalism in Britain as the true template for development along Marxian lines. So he decided that before embarking on a career of research in the economic history of Japan he ought to look into the model by which established Japanese economic historians judged the pattern of Japan's progress, the development of the British economy and society and their transition to industrialism. It was to provide him with a lifetime's work, based on immensely detailed and painstaking research in British archival and published sources covering everything from the relationship between medieval English boroughs and their agrarian hinterlands to the phenomena of industrial welfare, paternalism and child labour in nineteenth-century Britain.

Academics in the Japanese National university sector tend to retire earlier than their colleagues in the prefectural, municipal or private universities, and following retirement the more eminent frequently find employment in one of the other sectors. The phenomenon is sometimes referred to as 'descending from Heaven'. On retiring from Shizuoka National University in 1996, Prof Takei took up a post in the newly established Shizuoka Sangyo University – a joint prefectural/private institution – with the function not only of teaching but also of maintaining a general oversight of the new university's academic standards. He nevertheless continued to visit the UK every summer to follow his own research and keep in touch with his wide circle of friends among British academics. Manchester, of course, was the main focus of his affection for Britain and he had been one of the founders of the Tokyo-based Manchester Club in 1987, which provided a social forum for Japanese alumni of the University of Manchester as well as for Japanese academics who, like Prof Takei himself, had been visiting scholars in the University. He was elected President of the Club for 1993–4 and remained active in its successor organization, the Greater Manchester Club of Japan which enlarged the scope of the original body to include those Japanese people who had connections with UMIST, Manchester Metropolitan University and the University of Salford.

Prof Takei formed particularly close friendships with several members of Manchester University's Department of Economic History and greatly mourned the deaths of colleagues such as

W. H. Chaloner, A. E. Musson and, most recently, Douglas Farnie. Not long after his last visit to Manchester in the summer of 2006, his own health began to deteriorate and a planned visit in 2007 had to be cancelled to make way for a series of medical tests as a result of which cancer of the kidneys was diagnosed. In spite of his illness and the often difficult treatment he had to undergo, he maintained his contacts with, and interest in, Britain, and above all Manchester, until the very end. Indeed, one of his final acts before his own death in January 2009 was to write a brief memorial note on his friend Douglas Farnie, news of whose own death in late 2008 had only recently reached him.

*Alex J. Robertson*

**Note**

1. P. Hudson, ed., *Living economic and social history* (Glasgow, 2001), pp. 362–3.

# In memory of Professor Douglas Farnie

Professor Douglas A. Farnie passed away in August 2008. Although I had been acquainted with him for more than forty years, and we had promised to call each other by our first names more than ten years ago, here I would like to distance myself a little bit by calling him 'Farnie-san' in the Japanese style.

I came to regard Farnie-san as a genuine British gentleman of the old school. He was a very formal person who respected the distinction between official and private matters, and never talked about his own private affairs, whatever company he might be in. As a result, it was not until three years after his wife's death that his colleagues at Manchester University got to know about it, and the news of his own death did not reach his colleagues until three months after it had happened.

It was in 1965 when I met him for the first time, at an informal meeting of the staff of the Department of Economic History at Manchester University. Following a pattern established by W. H. Chaloner and presided over by the Head of the Department, Prof T. S. Willan, such meetings were held in the staff common room every Wednesday for two hours after lunch, there being no teaching commitments on Wednesday afternoons. Without any set theme, somebody picked up an interesting issue, and everybody taking part freely contributed from whatever knowledge he might have about the topic. Chaloner, exultantly, used to liken these meetings to those of the Lunar Society of eighteenth-century Birmingham. Although the meetings were open to all of the department's members, in those days in British universities there still existed some sense of hierarchy by which the younger men would give precedence to their elders – a major difference with the present, post-Beatles era. Not everyone found the rather conservative, almost Victorian, atmosphere entirely congenial, and A. E. Musson, for one, tended to bypass the group, albeit generally with a smile and a wave of the hand. Farnie-san, however, having just returned from Africa, took part in the meeting as the youngest of the participants, listening always with a smile.

Farnie-san was always one to wear his knowledge lightly and to share it freely. I think, for example, of the occasion at the turn of the century when he and I decided to take a walk in Salford's canal park, the redevelopment of which was about 80 per cent complete at that point. We went off in the car with Farnie-san driving, and as we got out in Salford two elegant Indian ladies stopped him to ask for directions to the road along the canal. He showed them the way to the road politely, and then having confirmed that they were interested in the canal's history, he began to explain the full story of the Salford Canal and its links with the cotton industry. He got quite animated, and his lecture went on for thirty minutes or so. The ladies were very pleased and asked diffidently, 'Why do you know so much about it?' Farnie-san joyfully replied that having been born in Salford, he had advanced his interest in its local history from his childhood when he started to visit the Salford Local History Library, and that he had kept up his interest ever since.

After leaving the local grammar school he went on to the University of Manchester as both an undergraduate and as a graduate student. It was a natural choice for a man who loved Manchester so much, that is to say, Manchester in the broad sense which included Salford, just across the river Irwell.

Farnie-san is very well known among economic historians in Japan as a leading historian of the British cotton industry, but in his own country and in Europe he is also known as a well informed scholar on the history of the cotton industry of the world at large. His studies ranged widely over various fields centring on the British cotton industry, with the Manchester Ship Canal and related areas, but here I should like to focus on the cotton industry and on South African economic history, the study of which he had been engaged in before his work on cotton. He started his academic career at the University of Natal in Durban, South Africa, and his article 'The mineral revolution in South Africa' (*The South African Journal of Economics*, vol. 24, no. 2 [1956], pp. 125–34) is a good example of what he produced at that stage. Its coverage is wide over various topics including gold-, coal- and diamond-mining, railway construction, fruit cultivation and so on, but its main focus is on the mining industry. His inimitable and exhaustive way of collecting documents and meticulous analysis is already evident in this article, examining the mining industry from the 1870s to the 1930s. Most of the firms were established by British capital, and with such capital investment South Africa deepened the connection with the British economy. Farnie-san also pointed out that while the industry in its early stages relied upon immigrants from the mines of Cornwall and Devon, as it developed it steadily grew more dependent on migrant labour from within southern Africa itself. This article shows that his work in and on Africa was never ephemeral but serious and strenuous.

Another work we must not forget is *The English cotton industry and the world market, 1815–1896* (1979). He emphatically stressed that capital for the cotton trade in Lancashire, especially in Oldham and Rochdale, came not from mighty capitalists as often imagined, but from 'yeoman capitalists' or what R. H. Tawney called 'capitalists in Lilliput'. Easy entry to the trade allowed them to tap small sources of capital, which eventually led to the emergence of big factories like the Sun Mill – that is why, he argued, the industry could raise the standard of living of labourers in Lancashire.

After his retirement from Manchester University, Farnie-san accepted a position as a visiting professor at Manchester Metropolitan University, where he continued his research even more energetically, and published one piece of work after another on the distribution branches of the cotton trade. His ceaseless effort widened his horizons to cover India, Japan, and the US. At the same time, he demonstrated his characteristic capability for making contact with foreign scholars to launch out joint projects. In Japan, he worked with the late Professor Shinichi Yonekawa and with other prominent economic historians in the Osaka area (the traditional centre of Japan's cotton industry). The latter project bore a fruit as a book co-edited with David J. Jeremy, *The fibre that changed the world: the cotton industry in international perspective, 1600–1990s* (2004).

I cannot go over all his achievements, but what I want to emphasize is that he was in the middle of his journey from the English cotton industry to the world trade of cotton products, then to the world economic history of the cotton industry. He himself, I am sure, must have been extremely disappointed that his sudden death from a heart attack meant he was unable to finish this journey. I just pray his soul may rest in peace.

*Yoshiteru Takei*
Translated by Makoto Akagi, Hitotsubashi University, Tokyo

# ARTICLES

# Capital ownership, capital structure, and capital markets: financial constraints and the decline of the Lancashire cotton textile industry, c1880–c1965[1]

D. M. Higgins and J. S. Toms

## Introduction

Two issues have dominated the historiography of the Lancashire textile industry in recent decades. These are whether entrepreneurs were rational or not in the light of the constraints they faced and, related to that issue, the causes of the industry's decline.[2] It is not the purpose of this article to review the intricacies of these debates. However, it does seek to comment upon them in the light of new evidence from recent research into the ownership of the industry and its financial performance.[3] Broadly, the argument that arises from these studies is that ownership and governance structures placed financial constraints on decision-makers. Also, the governance structure of the Lancashire cotton textile industry that developed during the nineteenth century had far-reaching consequences for its performance in the twentieth century.

This interpretation has some similarity with others that have contributed to the current state of the debates. For example, it acknowledges the importance of major variations in demand and that in other respects the cotton industry of Lancashire evolved in a path-dependent, incremental, fashion. However there are several important differences. First, it is not the case that the type of firm structure which evolved in the nineteenth century was inimical to progress and competitiveness in the twentieth century.[4] Indeed, an earlier paper demonstrated that the choice of structure was rational in the light of the profitability of alternatives.[5] Second, the pattern of firm structure did not restrict the range of profitable or feasible technological options available to firms in the twentieth century.[6]

Third, although Lazonick was correct to identify the managerial/entrepreneurial split as being at the crux of debate,[7] he did not directly examine the changing impact of governance structures on the evolution of the industry and its consequences for capital structure and business strategy.[8] However, as will be demonstrated, in this analysis, governance structures and their associated financial constraints were the crucial legacies of the nineteenth century.

Collapse in demand in export markets after 1920 and the emergence of excess capacity are well acknowledged aspects of the problems facing the industry. In addition, as shown below, the new owners of the industry placed demands on cash flow in the form of repayments of loan finance, and other capital, dividend and interest payments. After 1945, these problems were compounded by unhelpful taxation rules. When problems in export markets and over-capacity are combined with these governance-imposed constraints, the interpretation presented here provides new insight into the inability of entrepreneurs to formulate responses to external threats and industry decline. This interpretation is also a variant of the 'early-start' thesis that has been used to explain poor competitiveness for the British economy as a whole.[9] Unlike this thesis, the explanation here is based on the use of capacity created in the nineteenth century and its associated system of finance. These then formed a basis for a series of re-orderings in financial claims as the industry staggered from one crisis to another in the twentieth.[10] Previous studies have recognized the extent of this financial crisis and as a result have concentrated on its most prominent aspect, the intervention of the Bank of England and the formation of the Lancashire Cotton Corporation (LCC) during the period 1929–31.[11] The empirical aspect of the present study, which focuses on financing and dividend policies of typical firms (Tables 1, 2 and 3) concentrates on other major firms whose strategies have been neglected to a certain extent, especially in the inter-war period. These firms were also selected for comparability through time, whose records were consistently available from comparable sources during the major sub-periods of the study.[12]

The remainder of the paper is organized as follows. Section two examines the changes in governance structures and ownership that emerged in the industry during the pre-1914 period and analyzes how this led to an over-commitment of financial and physical resources in the industry. Section three evaluates the impact of pre-war governance structures on the ability of entrepreneurs to formulate recovery strategies after the onset of crisis in the 1920s and 1930s. Particular attention is paid to explaining how financial constraints limited the opportunities for increasingly urgent re-equipment. Section four re-examines this relationship in the period from the end of the Second

World War to the 1960s and shows that entrepreneurs remained subject to a similar set of financially induced constraints. Section five reassesses the current state of the debates on Lancashire textiles in light of the preceding discussion.

**Capital markets and governance before 1914**

The boom-slump cycle and continued underlying growth of the industry before 1914 led to important and decisive changes in corporate governance. There were several important aspects to this. First, capital market inefficiency followed directly from the vicissitudes of the trade cycle. Second, market imperfections enabled promotional speculators to engage in systematic wealth transfers. Third, as a consequence of the first two aspects, capital was misallocated in promotional booms and as a result there was always latent excess capacity. Finally, the new owners of the industry shunned corporate saving and instead accumulated wealth privately. Each of these aspects is discussed in more detail below. The discussion relies on evidence from previous studies and also evidence on the financial policies of typical Lancashire companies. Table 1 summarizes the dividend and borrowing policies for a sample of these firms.

For many modern economists, financial markets can only become more efficient as information flows faster and entry barriers break down.[13] Whether or not Britain had established efficient capital markets before 1914 has been the source of some debate, although research into this question is under-developed empirically.[14] As far as the capital markets of Lancashire were concerned some clear evidence has recently emerged. This evidence suggests that market efficiency *declined* during the period.[15] Centred on Oldham, the Lancashire stock market began in the early 1870s on the back of a flotation boom of dozens of companies underpinned by the mass participation of the local factory-based population.[16] In the first half of the 1890s, the system met with a crisis. Depressed demand was a function of the loss of the Indian and other eastern markets, which followed from the depreciation of silver relative to gold on the world market.[17] Capital market efficiency declined following this slump. A survey of annual returns has shown that whilst the typical company of the 1880s had hundreds of transactions in its shares, by the early 1890s the number of transactions fell to only a handful.[18] As the market could not match buyers and sellers, prices could not reflect true values.[19] As we shall see, this had important consequences for the allocation of capital.

Meanwhile, the 1890s slump in values also altered the social ownership of the industry. By the 1900s participation had narrowed, and large, wealthy dealers dominated the market.[20] Promotional

**Table 1:** Financial policies of Lancashire firms, 1884–1914

| Company | Period | Debt/Equity Ratio* Average for period | DPR† Average for period |
|---|---|---|---|
| Ashton Brothers | 1899–1913 | 0.86 | 0.72 |
| Barlow & Jones | 1900–1913 | 1.77 | 0.73 |
| Elkanah Armitage | 1891–1913 | 0.13 | 0.70 |
| FCSDA‡ | 1899–1913 | 1.66 | 0.58 |
| Horrockses§ | 1887–1914 | 0.85 | 0.57 |
| Rylands | 1884–1913 | 0.21 | 0.87 |
| Tootal | 1888–1914 | 1.48 | 0.49 |
| Sample average | | 0.99 | 0.67 |

*Notes*: *Debt divided by equity where: Debt is defined as all borrowing falling due in greater than 12 months; Equity is defined as called-up share capital plus reserves.
† Divided Pay-out Ratio, calculated as dividends payable divided by profits available for distribution to ordinary shareholders.
‡ Fine Cotton Spinners & Doublers Association
§ Main constituent firm of the Amalgamated Cotton Mills Trust (ACMT) from 1920.
*Sources*: Ashton Bros, Barlow and Jones, Elkanah Armitage, Fine Cotton Spinners & Doublers, Rylands, London Guildhall Library, Commercial Reports, half-yearly Balance Sheets, 1899–1913. Horrockses; Coats Viyella Records (held by the company), Detailed Accounts, half-yearly Balance Sheets and Profit and Loss Accounts, November 1887– October 1905 and Lancashire County Record Office, DDHs/53, Balance Sheets, half-yearly Balance Sheets and Profit and Loss Accounts, October 1905–April 1914. Tootal, Manchester Central Reference Library, M.461, Board Minutes, Yearly Balance Sheets and Profit and Loss Accounts, July 1888–July 1914.

booms facilitated this process. Such booms, for example in the late 1870s and mid 1880s provided opportunities for promoters to float companies at inflated prices and sell their holdings for large personal profits.[21] This was a rational strategy from their point of view since a rising efficient scale, particularly lengthening mule-spinning carriages, meant that it paid to build new mills in times of boom rather than extend existing buildings.[22] Meanwhile accumulation of private fortunes meant that next-generation mills could be floated using a narrower range of shareholders.[23] Thus subsequent booms compounded market inefficiency further and created new opportunities for systematic wealth transfers.[24] This was especially the case in the pronounced and protracted boom after 1896 that continued with brief interruptions until 1914. Accounting profit rates grew steadily from 1896 onwards and peaked in the boom of 1907.[25] In turn, this prompted an unprecedented mill-building boom in the period 1904–8, centred on the Oldham district.[26] By the 1900s, groupings of individually controlled mills became more clearly established.[27] The proprietors of these groups of mills possessed access to financial resources based on reputation and personal contact.[28] As a result they were individually involved in the flotation and directorships of up to a dozen mill companies.[29] These changes created a highly unusual system of governance based on diversified directors and non-diversified shareholders (in the conventional model of Anglo-Saxon economies it is the other way round). Hence the rise of powerful directors was not consistent with the rise of managerial capitalism, rather an unusual Lancashire variant of personal capitalism.[30] It was also persistent during the period of decline. The annual returns of these companies in the 1950s revealed similar interlocking directorships and a rump of residual small private shareholders.[31]

There were several important consequences of these changes in ownership. First, the activities of the mill promoters led to the centralization of capital ownership and the industry increasingly fell under the control of speculative entrepreneurs.[32] As the post-1896 boom developed, their skills at company promotion came to the fore. Profits from existing mills were channelled via the estates of these proprietary capitalists into personally administered flotations or acquisitions of other concerns.[33] They used individual contacts, cross directorships and shareholdings to develop 'empires' of otherwise un-integrated businesses.[34] The late 1890s witnessed the rise of cliques of directors and also the emergence of new combines, such as the Fine Cotton Spinners and Doublers Association.[35] Strategy formulation became the exclusive preserve of these individuals whilst managers became nominee officials at plant level, trusted only with routine. In other words, imperfections in the capital market led to the rise of owner-managed firms that precluded the emergence of professional managerial hierarchies.[36]

A second consequence was that ownership interests were able to impose limits on free cash flow available to managers. As equity holders they demanded high dividends and also used extensive loan finance to fund new flotations. As shown in Table 1, typical companies paid out 67 per cent of their available profits as dividends and the typical debt-to-equity ratio was close to one during this period. Although there is little comparable evidence of calculated dividend pay-out ratios for other industries, it is reasonable to suppose that divestment was higher in Lancashire than elsewhere, since equity capital growth rates were below national averages.[37] Much of the debt to finance new mills came from cash balances in existing mills, and were often used to underpin inter-firm control by cliques of directors.[38] Although these investments occurred without the consent of the residual shareholders,[39] they still reflected the dependence of the industry on local finance, a situation that changed after 1918. This system of finance depended on strong subsequent cash flow to repay loans and also on the willingness of entrepreneurs and promoters to recycle cash from dividends into new flotations.

A further consequence of ownership structure was that the new capacity created by these 'gangs of promoters' destroyed the profit margins of installed capacity and left the industry over-committed in subsequent slumps.[40] The activities of promotional speculators were important because as a result of the 1907 mill-building boom, capacity in the industry reached levels that subsequently proved unsustainable. One contemporary estimate was that by 1935, there were still 13.5 million surplus spindles in the industry of which 9.5 were in the American section and 4 million in the Egyptian section.[41] For 1935, this represents plant utilization of just 69 per cent in the spinning industry.[42] An alternative way of interpreting this figure is as follows: installed capacity in 1935 was approximately 47 million spindles, but there was only enough demand to keep 33.5 million spindles (installed capacity minus excess capacity) fully employed. Even as early as the 1880s the industry already contained over 40 million spindles.[43] In other words, the capacity that was installed by the promoters in the boom period of 1896–1914 was all potentially surplus in the light of the performance of the industry after 1920. However, if Lancashire's entrepreneurs had *not* responded to the rapid growth of export demand pre-1914 they may have been accused of 'failure'. Any expenditure on plant must be governed by the expectation that the future (but uncertain) returns will outweigh the cost of these assets. Where expectations differ it may be possible to recover these costs by selling the asset to other businessmen. For the first time this drew in significant finance from outside Lancashire. As one authority has suggested,[44] with the development of capital markets, capitalists shed their entrepreneurial role and entrepreneurs shed their financing function. The 1919–21 re-flotation boom provides a classic example of this divergence of interests. The over-capacity problem was compounded because corporate growth rates were strongest where private or family control was exercised and weakest where there was dependency on regional stock markets.[45] Yet it was the latter case, best exemplified by Oldham, that led to the greatest expansion of capacity at industry level.

The final important consequence of the industry's ownership

structure was for the technological development of the industry. Because the commercial and technical advantages of ring spinning and the automatic loom were not yet established,[46] entrepreneurs ploughed the resources from the pre-1914 booms into specialized establishments using traditional technologies. It was for this reason that whilst there were few advocates of integrated production before 1914, technical issues associated with disintegration came to the fore in the 1920s and 1930s. Thus the critique of specialization from within the industry, as presented by Lazonick, came from technical experts and managers rather than entrepreneurs.[47] The governance structure inherited from the nineteenth century meant the opinions of mill managers were much constrained by the actions of the directors. During the pre-1914 period, industry ownership and its consequences dominated the issue of technical choice.

**Financial paralysis, 1918–1939**

After a sharp and very important boom in 1919–21, Lancashire cotton lost ground in several important overseas markets. Particularly significant was the loss of the Indian market, and Japanese competition in third markets.[48] These facts are well known. When considered in conjunction with the ownership structure described in the previous section, together with further evidence on financial strategies (Table 2), new insights are offered.

There were several important consequences of this latest twist in the boom-slump cycle that prevented the industry from recovering, as it had been able to do before the war, for example, after 1896. The first consequence was that, to varying degrees, all firms were subject to high fixed charges as a result of the refinancing strategies adopted during the 1919–20 boom. In 1919 entrepreneurs faced boom conditions even more dramatic than those of 1907. However, unlike previous booms, it was wider margins rather than increases in demand which was instrumental.[49] Also a shortage of equipment and building supplies prevented a new wave of mill construction. These features deterred further investment in physical mill capital that could have only made the subsequent over-capacity problem worse. Instead, firms were re-capitalized such that the capitalization of the typical company increased by a factor of three. Much of the re-capitalization was supported by new long-term debt finance.[50] Table 2 provides examples of the typical ratio of debt to equity in 1920. For these firms debt represented two-thirds of the value of shareholders' assets. Levels of borrowing were lower in 1920 than it had typically been prior to 1914 although they increased to a comparable level, as the crisis of the 1920s and 1930s became more severe. Evidence is

| Company | Debt/Equity Ratio | | | | DPR Average |
| --- | --- | --- | --- | --- | --- |
| | 1920 | 1930 | 1938 | 1945 | 1920–45 |
| ACMT | 0.65 | 0.70 | 0.46 | 2.12 | 0.36 |
| Ashton | 0.41 | 0.94 | 0.91 | 0.30 | 0.41 |
| Barlow & Jones | 0.85 | 0.65 | 0.15 | 0.19 | 0.75 |
| Brierfield Mills | 0.51 | 0.39 | Nil | Nil | 2.54 |
| Crosses & Winkworth | 1.35 | 1.62 | 4.64 | 1.22 | −0.17 |
| Elkanah Armitage | Nil | Nil | Nil | Nil | 2.03 |
| FCSDA | 0.92 | 1.24 | 1.21 | 0.88 | 0.71 |
| Hollins Mill | 1.12 | 1.24 | 2.47 | 2.31 | 1.00 |
| Jackson and Steeple | Nil | Nil | Nil | Nil | 1.37 |
| Joshua Hoyle | 1.11 | 2.05 | 1.98 | Nil | 0.91 |
| Rylands | 0.51 | 0.57 | 1.17 | 0.35 | 1.27 |
| Tootal Broadhurst | 0.44 | 0.38 | 0.29 | 0.31 | 0.88 |
| Sample Average | 0.66 | 0.82 | 1.11 | 0.64 | 1.00 |

*Notes*: Calculations as described in Table 1. Debt equity ratios calculated at each point in time instead of an average for the period.
*Source*: Stock Exchange Official Intelligence.

Table 2: Financial policies of Lancashire firms, 1920–1945

presented in the discussion below, but it should be stressed at this stage that these valuations were based on dubious assumptions. Some companies, such as Crosses & Winkworth, borrowed to extreme levels in 1919–20 (Table 2). Ignoring the dividend requirements of ordinary shareholders for the moment, these refinancing strategies had the effect of also increasing fixed charges threefold. The annual cost increase represented by fixed interest and depreciation charges was £43,233 for a typical 100,000-spindle mill. On the basis of its average output, that translated into a 2.8d increase in cost per pound on 30s yarns and a 12.2d increase for 100s yarns.[51] To put these figures into context, the average net profit per company even at the height of the 1919 boom was only £14,786. Margins for 32s yarns were 29.88d per pound in 1920, but then fell sharply at first and then steadily to 2.98d by 1931.[52]

Linked to these increases in fixed charges was the second important feature of the boom: a further redistribution of ownership rights.[53] Money capital was invested through the re-capitalization of existing mills with bonus issues and new loan finance. Like the 1907 boom, these re-flotations were speculative and depended heavily on the reputations and contacts of the entrepreneur.[54] As in all previous booms, new capital was used to finance high dividends to equity shareholders, in particular those promotional capitalists who used stock market quotations as fast exit routes for their own investments.[55] Unlike previous booms, however, money was attracted from syndicates from outside the local area,[56] into what turned out to be a more fundamental mis-allocation of capital. When the boom turned to bust after 1921, as in 1892–5, calls were made on shareholders and exhortations made to lenders.[57] Whilst individuals were bankrupted, businesses survived under new owners. Specifically, the banks became the new owners of the industry in place of speculative capitalists.[58] Their priorities did not follow from any expertise in cotton, and were dictated by the recovery of capital rather than the strategic restructuring of the industry.[59] Even when original entrepreneurs remained, the financial claims of this new group effectively ended local control of a large section of the industry.[60] Again, as with the pre-war business cycle, market efficiency was reduced and the social ownership of capital was redistributed.

The consequences of the revised 1920 ownership structure of the industry were serious and made immediate recovery impossible. The first and most important aspect was that firms could not retrench due to their financial structures and were thus also prevented from pursuing re-equipment-based recovery strategies. Retrenchment meant stabilizing cash flows through cost cutting or asset disposals.[61] However, neither of these strategies was feasible in post 1920 conditions. Costs had been driven up by higher interest and depreciation charges and they were unalterable without a further re-ordering of the financial claims of equity and loan investors. Asset sales were the least attractive option to loan creditors. The main reason was that realizable values were low. These low values were due to a combination of factors. The collapse in export markets had created over-capacity and hence there was no second-hand market. The assets involved were highly specific, especially machinery, and in many cases had reached an old vintage by 1930.[62] New but more expensive technology was available. Book values were therefore well below replacement cost. Thus the only alternative valuation available to financial claim holders was the economic value of the assets in use. As a correspondent wrote, 'the real security for many outstanding loans in our depressed industries is little else but the earning power of the assets pledged'.[63] Such valuations require forecasts of the future earning capacity of the assets. Where realizable values are low, forecasts of the risk-adjusted present value of future cash flows do not have to be especially high for a rational decision-maker to support continued investment. Moreover, these forecasts were imbued with a degree of optimism as a result of prior experience of the trade cycle. For example some recalled the depression of the 1890s and argued that the causes of that depression (high world gold prices) were also part of the present difficulties. As one industry authority, writing in the 1930s, put it, 'though the circumstances and events of that depression (the 1890s) were different in a few respects, the essential causes were practically the same as the causes of the present depression'.[64] These commentators noted that when gold prices fell in the period 1897–1914, the cotton industry had experienced the greatest boom in its history.[65]

A second consequence of the 1920 ownership structure was that the re-distribution of ownership rights during the boom of 1919–20 reduced the competitiveness of those firms that might otherwise have been able to best compete in the revised world economic conditions. The newer the assets, the higher the revaluation and the higher the increase in fixed costs. Hence the best-equipped mills of 1920 became the most financially embarrassed by 1930.[66] As shown in Table 2, Amalgamated Cotton Mills Trust and Crosses & Winkworth became heavily over-borrowed as losses reduced the equity base of these companies still further. In 1919, these were both companies with relatively new assets and in markets not especially vulnerable to overseas competition. By 1930, their share values and market capitalizations had fallen to extreme levels.[67]

A further consequence was that industry leaders resorted to collusive behaviour. This behaviour followed from the restrictions on exit imposed by the revised governance structure. Price-fixing schemes were in operation between 1923–4, 1926–7, 1930, and then in every year from 1933.[68] Initially attempts were made to secure industry-wide schemes. However, because these failed to take into account the widely differing experiences of the industry's two major sections, American and Egyptian, they were only short lived.[69]

In addition, financial paralysis prevented Lancashire entrepreneurs from taking advantage of major opportunities offered by technical developments to restore competitiveness through re-equipment. Newer technologies were based on faster throughput and in particular the invention of high-speed drafting in 1914. The technical dominance of these new methods was not established until after 1914, and in British conditions investment in new technology only became a potential commercial option in the 1920s and 1930s. Prior to this breakthrough before the First World War productivity in ring and mule spinning increased at approximately equal rates.[70] Only in the spinning of very fine yarns did mule spinning retain its advantages, including the period after 1945.[71] From 1920, high drafting and other improvements in intermediate processes such as doffing and winding provided opportunities to speed up production[72] and offered savings in areas of traditional labour intensity.[73] A survey in 1932 noted three cases of ring-spinning mills replacing low-draft with high-draft spinning, resulting in average improvements in labour productivity of 49.3 per cent.[74] By now industry commentators recognized that 're-equipment was needed on a vast scale'.[75] From 1931, Japanese producers adopted these techniques. This, together with competitive de-valuations of the yen, explained the loss of Lancashire's traditional far eastern markets.[76] Without adequate finance, technological advances were always threats and never opportunities for Lancashire firms.

Finally, because profit streams were unable to cover fixed charges, the financial distress of many large firms had reached extreme levels by 1930, effectively ruling out new strategic investment. However, the tradition of independence of many cotton companies from bank finance[77] meant the financial institutions lacked the managerial expertise required to effect restructuring. In any case, as noted above, individualistic control of mills had long prevented the emergence of professional managerial hierarchies, and remaining businessmen instinctively favoured industry co-operation to closure and rationalization. As demonstrated earlier, the new financing structure of the industry placed restrictions on free cash flow through high fixed charges. When the dividend requirement was added, managers were left with no available cash to fund re-organization and re-equipment. Despite the collapse in profits and heavy indebtedness of the 1920s, dividends were slow to adjust to lower levels of average profits.[78] As Table 2 shows, the average dividend payout ratio was 84 per cent of available profits. Some companies in the sample, for example Brierfield and Rylands, paid dividends greater than the available profits whilst another, Crosses & Winkworth, paid dividends notwithstanding aggregate losses.[79] It was these restrictions on cash flow imposed by financial policies and governance structures that informed the response of the industry to its problems, especially the problem of over-capacity. A survey of the industry conducted by John Ryan, managing director of the LCC, estimated the average value of debt per company to be £108,350.[80] At these levels, assuming all the profits earned subsequently were applied to retire debt, the earliest year at which firms would be free of debt would have been 1947.[81] Meanwhile the level of debt remained a significant exit barrier at a time when restructuring became increasingly urgent.[82]

### The impact of equity and fiscal financial constraints, 1945–60

Lancashire firms did succeed in repaying the excess debt that had dominated their balance sheets in the aftermath of the 1920 re-constructions, notwithstanding the continuing demand for dividends profits, investment-decision-makers would have to be confident of sufficient profits to take advantage of them. For example, a company with profits of £1m per year subject to corporate taxation at 50 per cent could make investments in new fixed assets of £2m per year and avoid tax altogether. However, marginal expenditure over £2m would not be subject to any tax-based incentives.[92] For a company like the LCC, with uncertain pre-tax profits averaging £3.2m between 1949–64 and requiring capital expenditure in excess of £62m, there was no benefit in this scheme.[93] If the LCC was typical, profit levels for the industry, especially after 1952, were too low relative to the required investment. Unlike companies in other sectors of the economy where re-structuring was not a pre-requisite for growth, Lancashire firms had to bear high rates of tax, but without the compensatory relief of deductions from investment allowances. When combined with the dividend demands of shareholders discussed earlier, it is clear that there were financial constraints on investment behaviour in addition to those documented elsewhere in the previous literature.

**Discussion and conclusions**

By examining three neglected aspects in the current debate – capital ownership, capital structure, and capital markets – the previous discussion has aimed to offer a new perspective on the decline of the Lancashire textile industry. It is intended that these aspects will be seen as incremental to other causes of decline highlighted elsewhere. Monetary conditions and changes in world demand were of obvious importance but beyond the control of the typical entrepreneur. It is therefore appropriate to concentrate the discussion on entrepreneurial responses to externally driven crises.

Much prior debate has revolved around the definition of the entrepreneur, and the scope of and constraints on entrepreneurial activities. Whilst it is possible to agree that constraints existed, the question is, which were the most important? Sandberg argued that entrepreneurs operated rationally within the constraints imposed upon them, for example by the structure of the industry. Taking a Schumpeterian view, Lazonick argued that it was up to entrepreneurs to remove these constraints but that they had a problem in Lancashire because *ex ante* horizontal specialization prevented co-ordinated decision making.[94] There are two problems with this view. First, although not dealt with in the discussion above, there is a presupposition about the desirability of vertical integration.[95] Secondly, if for the moment the desirability of vertical integration is accepted, it is not clear how the *ex ante* horizontal structure of the industry prevented this happening.[96] As the evidence discussed earlier shows, during their careers, some promoters floated over a dozen mills in the booms before 1920. Through their contacts they were able to raise large amounts of equity finance and additional debt finance through further borrowing. In most cases they built brand new mills rather than extending existing factories. It is difficult to understand why, if the advantages of vertical integration were overwhelming, they did not build integrated plants from scratch. They could have gone further and invested in ring-spinning and automatic looms and deployed them in these new factories. Instead, they stuck to mules and power looms in specialized mills. Yet they still demonstrated rational, profit-maximising tendencies, as their demand for dividends suggests. Up to 1920, these dividends made them richer, and even more capable of overcoming the constraint of industry structure had this constraint been problematic.

The evidence presented here suggests an alternative view. Ring spinning and automatic weaving established their commercial advantages in the 1920s. Meanwhile a new constraint on investment was dramatically imposed by the financial paralysis of the 1920s and 1930s. This placed constraints on retrenchment and hence reinvestment. In the Lancashire case and in the general case it is sensible to consider the corporate governance structure as the ultimate constraint on the entrepreneur. Financial stakeholders have considerable power to restrict the options available to the entrepreneur.[97] Although 'creative destruction' may be required, for example through the scrapping of surplus capacity, it is within the remit of lenders and equity holders to deny the required freedom of action to corporate decision-makers. It is significant that large-scale vertical integration in the industry occurred only from the mid 1960s, *after* the elimination of so many firms and their capacity as a result of the Cotton Industry (Re-equipment) Act (1959).[98]

From the 1890s especially, managerial power was limited by the governance structures imposed by the mill promoters, notwithstanding the continuing expansion of the industry. The promoters performed an entrepreneurial role that was of its nature unconstrained. After 1920, when ownership was transferred to outside financial stakeholders, genuine restrictions were imposed on action at the corporate level. In this sense the pattern of the industry's development in the nineteenth century adversely affected its development in the twentieth. It could also be said, paraphrasing an earlier debate,[99] that the governance constraint was non-problematic in the nineteenth century but problematic in the twentieth when Lancashire hit the problems of changed world-trading conditions. It would be more accurate to argue that the constraint did not exist at all before 1920. As in the general case, in the life cycle of an industry, entrepreneurial power peaks when forecast returns facilitate raising venture finance but before the sale of claims dilutes control. Beyond a certain point the dilution process brings the requirement to satisfy outside stakeholders to the fore and may coincide with the onset of maturity. The same happened in Lancashire. The important difference here, though, was that the effects of transferring financial claims coincided with extraordinary vicissitudes in world-trading conditions to produce a crisis and decline of spectacular proportions. Like the industry, the reputation of Lancashire entrepreneurs never recovered.

**Notes**

1. This paper was first published under the same title in the *Journal of Industrial History*, 4 (2001), pp. 48–64. Since the original publication, further papers have been published by the authors that are complementary to, but do not overlap directly with, the ideas and evidence presented here. In some cases they supersede the works referred to in n. 3 below. These are: S. Toms, 'Information content of earnings announcements in an unregulated market: the co-operative cotton mills of Lancashire, 1880–1900', *Accounting and Business Research*, 31 (2001), pp. 175–90; S. Toms, 'The rise of modern accounting and the fall of the public company: the Lancashire cotton mills, 1870–1914', *Accounting Organizations and Society*, 27 (2002), pp. 61–84; D. M. Higgins and S. Toms, 'Financial distress, corporate borrowing and industrial decline: the Lancashire cotton textile industry, 1918–1938', *Accounting Business and Financial History*, 13 (2003), pp. 207–32; I. Filatotchev and S. Toms, 'Corporate governance, strategy and survival in a declining industry: a study of Lancashire textile companies', *Journal of Management Studies*, 40 (2003), pp. 895–920; S. Toms and I. Filatotchev, 'Corporate governance, business strategy and the dynamics of networks: a theoretical model and application to the British cotton industry, 1830–1980', *Organization Studies*, 25 (2004), pp. 629–51; S. Toms, 'Financial control, managerial control and accountability: evidence from the British cotton industry, 1700–2000', *Accounting Organizations and Society*, 30 (2005), pp. 627–53; D. Higgins and S. Toms, 'Financial institutions and corporate strategy: David Alliance and the transformation of British textiles, c1950–c1990', *Business History*, 48 (2006), pp. 453–78; S. Toms and I. Filatotchev, 'Corporate governance and financial constraints on strategic turnarounds', *Journal of Management Studies*, 43 (2006), pp. 407–33; S. Toms and M. Beck, 'The limitations of economic counterfactuals: the case of the Lancashire textile industry', *Management and Organizational History*, 2 (2007), pp. 315–30; D. M. Higgins, 'Was the Lancashire cotton textile industry competitive? An alternative analysis', in J. Wilson, ed., *King Cotton: a tribute to Douglas Farnie* (Lancaster, 2009),

pp. 83–92; S. Toms, 'The English cotton industry and the loss of the world market', in Wilson, ed., *King Cotton*, pp. 58–76.

2. For summaries of these debates see W. Mass and W. Lazonick, 'The British cotton industry and international competitive advantage: the state of the debates', *Business History*, 32 (1990), pp. 9–65; and A. V. Marrison, 'Indian Summer', in M. B. Rose, ed., *The Lancashire cotton industry: a history since 1700* (Preston, 1996). One authority on the industry has gone so far as to argue that the progress of the product cycle meant it should have become obvious to government and industry leaders in the 1930s that the industry simply was not worth saving: J. Singleton, *Lancashire on the scrapheap* (Oxford, 1991), p. 232.

3. For detailed analysis of this evidence, see D. M. Higgins, 'Rings, mules, and structural constraints in the Lancashire textile industry, c1945–c1965', *Economic History Review*, 46 (1993), pp. 342–62; D. M. Higgins, 'Re-equipment as a strategy for survival in the Lancashire spinning industry, c1945–c1960', *Textile History*, 24 (1993), pp. 211–34; J. S. Toms, 'Financial Constraints on economic growth: profits, capital accumulation, and the development of the Lancashire cotton spinning industry, 1885–1914', *Accounting Business and Financial History*, 4 (1994), pp. 364–83; J. S. Toms, 'The finance and growth of the Lancashire textile industry, 1870–1914' (PhD thesis, University of Nottingham, 1996); D. M. Higgins and J. S. Toms, 'Firm structure and financial performance: the Lancashire textile industry', *Accounting Business and Financial History*, 7 (1997), pp. 195–232; J. S. Toms, 'Windows of opportunity in the textile industry: the business strategies of Lancashire entrepreneurs 1880–1914', *Business History*, 40 (1998), pp. 1–25; J. S. Toms, 'Growth, profits and technological choice: the case of the Lancashire cotton textile industry', *Journal of Industrial History*, 1 (1998), pp. 35–55; J. S. Toms, 'The demand for and the supply of accounting information in an unregulated market: examples from the Lancashire cotton mills, 1885–1914', *Accounting, Organizations and Society*, 23 (1998), pp. 217–38; S. Bowden, and D. Higgins, 'Short-time working and price maintenance: collusive tendencies in the cotton-spinning industry, 1919–1939', *Economic History Review*, 51 (1998), pp. 319–43; S. Bowden and D. M. Higgins, 'Quiet successes and loud failures: the UK textile industries in the inter-war years', *Journal of Industrial History*, 3 (2000), pp. 91–111; S. J. Procter and J. S. Toms, 'Industrial relations and technical change: profits, wages and costs in the Lancashire cotton industry, 1880–1914', *Journal of Industrial History*, 3 (2000), pp. 54–72; D. M. Higgins and J. S. Toms, 'Public subsidy and private divestment: the Lancashire cotton textile industry', *Business History*, 42 (2000), pp. 59–84; J. S. Toms, 'The rise of modern accounting and the fall of the public company', *Accounting Organizations and Society*, 27 (2000), pp. 61–84. For preliminary results of further surveys in this area, see D. M. Higgins and J. S. Toms, 'Corporate borrowing, financial

distress and industrial decline: the Lancashire cotton textile industry, 1918–1931', *Accounting, Business and Financial History*, 13 (2003), pp. 1–26; Filatotchev and Toms, 'Corporate governance, strategy and survival in a declining industry'; J. S. Toms, 'Information content of earnings in an unregulated market: the co-operative cotton mills of Lancashire, 1880–1900', *Accounting and Business Research*, 31 (2001), pp. 175–91. In view of the preliminary nature of the later citations, where appropriate, relevant evidence from them is also presented in the current paper.

4. The view that the pattern of development in the nineteenth century adversely affected performance in the twentieth is advocated most strongly by Lazonick. See, especially, W. Lazonick, 'Competition, specialisation, and industrial decline', *Journal of Economic History*, 41 (1981), pp. 31–8; W. Lazonick, 'Industrial organization and technological change: the decline of the British cotton industry', *Business History Review*, 57 (1983), pp. 195–236.

5. Higgins and Toms, 'Firm structure and financial performance'.

6. Higgins, 'Rings, mules and structural constraints'; G. Saxonhouse and G. Wright, 'New evidence on the stubborn English mule and the cotton industry, 1878–1920', *Economic History Review*, 37 (1984), pp. 507–19.

7. Lazonick, 'Competition, specialisation, and industrial decline'; Lazonick, 'Industrial organization and technological change'; W. Lazonick, 'The cotton industry', in B. Elbaum and W. A. Lazonick, eds., *The decline of the British economy* (Oxford, 1986), pp. 39–45.

8. In the ensuing discussion it is accepted that there is a distinction between managers and entrepreneurs. Managers are concerned with the day-to-day running of the business, whereas entrepreneurs are concerned with strategic issues.

9. For example, S. Pollard, *Britain's prime and Britain's decline* (London, 1990).

10. The central importance of capacity acquired during the nineteenth century and the problems of maladjustment it posed in the twentieth when demand collapsed, has recently been emphasized for another staple industry, shipbuilding, during the inter-war years: F. Geary, 'The emergence of mass unemployment: wages and employment in shipbuilding between the wars', *Cambridge Journal of Economics*, 21 (1997), pp. 303–21.

11. For example, J. Bamberg, 'The government, the banks, and the Lancashire cotton industry, 1918–1939' (PhD thesis, University of Cambridge, 1984); J. Bamberg, 'The rationalization of the British cotton industry in the inter-war years', *Textile History*, 19 (1988), pp. 83–102; R. S. Sayers, *The Bank of England, 1891–1944* (Cambridge, 1976); H. Sjogren, 'Financial reconstruction and industrial reorganisation in different systems: a comparative view of British and Swedish institutions during the inter-war period', *Business History*, 40 (1998), pp. 84–105.

12. The principal sources were the Companies Archive at the London Guildhall Library, the *Stock exchange official year-book* and the Cambridge University Companies Database. To a certain extent, therefore, the evidence and argument presented here only relate to large publicly quoted companies.
13. I. Walter and R. Smith, *Global capital markets and banking* (London, 1999), pp. 198–200.
14. D. McCloskey, *Knowledge and persuasion in economics* (Cambridge, 1994), p. 154.
15. Toms, 'The rise of modern accounting and the fall of the public company'; and Toms, 'Information content of earnings in an unregulated market'.
16. W. Thomas, *The provincial stock exchanges* (London, 1973), p. 147.
17. For a discussion of the political economy of silver depreciation, see A. Howe, 'Bimetallism, c1880–1898: a controversy re-opened?', *English Historical Review*, 55 (1990), pp. 377–91; E. Green, 'Rentiers versus producers? The political economy of the bimetallic controversy, c1880–98', *English Historical Review*, 53 (1988), pp. 588–612; E. Green, 'The bimetallic controversy: empiricism belimed or the case for the issues', *English Historical Review*, 55 (1990), pp. 674–83. An econometric analysis of gold prices and cotton profits shows a strong association: see Toms, 'The finance and growth of the Lancashire cotton textile industry', ch. 11.
18. Toms, 'The rise of modern accounting and the fall of the public company'.
19. In 1891 the *Oldham Standard* reported that 'the published list of market prices is not a very reliable guide just now, as they are either nominal or too wide in price to be of practical use': *Oldham Standard*, 1 Aug. 1891.
20. As illustrated by an analysis of the share registers of Lancashire companies. For details see Toms, 'The rise of modern accounting and the fall of the public company'.
21. D. Farnie, *The English cotton industry and the world market* (Oxford, 1979).
22. G. Wood, 'The statistics of wages in the nineteenth-century cotton industry', *Journal of the Royal Statistical Society*, 73 (1910), pp. 585–626; R. Tyson, 'The cotton industry', in D. H. Aldcroft, ed., *The development of British industry and foreign competition, 1875–1914* (London, 1968), p. 123.
23. Toms, 'The rise of modern accounting and the fall of the public company'.
24. Ibid.
25. Toms, 'Growth, profits and technological choice', pp. 39, 44.
26. During the period 1897–1913, installed spindleage increased by 2 per cent per annum in Lancashire but by 2.7 per cent in Oldham (calculated from R. Robson, *The cotton industry in Britain* [London, 1957], Tables 2

and 5, pp. 334, 340; and Farnie, *English cotton industry*, p. 42.) The higher rate in Oldham was a function of the extraordinary boom of the middle years of the 1900s. For details of the mills constructed, see F. Jones, 'The cotton spinning industry in the Oldham district, 1896–1914' (MA thesis, University of Manchester, 1959), pp. 221–3.

27. Toms, 'The supply of and the demand for accounting information', p. 228.
28. R. E. Tyson, 'Sun Mill: a study in democratic investment' (MA thesis, University of Manchester, 1962); W. Thomas, *The provincial stock exchanges* (London, 1973); Toms, 'The supply of and the demand for accounting information', p. 228.
29. For examples of individual entrepreneurs see Toms, 'The supply of and the demand for accounting information', p. 228; Toms, 'The rise of modern accounting'; D. Gurr and J. Hunt, *The cotton mills of Oldham* (Oldham, 1985), pp. 9–10. In the 1873–5 boom alone William Nuttall was involved in the flotation of twelve mills: Thomas, *The provincial stock exchanges*, p. 146. During the period 1899–1914, one firm of accountants floated twelve mills: Jones, *The cotton spinning industry*, p. 13.
30. Managerial capitalism refers to a managerial hierarchy facing a diversified group of equity investors; personal capitalism refers to owners treating their businesses as personal estates: A. Chandler, *Scale and scope: the dynamics of industrial capitalism* (Cambridge, MA; 1990).
31. Filatotchev and Toms, 'Corporate governance, strategy and survival in a declining industry'. This conclusion is based on a survey of the Annual Returns (Form E) of a sample of twenty-nine companies from the period 1950–1965 from the BT31 file at the Public Record Office.
32. Toms, 'The finance and growth of the Lancashire cotton textile industry', pp. 226–31.
33. Toms, 'Financial constraints on economic growth', p. 380; Toms, 'The finance and growth of the Lancashire cotton textile industry', pp. 328–9; Toms, 'Windows of opportunity in the textile industry', p. 16.
34. Typically, there were no stock market-based acquisitions and mergers in the Oldham district. Instead entrepreneurs preferred to float and build new mills: Toms, 'The finance and growth of the Lancashire textile industry', p. 231; Toms, 'The supply of and demand for accounting information', p. 230.
35. Toms, 'The demand for and supply of accounting information', pp. 226–31; H. Macrosty, *The trust movement in British industry* (London, 1907), pp. 124–5.
36. Toms, 'Financial constraints on economic growth', p. 380; Toms, 'The finance and growth of the Lancashire textile industry', pp. 217–38; Toms, 'Windows of opportunity in the textile industry', p. 10.
37. For further evidence on debt and dividend policies see Toms, 'Windows of opportunity in the textile industry', pp. 3–9. See Table 1, p. 4, for a

comparison between sections of the Lancashire textile industry with national average rates of capital accumulation.

38. Jones, 'The cotton spinning industry', pp. 38, 88.
39. Tyson, 'Sun Mill', p. 295.
40. Jones, 'The cotton spinning industry in the Oldham district', p. 3.
41. T. Barlow, 'Surplus capacity in the Lancashire cotton industry', *Manchester School*, 6 (1935), p. 35.
42. Robson, *The cotton industry*, Table 8, p. 344.
43. Calculated from Robson, *The cotton industry*, Table 5, p. 340.
44. S. Wu, *Production, entrepreneurship and profits* (Oxford, 1988).
45. Toms, 'Windows of opportunity in the textile industry', p. 3.
46. See, for example, Saxonhouse and Wright, 'New evidence on the stubborn English mule', p. 519. A more recent discussion of the commercial and technological factors which affected the adoption of ring spinning during the inter-war years is contained in Higgins and Toms, 'Firm structure and financial performance', pp. 212–14.
47. Developments in intermediate processing, principally high drafting, doffing and winding that were developed and available commercially after 1914 gave a decisive advantage to the ring and automatic loom combination by the 1930s: Toms, 'Growth, profits and technological choice'. For examples of technicians' criticisms of industry structure, see Lazonick, 'Industrial organization and technological change'; B. Robinson, 'Business methods in the cotton trade', *Journal of the British Association of Managers of Textile Works*, 9 (1918–9); and F. Holt, 'High speed winding and warping', *Journal of the National Federation of Textile Managers' Associations*, 9 (1929–30), pp. 104–5.
48. A. Burnett-Hurst, 'Lancashire and the Indian market', *Journal of the Royal Statistical Society*, 95 (1932), pp. 395–454; B. Ellinger and H. Ellinger, 'Japanese competition in the cotton trade', *Journal of the Royal Statistical Society*, 93 (1930), pp. 185–218.
49. Ibid., p. 170.
50. Thomas, *The provincial stock exchanges*, pp. 159–60.
51. For example see the calculations in T. Thornley, *Modern cotton economics* (London, 1923), pp. 187–9.
52. Robson, *The cotton industry*, pp. 336, 338.
53. Thomas, *The provincial stock exchanges*, p. 156.
54. Samuel Firth Mellor and Frank Platt were typical of the entrepreneurs involved: Thomas, *The provincial stock exchanges*, p. 157; Bamberg, 'The government, the banks, and the Lancashire cotton industry', p. 6.
55. For example the premature retirement of Frank Platt: Bamberg, 'Sir Frank Platt', in D. Jeremy, ed., *Dictionary of Business Biography* (London, 1984–6); Thomas, *The provincial stock exchanges*, p. 158.
56. Thomas, *The provincial stock exchanges*, p. 157.
57. As in the 1890s, when calls were made on share capital, equity investors

responded by withdrawing loan money from other companies: G. Daniels and J. Jewkes, 'The post-war depression in the Lancashire cotton industry', *Journal of the Royal Statistical Society*, 91 (1928), pp. 179–80.

58. By 1926 it was claimed, a large section of the industry was 'practically in the hands of the banks': Ibid., p. 161.
59. Keynes recognized that the need of the banks to secure their original advances with fresh advances reduced the exit of inefficient firms and increased the need for short-time working: J. M. Keynes, 'Industrial reorganisation: cotton', in D. M. Moggridge, ed., *The collected writings of John Maynard Keynes*, vol. 19 (London, 1926), p. 584.
60. Ibid., p. 162.
61. Strategic management theory suggests that firms responding to crisis should follow these strategies as precursors to further action. See, for example, J. A. Pearce and K. D. Robbins, 'Towards improved theory and research on business turnaround', *Journal of Management*, 19 (1993), pp. 613–36; F. Zimmerman, *The turnaround experience* (New York, 1991).
62. J. Ryan, 'Machinery replacement in the cotton trade', *Economic Journal*, 40 (1930), pp. 568–80.
63. *Economist*, 30 Aug. 1930, p. 394.
64. Federation of Master Cotton Spinners' Associations [FMCSA], *Measures for the revival of the Lancashire cotton industry* (Manchester, 1936), p. 7.
65. *Economist*, 20 Sep. 1930, p. 520; FMCSA, *Measures for the revival*.
66. Bowden and Higgins, 'Short-time working and price maintenance', pp. 326–7.
67. *Stock Exchange Official Year Books*, 1930 and 1931.
68. Collusive policies were recognized by Keynes: '[they] are founded on the belief that, if only industries hang on, "normal" times will return when they may again hope to employ plant and capital on profitable terms': J. M. Keynes, *Collected writings*, vol. 19: *Activities, 1922–1929: The return to gold and industrial policy*, II: *Industrial reorganisation: cotton*, p. 579.
69. Bowden and Higgins, 'Short-time working and price maintenance', pp. 330–1.
70. Higgins and Toms, 'Firm structure and financial performance', p. 213.
71. Higgins, 'Rings, mules, and structural constraints'; Higgins, 'Re-equipment as a strategy for survival'.
72. H. Catling, *The spinning mule* (Newton Abbot, 1970), p. 189; S. Noguera, *Theory and practice of high drafting* (privately published, 1936), pp. 20–3; L. Tippett, *A portrait of the Lancashire cotton industry* (Oxford, 1969).
73. Procter and Toms, 'Industrial relations and technical change'.
74. Board of Trade, *An industrial survey of the Lancashire area (excluding Merseyside)* (London, 1932), p. 135.

75. *Economist*, 1930, p. 394.
76. D. Farnie and T. Abe, 'Japan, Lancashire and the Asian market for cotton manufactures, 1890–1990', in D. Farnie, T. Nakaoka, D. Jeremy, J. Wilson and T. Abe, eds., *Region and strategy in Britain and Japan* (London, 2000).
77. Toms, 'Windows of opportunity in the textile industry', p. 8.
78. Most companies avoided liquidation and indeed some continued to pay dividends; see the example of the large dividends paid by Lilac Mill in 1925 and 1926, in Thomas, *The provincial stock exchanges*, p. 160.
79. In both cases this amounted to funding dividends by running down reserves, a strategy likely to damage the interests of loan creditors.
80. Bamberg, 'The government, the banks, and the Lancashire cotton industry', app. 4.1, p. 122. Unfortunately, this data does not give the exact amount of debt owned by each company entering the LCC. It does, however, give a range of the amounts owed to creditors. By taking the mid point of each range, it is possible to calculate the average indebtedness of the 321 companies surveyed by Ryan and the average indebtedness of companies entering the LCC.
81. Robson, *The cotton industry*, Table 4, p. 338. Summing all the profits from 1935 to 1947 yields £109,339. This calculation makes no allowance for trading losses accumulated throughout the 1920s.
82. In this context our interpretation of the industry's twentieth-century performance does have some similarities with those recently advanced by Lorenz. However, while we agree that there was 'excess inertia', we view this as a rational strategy by the industry's businessmen to preserve their physical assets in order to be able to divest money capital as fully as possible, rather than simply as conservatism: E. Lorenz, 'Organisational inertia and competitive decline: the British cotton, shipbuilding and car industries, 1945–1975', *Industrial and Corporate Change*, 3 (1994), pp. 387–88.
83. J. Singleton, 'The decline of the cotton industry since 1940', in Rose, ed., *Lancashire cotton industry*, pp. 300–1.
84. For example, Barlow and Jones; Crosses and Winkworth; FCDSA; and Jackson and Steeple carried out schemes in 1936, 1944, 1942 and 1943 respectively: *Stock exchange official year-book*.
85. Filatotchev and Toms, 'Corporate governance, strategy and survival in a declining industry'. This conclusion is based on a survey of the Annual Returns (Form E) of a sample of twenty-nine companies from the period 1950–1965 from the BT31 file at the Public Record Office.
86. For evidence of capital market inefficiency in this period, see Higgins and Toms, 'Public subsidy and private divestment', p. 72, esp. n. 74.
87. Ibid., Fig. 1, p. 64.
88. [Political and Economic Planning], *Growth in the British economy* (London, 1960), p. 123.

89. Higgins and Toms, 'Public subsidy and private divestment', pp. 66–7.
90. Filatotchev and Toms, 'Corporate Governance, strategy and survival in a declining industry'. The evidence refers to a sample of twenty-nine firms taken from PRO BT31, 1950–65.
91. Annual Report and Accounts, 1950, Companies House.
92. Higgins and Toms, 'Public subsidy and private divestment', p. 68.
93. Average profits calculated from Cambridge University Companies Database. See also Greater Manchester County Record Office, LCC Annual Reports, 1953/4 for details of capital expenditure requirement.
94. L. Sandberg, *Lancashire in decline* (Columbus, OH; 1974); Lazonick, 'Competition, specialisation, and industrial decline'; Lazonick, 'Industrial organization and technological change'; Lazonick, 'The cotton industry'.
95. A comparative empirical study has shown that profit signals did not suggest the superiority of vertical integration. Higgins and Toms, 'Firm structure and financial performance'.
96. For an additional perspective on this point, see G. Saxonhouse and G. Wright, 'Stubborn mules and vertical integration: the disappearing constraint', *Economic History Review*, 40, 2nd. ser. (1987), pp. 87–94.
97. V. Barker, and I. Duhaime, 'Strategic change in the turnaround process: theory and empirical evidence', *Strategic Management Journal*, 18 (1997), pp. 13–38.
98. A number of contemporaries, especially during the inter-war years, were well aware of the vital importance of *first* removing excess capacity: G. C. Allen, *British industries and their organisation* (London, 1959), pp. 239–40; H. Clay, *Report on the position of the English cotton industry*, Confidential Report for Securities Management Trust (1931), p. 83. For Keynes, policies of short-time working and price maintenance merely delayed the introduction of much needed measures to reduce capacity: Keynes, 'Industrial reorganisation', pp. 590–98.
99. Mass and Lazonick, 'The British cotton industry and international competitive advantage'.

# Lancashire and the New Zealand market in the mid twentieth century: cotton, glass and locomotives

*John Singleton*

New Zealand was a distant but significant market for a number of Lancashire firms during the twentieth century. After discussing the salient features of the New Zealand business environment after the Second World War, three case studies will be presented. The first shows how the New Zealand government treated the interests of the Lancashire cotton industry during trade negotiations with Japan in the 1950s. The second examines the New Zealand investments of Pilkington Brothers, the famous glass-making firm from St Helens. The final case study deals with exports of electric and diesel-electric multiple units and locomotives to New Zealand from the English Electric plant at Preston.

While it would be unrealistic to make definitive judgments on the basis of three examples, the approach taken here highlights some of the commonly mentioned strengths and weaknesses of British and Lancashire manufacturing in the post-war decades. Old industries, including cotton, were unable to hang on to international markets; firms in apparently more dynamic industries, such as engineering, often struggled to develop reliable new products and deliver them on time in the face of stiff competition; yet some manufacturing firms continued to prosper, especially in commonwealth markets. It is difficult to weigh failures against successes. Debate on the overall performance of British industry after 1945 continues, with new contributions appearing at regular intervals.[1]

### Features of the New Zealand market

What was the attraction of the New Zealand market to companies from Britain, and from Lancashire in particular? New Zealanders

**Table 1:** Per capita GDP in New Zealand compared with the US and Australia (in 1990 international dollars)

|      | US    | Australia | New Zealand | NZ as % of US | NZ as % of Australia |
|------|-------|-----------|-------------|---------------|----------------------|
| 1900 | 4091  | 4013      | 4298        | 105           | 107                  |
| 1950 | 9561  | 7412      | 8456        | 88            | 114                  |
| 2000 | 28129 | 21540     | 16010       | 57            | 74                   |

Source: Angus Maddison, *The world economy: historical statistics* (Paris, 2003), pp. 85–7.

were very prosperous compared with the citizens of most empire or commonwealth countries. In 1950, moreover, real incomes in New Zealand were still above the Australian level. The New Zealand legal system was familiar, and there were many similarities between British and New Zealand tastes and ways of doing business. In an article on regional trading blocs, the economists Anderson and Norheim concluded that 'national languages, customs, and legal systems' have an important impact on the 'transactions costs of doing business with other nations'.[2]

There were and remain links between New Zealand and north-west England. One of New Zealand's most admired prime ministers, Richard 'King Dick' Seddon (1845–1906), came from Eccleston near St Helens. Seddon worked as an apprentice in the engineering industry in St Helens before emigrating to Australia and then New Zealand.[3] Shops in New Zealand continue to advertise 'Manchester' goods, meaning cotton textiles, even though they have been made in Asia for fifty years. *Coronation Street* was top of the New Zealand television ratings in early 2008 – a contemporary example of a successful Lancashire-made export.

At the same time, however, New Zealand was by no means a mass market. The population was small, growing from one million in the early years of the twentieth century to almost four million by the end. Though New Zealanders enjoyed an enviable standard of living and purchasing power for the first three-quarters of the twentieth century (Table 1), the economy faltered badly between the mid 1970s and early 1990s. New Zealand, Switzerland, and Mexico were the most sluggish economies in the developed world between 1970 and 2000, comparing actual performance with their long-term trends.[4] A substantial gap emerged between incomes in New Zealand and in Australia and western Europe.[5] Australia benefited from the discovery and exploitation of mineral wealth, especially in Western Australia, from the 1960s onwards. New Zealand had nothing to match this natural wealth, and became the poor relation.

Several institutional factors worked in favour of trade with Britain

|  | \multicolumn{7}{c}{*Destination (percentage of total exports)*} |
| --- | --- | --- | --- | --- | --- | --- | --- |
|  | *Australia* | *New Zealand* | *Canada* | *South Africa* | *United States* | *EEC (Six)* | *EFTA* |
| 1938 | 7.3 | 3.7 | 4.6 | 7.5 | 5.4 | – | – |
| 1946 | 5.8 | 2.9 | 3.6 | 7.8 | 4.1 | 14.6 | 11.8 |
| 1950 | 11.4 | 3.8 | 5.7 | 5.4 | 5.6 | 12.3 | 11.4 |
| 1955 | 9.6 | 4.7 | 4.8 | 5.6 | 6.6 | 14.1 | 10.4 |
| 1960 | 7.1 | 3.3 | 6.0 | 4.2 | 9.3 | 15.3 | 10.7 |
| 1965 | 5.8 | 2.6 | 4.2 | 5.4 | 10.5 | 20.0 | 12.5 |
| 1970 | 4.3 | 1.6 | 3.6 | 4.1 | 11.6 | 21.7 | 15.9 |

*Note*: EEC (Six) comprises Belgium, France, Germany, Italy, Luxemburg, and the Netherlands. East Germany is excluded after 1950; EFTA comprises Austria, Denmark (including the Faroes and Greenland), Liechtenstein, Norway (including Spitzbergen), Portugal (including Azores and Madeira), Sweden, and Switzerland.

*Source*: B. R. Mitchell, *British historical statistics* (Cambridge, 1988), pp. 453–4, 507–15.

**Table 2:** Britain's main export markets, 1938–70 in the mid twentieth century. Between the 1930s and 1970s tariff preferences gave some protection to imports from Britain and the commonwealth. Reciprocal concessions safeguarded the UK market for New Zealand dairy and meat exports. This system was known as imperial or commonwealth preference. The Lancashire cotton industry benefited considerably from protection in dominion markets – Australia, New Zealand, South Africa, and Canada – between the wars. Cotton textile exports from Lancashire to the dominions did not fall between 1909–13 and 1938 – an astonishing fact considering Lancashire's rout elsewhere – and their combined share of British cotton cloth exports increased from 6 per cent to 28 per cent over this period.[6] British preference remained important in New Zealand after it had dwindled in most other commonwealth countries, and did not disappear until after Britain's entry into the European Economic Community in 1973. The average percentage margin in New Zealand between the British preferential tariff and the most favoured nation (MFN) tariff was almost unchanged between 1952 and 1967.[7] Between 1945 and the late 1950s, New Zealand also used exchange controls and import licensing to discriminate against US products, on the grounds that US dollars were scarce; and against Japanese goods, since Japan was a former enemy and many of its products were deemed to be priced unfairly. Dollar discrimination was practiced throughout the sterling area, which consisted of countries that in effect pooled their foreign exchange reserves with Britain.

Table 2 shows that in the 1950s and early 1960s, the New Zealand market mattered considerably to British industry. Remarkably, sales of British products to New Zealand in 1955 were worth 70 per cent of sales to the US and 33 per cent of sales to the European 'Six' (France, West Germany, Italy, the Netherlands, Belgium and Luxemburg). However, New Zealand and other commonwealth countries became less important as trading partners when Britain was drawn into the European orbit in the 1960s and 1970s. Trade discrimination enabled British firms to achieve a higher initial market share in commonwealth markets after 1945, but did not affect the rate at which this market share was eroded during the 1950s. British industrial competitiveness was sliding throughout the world across an array of product groups. The rate at which markets were lost was quite similar in the sterling area (and imperial preference area) and in the rest of the world. Commonwealth markets seemed to be safe havens because they were disproportionately large at the start of the 1950s, but competition was becoming fierce.[8]

British penetration of the New Zealand market in the mid twentieth century would have been even greater in the absence of measures to encourage and safeguard the domestic manufacturing sector. For New Zealand manufacturers with small production runs and high costs, there was little hope of survival without government support and protection. In many product lines, the British preferential tariff was set at the level required to protect local industries. Quantitative restrictions were applied to the entry of British as well as foreign goods. Unlike Australia, the UK, and other developed countries, New Zealand retained quantitative import controls until 1984, though by the 1960s it no longer discriminated between suppliers. The purpose of these measures was to bolster the balance of payments, and create sufficient industrial jobs to maintain full employment, there being pessimism about the ability of the farming sector to absorb the growing workforce.[9]

Protectionism begot inward foreign direct investment. Official attitudes to foreign investment were ambivalent for nationalistic reasons, but New Zealand was short of capital, and British, Australian and American (but not Japanese) firms were made relatively welcome. As Jones has shown in his article on Cadburys between 1918 and 1939, British firms had a bias towards direct investment in empire countries, which was felt to be less risky. Cadburys established a successful manufacturing joint venture with a local firm in New Zealand, in 1930, after tariffs had been raised on chocolate products.[10] The performance of overseas subsidiaries and joint ventures in New Zealand was on average superior to that of local firms. Even so, few such establishments were able to achieve a minimum efficient scale of production because of the inadequate size of the domestic market.[11]

British tariff preferences had disappeared by the late 1970s. In the second half of the 1980s, New Zealand industries and overseas subsidiaries operating in New Zealand were exposed to the rigours of international competition. Quantitative import controls were scrapped and tariffs reduced as part of a wide-ranging package of free market reforms.[12] British firms no longer enjoyed any favours in New Zealand.

**Cotton**

As the New Zealand authorities began, albeit tentatively, to cultivate new trading partners in Asia, the safeguards enjoyed by British exporters were called into question. In the 1950s, Japan was the Asian market with the greatest potential as a destination for New Zealand primary commodity exports – wool, meat and dairy products.[13] Since agriculture was an influential sector in Japan, it was inevitable that New Zealand would be asked for significant reciprocal concessions on industrial items such as cotton textiles. New Zealand did not as yet accord MFN status to Japan. Japanese goods faced the general (or highest) level of tariff in New Zealand, western European and American goods encountered the MFN or intermediate level of tariffs, and imports from commonwealth countries benefited from low preferential rates. Quantitative controls also discriminated against Japan.

Japanese demands for improved access for their cotton textiles were a sticking point during the trade talks held in Wellington in June 1954. The Japanese argued that 'cotton piece goods would be the first item the Diet would look for when the approval of the agreement was under consideration', but New Zealand offered concessions on yarn alone.[14] Tokyo demanded that the tariff on Japanese cotton textiles be reduced to the MFN rate, and that quantitative discrimination against Japanese exports be abolished. (This would have reduced the margin between the general tariff and the British preferential tariff.) Cotton was one of the few industries in which the Japanese considered their firms to be competitive vis-à-vis Britain in the mid 1950s. After the loss of the massive Chinese market, which was denied to Japan after the Korean War and the imposition of US-inspired sanctions, Tokyo embarked on a desperate search for new markets, of which New Zealand, though small, was potentially one.[15]

New Zealand negotiators were embarrassed by Japanese demands and pointed out that 'the United Kingdom [cotton] manufacturers had strong agents in New Zealand who could cause political difficulties for the Government'.[16] Offending Britain would be dangerous in view of the importance of the UK food market, and the need for

The business of McGruer's household drapery & apparel store, Devon Street, New Plymouth; New Zealand was heavily reliant on imports for supplies of cotton textiles. 1920s–1930s. Photographer: William Stanley Oakley (W. S. Oakley Collection, Alexander Turnbull Library, Wellington, NZ)

British co-operation in regulating competition from suppliers such as Argentina in meat and Denmark in dairy produce. Ministers were equally concerned about the domestic political reaction to concessions that could undermine New Zealand jobs. Although the New Zealand treasury felt that Lancashire no longer merited special protection, and referred to the desirability of more consumer choice, more cautious counsels prevailed. New Zealand merely offered to apply existing import-licensing arrangements to Japanese cotton goods in a 'liberal' spirit, while leaving the tariff on woven cottons at the general level. The British did not participate directly in the June 1954 negotiations, but they were lurking in the background. The Commonwealth Relations Office wrote to the New Zealand government after these talks to say that Britain would oppose tariff concessions on cotton yarn and piece goods, silks, rayon, and certain other products. At that time, New Zealand was the fourth-largest export market for the Lancashire cotton industry. Wellington was invited to list the items on which it proposed to reduce tariffs, so that the British could 'examine the whole matter thoroughly'.[17] The government continued to hesitate and the opportunity to reach a settlement with Japan was lost, albeit temporarily.

By 1958, New Zealand's bargaining position had deteriorated, and ministers were more willing to make concessions. Australia concluded a trade agreement with Japan in 1957, obtaining better access for its wool and foodstuffs, and thus placing New Zealand exporters at a disadvantage.[18] In renewed talks with New Zealand, the Japanese demanded MFN tariff treatment and 'non-scheduled country' import-licensing status across the board. At first, New Zealand hoped to restrict concessions to selected goods, while excluding sensitive textile items, engineering goods, and motor vehicles. But Tokyo insisted on 'more reasonable treatment [of] Japanese textiles having regard to the United Kingdom supplies'.[19] When it became clear that the Japanese would make no agricultural concessions without an improved offer, New Zealand caved in and accepted their industrial demands in their entirety. Henceforth the only protection for British exports, including cotton goods, would be the margin between the MFN and preferential tariff rates. A British Cotton Board mission visited Wellington in 1959 to protest against increased imports from Japan, but such complaints were in vain.

By the late 1950s, the British government was losing interest in fighting for cotton-industry survival in external markets.[20] The New Zealand market was lost in the 1960s, though not entirely because of Japanese competition. British exports of cotton cloth to New Zealand fell from 35 million square yards in 1955 to 25 million in 1960, and 13 million in 1965.[21] By 1965–6, Japan supplied 35.5 per cent of New Zealand's imports of cotton fabrics suitable for the manufacture of apparel, while Hong Kong supplied 25.7 per cent, and the UK 10.4 per cent.[22] As was the case in the UK market itself, competition was now coming from other parts of the commonwealth.

**Pilkington Brothers**

One of Lancashire's most prominent and consistently successful firms, Pilkington Brothers,[23] made the most of the protected conditions on offer in the New Zealand market in the 1950s and 1960s. A wholly-owned subsidiary, Pilkington Brothers (New Zealand) Ltd, opened a safety-glass factory at Taita near Wellington in 1953. In association with their Australian partners, Australian Consolidated Industries (ACI), Pilkingtons also bought a sheet-glass factory under development at Whangarei, north of Auckland, in 1963. By such moves the St Helens firm consolidated its position in New Zealand.

Foreign direct investment (FDI) by Lancashire firms is a neglected topic. Timmins's survey of Lancashire's industrial history looks inward rather than outward, as does the work by Wilson and Singleton on the Manchester industrial district. In a volume comparing Lancashire and the Kansai region of Japan, Jeremy, Abe and Sasaki pay scant attention to outward FDI by Lancashire firms. Clearly this is an area to Pilkingtons and ACI, who then proceeded to make technical modifications and brought in an English start-up team. New Zealand Window Glass, as the new joint venture was called, began operating in 1964, after receiving assurances from the government of protection from domestic and import competition.[32]

Pilkingtons dug in with the intention of staying in New Zealand for the long term, as Cadburys had done in the 1930s. In 1974, Sir Alistair Pilkington reported to shareholders that the company's New Zealand businesses were thriving,[33] though conditions in the later 1970s and 1980s would be more troublesome. Other investments followed, including factories in Auckland, Christchurch, and Hamilton. However, protection was gradually withdrawn from local manufacturing after 1984, under a new free-market policy regime. Tight monetary policy created additional problems for firms attempting to compete with imports. The Whangarei plant of New Zealand Window Glass – the last of its type in operation in the developed world – closed in 1991, being unable to resist Chinese competition.[34] The Taita safety-glass plant continued in production, despite the gradual disintegration of the New Zealand auto industry, surviving by concentrating on exports, and serving other users. A NZ$15 million (about £6m) upgrade to Pilkingtons' New Zealand facilities was underway in 1997.[35] Taita finally closed in 2003 but other facilities stayed open.

Furnace operator Gary Collins at the Pilkington Brothers glass factory, Wingate, Lower Hutt, Wellington, where a fire had broken out the previous evening. 1984. Photographer: Mervyn Griffiths (*Dominion Post* Collection, Alexander Turnbull Library, Wellington, NZ)

Pilkingtons arguably ceased to be a 'Lancashire' firm in 2006, when the company de-listed from the London Stock Exchange and was taken over by Nippon Sheet Glass (NSG).[36] NSG was not interested in the Australian and New Zealand operations, and Pilkington Australasia was sold to CSR, an Australian conglomerate, in 2007.[37] Pilkingtons had not failed in New Zealand. Unlike many firms that had come to New Zealand during the import substitution era, Pilkingtons weathered the storm accompanying economic liberalization after 1984. Notwithstanding the collapse of the New Zealand auto industry, they were able to introduce new products and develop new markets both domestically and abroad.

## English Electric

English Electric, a product of the merger boom after the First World War, included facilities in Yorkshire and the Midlands as well as in Lancashire. The Lancashire side of the business grew out of the former United Electric Car Company (later Dick, Kerr & Co.) of Preston, which was best known for its trams.[38] English Electric was a diversified electrical-engineering company by the 1940s and 1950s, with involvement in the production of diesel and electric railway locomotives, aircraft, heavy electrical plant, and, for a time, computers. The company's main Preston works sought to become a leading producer of diesel and electric locomotives. New Zealand was an early, and one might say experimental, market.

New Zealand was anxious to obtain secure access to British railway technology and production capacity in the 1940s. Post-war governments hoped to reduce coal imports, contain labour costs, and increase traffic density by modernizing the state-owned New Zealand Railways (NZR).[39] As the design and construction of electric and diesel-electric power units were beyond the capabilities of NZR workshops, the government required an overseas supplier, and entered into an exclusive arrangement with English Electric. When this British firm failed to deliver, NZR switched their custom to General Motors (GM).[40]

Acting through the consulting engineers Cory-Wright & Salmon, NZR signed an exclusive ten-year contract with English Electric to supply 'electric rolling stock' in 1946. NZR intended to purchase electric locomotives and electric multiple units for Wellington and Hutt suburban services. English Electric had already supplied this type of equipment to New Zealand (as well as to Southern Railways in the UK) in the 1930s. The New Zealanders were open to an exclusive contract because British industry was inundated with orders after the war, and desperately short of labour, materials, and capacity.[41]

New-class DE diesel-electric locomotive being unloaded at the Wellington wharves. 1951. Photographer unidentified (*Evening Post* Collection, Alexander Turnbull Library, Wellington, NZ)

New Zealand was reluctant to turn to North America for supplies because of the dollar crisis facing the sterling area. The government was under British pressure to reduce dollar purchases to a minimum. Without an exclusive agreement with a British firm, it was feared that NZR would be unable to obtain a secure supply of motive power. English Electric's chairman, Sir George Nelson, promised that NZR would not be charged more than any other customer for comparable products. The first order under this arrangement was for electric locomotives and electric multiple units (EMUs) for suburban services around Wellington.

In the late 1940s, there was growing interest in the possibility of electrifying the North Island Main Trunk (NIMT) between Auckland and Wellington. Although English Electric had limited experience in the manufacture of main-line electric and diesel-electric locomotives, the Solicitor-General of New Zealand advised that the 1946 agreement probably applied to all types of electric and diesel-electric locomotives.[42] In short, the government's freedom to

An A-class locomotive towing multi-unit train coaches for the Hutt Valley electrical rail. 1951. Photographer unidentified (*Evening Post* Collection, Alexander Turnbull Library, Wellington, NZ)

choose another supplier was constrained by the drafting of the 1946 agreement.

While the government pondered NIMT electrification, the overall shortage of motive power on NZR became acute. As an interim solution, an order was placed with English Electric in 1951 for thirty-one 1500-horsepower (hp) diesel-electric locomotives. English Electric had supplied two main-line 1600-hp diesels to the London Midland and Scottish Railway in 1947,[43] but this form of traction was still an experimental technology in Britain. Fears were expressed that English Electric would struggle to adapt their power units for use on NZR's narrow three-foot-six-inch gauge. With the Solicitor-General's ruling still in ministerial minds, however, the treasury's suggestion that a more experienced French manufacturer be approached was rejected, and the government resolved to stick with English Electric.

Difficulties with the diesel-electrics ordered in 1951 tarnished the reputation of English Electric in New Zealand. NZR was told that the entire order would be fulfilled within twenty-eight months, but English Electric made slow progress with design and construction. (To be fair to the company, NZR changed the order to a mixture of 1500-hp and 750-hp locomotives.) The first locomotive was not completed until April 1954, almost two years behind schedule. The English Electric locomotives proved unreliable in service. Although the New Zealand Treasury recommended the cancellation of the final eleven locomotives, the Solicitor-General insisted that, despite poor performance, English Electric's contract should not be broken.

In September 1954, W. E. Hodges, chairman of the New Zealand Railways Commission, recommended that, in view of English Electric's shortcomings, the ten-year agreement should be treated as no longer binding. He said that tenders should be requested globally for the manufacture of additional diesel-electrics. After consulting the Solicitor-General again, the government endorsed Hodges's strategy, and English Electric offered no objection. NZR still faced a chronic shortage of motive power. According to the chief mechanical engineer (CME), the 'protracted delivery of the orders already given to this company is the main factor in our present desperate power position ... I cannot but feel that this Company has let us down badly and is mainly responsible for the present mess we are in.'[44]

In October 1954, NZR invited tenders for the production of diesel-electric locomotives for the NIMT, the earlier electrification plans having been postponed indefinitely. Firms in the US, Britain, Canada, Belgium, Italy, and Australia submitted tenders. The Canadian, Australian, and British tenders were exempt from duty, but a 20 per cent notional tariff was applied to the American and European tenders. GM still submitted the three lowest tenders, offering to supply locomotives from their US and Canadian plants, and also, through their Australian licensee, Clyde Engineering.[45] The North American GM plants offered delivery within eight months. English Electric's tender was only the third-lowest from a British firm. The CME commented that the English Electric submission 'compare[d] very unfavourably in manufactured cost against all the North American tenders'. Moreover, it was 'preposterous' of English Electric to promise that delivery would commence in February 1956, given past experience.[46] NZR ordered fifteen locomotives each from GM in Canada and the US. GM diesel-electric locomotives became the standard on NZR.

English Electric achieved creditable results when producing diesel-electric locomotives for the modernization of British Railways in the late 1950s and 1960s.[47] In the 1950s, however, new entrants, including English Electric, were at a considerable disadvantage vis-à-vis GM, which had been making large numbers of diesel-electric locomotives since the 1930s. In 1954 GM built approximately 750 diesel units,[48] which amounted to a 75 per cent market share in the US. GM's success was based on size, modern management, aggressive marketing, and technical expertise with the internal combustion engine. Designs were simplified to facilitate bulk production.[49] Smaller British and European producers could not offer equivalent value for money. (It was a similar story in the aircraft industry.) NZR noted that GM diesel-electric locomotives were the cheapest and most reliable in the world, and already provided excellent service in Australia. Unlike English Electric, GM had successfully modified their basic product to suit narrow-gauge operation.

While the long-term contract between NZR and English Electric had given this firm a protected market in New Zealand, teething troubles and delays undermined their reputation, and in the mid 1950s the New Zealand authorities transferred their business to the more reliable GM. Other Lancashire engineering firms were somewhat more successful in meeting the expectations of New Zealand customers. For example, Walmsleys, a Bury firm, supplied the newsprint machine for the giant Murupara pulp and paper mill in the 1950s. The owners, Tasman Pulp and Paper, were sufficiently pleased with this equipment to order another from the same source in the early 1960s.[50] As NZR and the New Zealand government had anticipated in the 1940s, fulfilling their demands was not always high on the priorities of the British. For example, Cammell Laird (Birkenhead) put in the lowest tender in 1962–3 to build a frigate for New Zealand, but the admiralty insisted that work on the Polaris nuclear submarine programme should take precedence, and the frigate order was allocated to Harland & Wolff instead.[51]

## Conclusion

Lancashire's economic and business ties with New Zealand in the mid twentieth century were not insignificant. New Zealand had been a refuge for British cotton textile exports in the 1930s, and remained important to this industry in the mid 1950s. But it was unrealistic to expect that the New Zealand market for cotton goods could be retained permanently in the face of stiff Asian competition. New Zealand looked to Britain for heavy-engineering products, especially in the 1940s and early 1950s, when dollar rationing meant that US alternatives were passed over. Although firms such as English Electric established strong positions in the New Zealand market, they could not sustain them in the event of failure to perform. For companies willing to invest and remain in New Zealand, including Pilkingtons, there were even better prospects, especially in the protectionist era before 1984, but few Lancashire firms were multinationals. In conclusion, it would be worth paying more attention to the business and investment links between Lancashire and the old commonwealth. Examining these markets would add to our knowledge of Britain's international economic relations, and enable us to observe the successes and failures of Lancashire business from an unfamiliar perspective.

32. The *Dominion*, 5 Dec. 1963, 28 May 1964; [Wellington] *Evening Post*, 2 Dec. 1963, 22 Apr. 1964; Detailed terms of glassworks sale released: press statement by the Prime Minister, 29 May 1963, ANZ, IC, W1955, record 69/1, pt 3.
33. A Review by Sir Alistair Pilkington, Chairman of Pilkington Brothers Limited, circulated with the company's report and accounts for the year ended 31 Mar. 1974.
34. *New Zealand Herald*, 13 Feb. 1991.
35. *Evening Post*, 25 Feb. 1997.
36. http://www.pilkington.com/about+pilkington/company+briefing/company+history/2000+onwards.htm, accessed 23 Jan. 2008.
37. http://www.pilkington.com.au/pilkington+in+australia/default.htm, accessed 23 Jan. 2008.
38. Robert Jones and Oliver Marriott, *Anatomy of a merger: a history of G.E.C., A.E.I. and English Electric* (London, 1970); John F. Wilson, 'A strategy of expansion and combination: Dick, Kerr & Co., 1897–1914', *Business History*, 37 (1985), pp. 26–41.
39. David Leitch and Bob Stott, *New Zealand Railways: the first 125 years* (Auckland, 1988).
40. John Singleton, 'British engineering and the New Zealand market, 1945–60', *Business History*, 44 (2002), pp. 121–40.
41. Alec Cairncross, *Years of recovery: British economic policy 1945–51* (London, 1985); Helen Mercer, Neil Rollings and Jim Tomlinson, eds., *Labour governments and private industry: the experience of 1945–1951* (Edinburgh, 1992).
42. Singleton, 'British engineering', p. 125.
43. Michael Bonavia, *The birth of British Rail* (London, 1979), p. 63.
44. Singleton, 'British engineering', p. 126.
45. There was also a joint bid from General Electric and the New Zealand rolling-stock manufacturer A. G. Price.
46. Singleton, 'British engineering', p. 127.
47. Terence R. Gourvish, *British railways, 1948–73* (Cambridge, 1986), pp. 285–8.
48. A locomotive could consist of several units.
49. Thomas G. Marx, 'Technological change and the theory of the firm: the American locomotive industry, 1920–1955', *Business History Review*, 50 (1976), pp. 1–24; John K. Brown, *The Baldwin locomotive works, 1831–1915* (Baltimore, 1995), pp. 231–3.
50. Morris Guest and John Singleton, 'The Murupara project and industrial development in New Zealand, 1945–63', *Australian Economic History Review*, 39 (1999), pp. 54–5, 60, 63.
51. John Singleton, 'Vampires to Skyhawks: military aircraft and frigate purchases by New Zealand, 1950–70', *Australian Economic History Review*, 42 (2002), pp. 197–8.

# Freemasonry and civic identity: municipal politics, business and the rise of Blackpool from the 1850s to the First World War

*David Martín López and John K. Walton*

Freemasonry is obviously important to British business history, given the significant part Freemasons played in economic activity in practically every town and city, especially from the mid nineteenth century to the mid twentieth; but it has been systematically neglected by business historians. Andrew Prescott has argued that, 'It was at this point (the mid 1850s) that freemasonry becomes an overwhelmingly middle-class vehicle', important to 'the cohesion of the social elites in provincial towns and cities', and acquiring by 1890 'its multiplicity of orders, its lavish masonic halls, its newspapers and burgeoning professional membership.' By the end of the century freemasonry 'was settled in its position in society', with lodges represented prominently in civic ceremonial processions, a 'formidable commercial infrastructure' supporting its activities, and growing involvement in philanthropy. Its middle-class membership was extending to include professional groups in public services, such as town hall administrators, police officers and teachers.[1]

Freemasonry was undoubtedly a power in the land, although the geographical and chronological distribution and patterning of its lodges, their social composition, and their influence on business relationships and the policies of (especially) local government have yet to be mapped. Peter Clark's work on associational culture before 1800 has helped to lay the early modern groundwork.[2] But much of the recent academic work on the history of freemasonry is grounded in histories of science and ideas, radical politics and the emergence of the 'public sphere' in eighteenth-century Europe, and in examining its role in the expansion of the British empire, rather than in the growth of business networks or the development of urban economic and social institutions.[3]

Freemasonry is also almost invisible in histories of local government. Hennock's pioneering *Fit and proper persons* examines the economic background and cultural formation of Victorian and Edwardian civic elites but is almost silent about freemasonry. The same applies to subsequent reconstructions of Victorian and Edwardian municipal politics and urban middle-class culture. Gunn acknowledges freemasonry's importance in this period, but emphasizes its decreasing visibility and how its 'activities became increasingly closed and secretive in the course of the nineteenth century', while McKibbin delineates the pervasive, if low-key, influences of masonic sociability in small towns and suburbia during the inter-war years.[4] Close masonic social links between municipal councillors and officials have been noticed in, for example, Wolverhampton and Norwich.[5] The evidence for Freemasons' involvement in local government, whether as elected representatives or municipal officials, is well worth pursuing. Scott's reinterpretation of Glasgow's Necropolis cemetery has recently drawn attention to masonic influences on its layout and iconography, and thereby to the strength of freemasonry among the city's Victorian civic and business elite. Glasgow cannot have been alone in this.[6] On some assumptions it is interesting that recent investigations of 'corruption' in Victorian and early twentieth-century municipal government mention Methodists but not Freemasons.[7] There were extensive connections between business and urban government during this period of rapid urban and industrial development, strong civic pride, deep municipal penetration of urban economies, and expansion of freemasonry through the English provinces. These themes should not be considered in isolation.

This examination of the relationship between freemasonry and the growth of Blackpool makes a significant contribution to this story. It examines the extent to which Freemasons were present and involved in the town's public companies and municipal corporation, and investigates the iconography of freemasonry in Blackpool's public spaces and buildings.[8] Blackpool was neither a great city nor a typical industrial centre; but it was prominent among the fastest-growing towns of Victorian and Edwardian England. When the railway arrived in 1846 it was a mere village; in 1851 it had just over 2,500 April residents. By 1911 it was Britain's sixth most populous seaside resort (if we include Birkdale with Southport), with around 60,000 off-season residents. It attracted around four million visitors per year, far more than any rival. Most would stay for up to a week in one of over 4,000 unpretentious lodging- or boarding-houses. The story of its late Victorian and Edwardian growth, reaching a crescendo in the 1890s, has been fully examined elsewhere. A feature of its development was sustained investment in the 'pleasure palaces' of popular entertainment, especially the three piers, the Winter Gardens and, from 1894, the emblematic Tower. These initiatives were funded by 'popular capitalism' or 'shareholder democracy', with lengthy shareholders' registers listing hundreds of small investors from all over northern England. The companies were run by a mixture of local and external directors, drawn especially from Blackpool, Manchester and London.[9]

Blackpool's rise also depended on the proactive role of local government, through the Local Board of Health of 1851, the Improvement Commission of 1853, and the incorporation of the town as a municipal borough in 1876, with an elected council of twenty-four (including aldermen) whose numbers were doubled in 1898. The local authority moved from providing the basic utilities and civic improvements that were (eventually) common to almost all Victorian urban governments, to investing in amenities and attractions to enhance the growing resort's attractiveness and competitiveness. Particularly important were the expensive investments in building, widening and maintaining Blackpool's marine promenade from the mid 1860s onwards, and the securing in 1879 of the right to levy an advertising rate, which also funded special attractions to extend the season, culminating in the autumn illuminations which were inaugurated in 1912.[10]

This was not 'municipal socialism' in the usual sense: it was also 'municipal capitalism', using the local authority to provide services and amenities that underpinned the attractions of the resort and made it competitive, thereby subsidizing holiday businesses, from piers and pleasure palaces to seaside landladies, by providing necessary services that were unlikely to generate a profit on their own account. This was an early, local and successful form of public-private partnership, depending on overlapping membership between businesses and the council. Relevant business expertise was often valued, indeed viewed as essential, on the local authority committees that made the key decisions.[11] A by-product of this might be mutual agreements among interested parties to relax regulatory regimes to serve their purposes: an investigation into the workings of the Building Plans Committee during the late 1880s and early 1890s suggested that not only did building-industry representatives dominate its workings, but they colluded in infringing the building by-laws. Similar suspicions were voiced about the power of the 'drink interest' over the Watch Committee, which oversaw licensing issues.[12]

Blackpool enjoyed an alliance between locally-run businesses, friendship and interest groups, and the local authority. This pattern was particularly important for health and pleasure resorts, which needed to sustain an attractive and well-policed environment to attract and retain visitors. Success depended on collaboration between local businesses and municipal government, when most entertainment and catering businesses were locally based and municipalities had considerable autonomy, subject to central government approval for major capital projects, public order and policing initiatives such as local by-laws, and new fields of municipal expenditure.[13] Links between business and government were close and sustained, with business leaders actively engaged in urban government and voluntary organizations, providing opportunities for social interaction and networking.[14] The sense in which towns and cities were seen to be masters of their own destiny gave added purpose and drive to civic institutions. Freemasonry fitted neatly into this broader picture.

We have satisfactory explanations for the rise of Blackpool as the world's first working-class seaside resort, involving the interaction between demand from a populous, prosperous and expanding industrial hinterland, local openness to innovation and enterprise, and the early availability of mass transport systems.[15] Central to our understanding is the nature of Blackpool's business model and its successful pioneering of a form of public-private partnership, lubricated by the connections between business interests and council membership, which extended to holiday industry infrastructure, attractions (where they complemented private enterprise rather than competing with it), and publicity. Comparisons can be made with development patterns elsewhere, especially in the US (including Coney Island and Atlantic City).[16] But there is a further dimension to the story.

The missing link in explanations for Blackpool's spectacular late-Victorian and Edwardian growth is the role of freemasonry. Not only were Masons prominent among local business and political elites, acting together to promote their own interests and the growth of the town and its holiday industry; they were also involved in creating important parts of the urban fabric, and in presenting Blackpool's image to a wider public, through their contribution to the town's motto and original coat of arms, to its advertising and to its architecture. We trace this missing thread in Blackpool's history through council membership and positions of municipal power, entertainment company promoters and interlocking directorships, and surviving visual and architectural traces. Finally, we speculate on the opportunities this approach presents for a fuller understanding of the inter-relationships between business and municipal history.

Freemasonry came to Blackpool early. Two early initiates of the first lodge in the area, constituted in 1825, were Blackpool freeholders. In 1847 the revived and transferred Lodge of Economy, founded in Garstang in 1830, met for the first time at the new Beach

Hotel, and early recruits included two hoteliers, the physician John Cocker, and Blackpool's controversial first vicar, William Thornber, all of whom were to be active on the Improvement Commission and Local Board of Health. But this initiative failed to prosper, and in 1857 several of its members joined the new Clifton lodge (No. 703), set up by members of the Concord lodge in Preston. The first annual masonic ball was held in 1859 at the Clifton Arms Hotel.[17] Clifton lodge was supplemented in 1873 by Blackpool lodge (No. 1476), by West Lancashire Century lodge (No. 2349) in 1890, and by St John's lodge (No. 2825) in 1900. Further foundations followed the First World War, and Blackpool became a stronghold of the craft. A history of Clifton lodge suggests that its mid Victorian membership 'must have read like a "Who's Who" of Blackpool'. In 1888 local Freemasons acquired land in the town centre for a masonic hall, which opened ten years later to amused commentary on the inaugural procession in the local *Blackpool Gazette*, whose editor was himself a Mason: 'Who will number themselves among the detractors of Freemasonry when the Craft can turn out such a gathering of good looking, prosperous and paunchy gentlemen as paraded our streets on Saturday afternoon?' Blackpool's Freemasons already had a conspicuous record of processional activity on public occasions, including the laying of the North Pier foundation stone in 1863 and the Promenade opening ceremony in 1870. The foundation stone ceremony of the masonic hall in May 1898, combined with that of St Paul's Church on the North Shore, was a spectacular occasion for the local establishment. Among the 300 people in attendance at the service at the St Paul's site that preceded the masonic hall opening was Blackpool's Chief Constable, J. C. Derham; two of his inspectors had to marshal the procession. The Provincial Grand Lodge had already met at the central Christ Church schools, and the vicar of Christ Church, Revd C. H. Wainwright, led the service at St Paul's. Wainwright was the father of a recently deceased local councillor and Conservative parliamentary candidate, H. H. Wainwright, after whom the main Blackpool Conservative Club was named. Tom Gallon Lumb, an important figure in Blackpool's business and entertainment worlds and a future mayor and freeman of the borough, represented the architects Garlick and Sykes, who had their fingers in many Blackpool pies, while Fielding Brothers, the contractors, were among Blackpool's biggest building firms, constructed many of the residential streets around the church, and had contributed to its building fund. On this high-profile occasion we can see how senior Masons were present among, and interacted with, business leaders from the powerful entertainment and building industries, and with the Church of England, the Conservative Party, and the local forces

Freemasons were disproportionately involved in the two biggest entertainment companies, the Winter Gardens of 1875 and Tower of 1891. At least six Winter Gardens directors, including the prime mover Dr W. H. Cocker, were Freemasons and local councillors. So were John Bickerstaffe, the central figure in completing the Tower, and his ally on the board Dr A. J. Anderson. The close relationship between the Tower and its abortive Manx counterpart the Douglas Head Suspension Bridge Company, with four directors and ten foundation shareholders in common, is significant given the latter's close identification with freemasonry, as demonstrated by the foundation stone ceremony in October 1890 for which over 300 Masons sailed to the Isle of Man.[26] But neither the Tower nor the Winter Gardens had a formal masonic presence at their lavish processional foundation stone and opening ceremonies.[27] Sir Matthew White Ridley, who officiated at the Tower ceremony, was a prominent Freemason, but also the MP for the Blackpool division of Lancashire. Further Freemasons active in entertainment companies were the controversial builder and land speculator James Cardwell, a director of the Grand Theatre, and the waxworks proprietor Elias Fletcher. W. G. Bean, the moving spirit behind the Edwardian development of the Pleasure Beach amusement park, was also a Freemason, as was Thomas Sergenson, the founder of the Grand Theatre, who was never a councillor but had close friendship links with John Bickerstaffe and his allies.[28] Alderman Joseph Heap was the long-serving Chairman of the Finance Committee. Sir Albert Lindsay Parkinson (as he became), builder, government contractor, three-times mayor of Blackpool and later MP for the town, was another prominent Freemason, whose contributions to Blackpool's development included a central role in organizing the pioneer Aviation Meeting of 1909 and the purchase (in 1920) of the land for what became Stanley Park.[29] Several high-ranking municipal officials were also Freemasons, including the long-serving and influential Town Clerk Thomas Loftos, an equally long-serving Borough Treasurer, and the Advertising Manager.[30] This will be the tip of the iceberg.

The Freemasons on the council were longer-serving and more influential than their peers. They served on the council for longer than average (thirteen and a half years against twelve and a half), and many achieved civic honours. Fourteen of the first forty-two mayors of Blackpool were Freemasons active on the council. Some, such as Cocker, Cardwell and James Fish, served multiple terms. Half of those local men who were granted the Freedom of the Borough before 1950 were also Freemasons whose service on the council dated from before the First World War.[31]

The environments of council decision-making also furthered

Masonic influence. The Blackpool lodge, No. 1476, met at the Clifton Arms from its consecration in 1874 until 1899, when the new masonic hall opened. It is probably no coincidence that an inner elite of local councillors used to meet at the same premises before each council meeting, to discuss the agenda and decide on favoured courses of action.[32] In the late nineteenth century, the council chamber itself was dominated by an inner circle of aldermen and senior councillors, with distinctive dress codes and assertive ways of contributing to debate, among whom the friendship groups surrounding the Freemason W. H. Cocker and the Winter Gardens in the late 1870s and early 1880s, and his fellow Mason John Bickerstaffe and the Tower Company in the 1890s, contained strong masonic cores. The latter group included the Roman Catholic R. B. Mather, and it was not necessary to be a Freemason to become (informally) attached to either of them. Moreover, the doubling in numbers of the council from 1898 onwards diluted the intimidatory power of such groups. We can draw attention to these matters, but we cannot assume that they operated either universally or mechanistically. They were part of a wider web of shifting influences and relationships, alongside (for example) the Conservative clubs, the Literary and Philosophical Society or the Tradesmen's Association, all of which were as powerful numerically as the Freemasons.[33] This brings us to the wider cultural influence of freemasonry in Blackpool, as expressed through art and architecture.

## The aesthetics of freemasonry

Freemasonry in nineteenth-century England was unusual in its visible participation in the active social, economic and cultural life of the country. Elsewhere in Europe, for political and religious reasons, masonic activity was confined to the private sphere. In some countries it was the object of severe governmental repression; but in Britain it benefited from an atmosphere of freedom of thought and association. This distinctive situation of free masonic association encouraged an unusual openness towards lay society in Britain throughout the Victorian and Edwardian period, with highly visible participation in public events, philanthropy, processions and opening ceremonies for public buildings. This allowed the display of masonic art, architecture and iconography to take a very different form from the rest of Europe.

Thus, in England, the distinctive masonic aesthetic associated with architecture, urban design and the arts did not need to challenge the established order. The freedom enjoyed by freemasonry meant that it could and indeed *must* interact with contemporary British society through its buildings, funerary monuments, paintings and furniture. This masonic aesthetic was expressed by symbolic elements through which the internal workings of lodge meetings made themselves visible to communicate an understanding of freemasonry's purpose.

The town of Blackpool can be understood as an articulated expression of masonic aesthetics, in the context of the high level of public masonic activity in Victorian and Edwardian society, closely bound up with commerce, education, industry and politics. While in Catholic countries like Italy, Spain or Portugal the public display of masonic symbols required a certain secrecy or disguise, in Britain there was no need for the subversive encoding of such symbols. Indeed, the ease with which masonic expression fitted into places like Blackpool meant that it was not necessary to put on a forced display of masonic features to indicate the presence of the Order. The symbols were deployed in a more restrained manner, precisely expressing their intentions, and displayed in a cross-section of public places: cemeteries, churches, libraries, schools and town halls. An example is the eclectic simplicity of the masonic hall in Adelaide Street, a work by John Nuttall whose foundation stone was laid in

*Masonic Hall, Upper Adelaide Street, Blackpool, by J. A. Nuttall, 1898. This was built to provide a common meeting place for all the town's Lodges. The rational composition, partly compromised by the additions of the 1950s, embodies a functional simplicity unusual in projects of this kind, which at that time normally went in for Gothic eclecticism, or allusions to the Temple of Jerusalem or the English Gothic past*

1898. A square and compass, in the frieze that takes the place of a pediment, provide the only direct external reference to the symbols of the Order.

We shall return to this building; but before examining the nature of masonic symbolism and involvement in several important public Blackpool locations, we need some background and context. From its beginnings, masonic architecture drew upon numerous symbols from different cultures, professions and religions. The enormous syncretic growth of masonic symbolism since the eighteenth century, drawing on oriental influences and the cultural mingling of hitherto exotic regions, was accompanied by a diversity of interpretations.[34] As Cirlot points out, 'In immersing ourselves in symbolism, […] one of our essential concerns is […] to avoid the confusion of phenomena which might seem identical when they only look similar or are merely superficially related.'[35] This occurs in masonic symbolism because it acts as a double language, for the uninitiated and for members of the Brotherhood. Many symbolic elements of freemasonry are not only drawn from speculative masonry but also from a multiplicity of aesthetic influences, whether oriental, religious, mythological, alchemical or founded in craft skills. But such motifs retain an explicit meaning in the hands of a masonic artist or architect who is aware of their iconographic and formative context, or of a committed Freemason who grasps their symbolic importance within the lodge. This applies even more to precise masonic symbolism, even when it can still be read in other ways by an outsider.

Nothing in freemasonry is arbitrary.[36] Although the symbols varied according to the country or specific lodge, the aesthetic grammar of rules and rituals was shared by all. Universal symbols included (for example) the triangle, the five-pointed star, the hammer or mallet, the square, the compass, the acacia branch and the columns, although the triangle and square were always the most prevalent, along with the compass, the latter two joined together and often displaying a 'G' in the middle of the space left by the combination of the figures,[37] understood as denoting Geometry or the initial letter of the word 'God'.

## Masonic art and architecture in Blackpool

Excellent illustrations of the openness of Victorian society to freemasonry can be found in Blackpool. We begin with the tombs of the municipal Layton cemetery, a popular Sunday afternoon promenade in the absence of a public park, where many councillors who were Freemasons, and other members of local lodges, were buried from 1873 onwards. The local monumental mason, John Wray,

Blackpool Town Hall. As the flagship building of the town's local authority, it deploys emblems alluding to power and justice, to the sea and the sun, which had a double meaning because of their masonic significance

was himself a Freemason, and tombstone patterns were adapted to display a sequence of masonic emblems: Pythagoras' Theorem, the square and compass denoting the grade of master, the masonic handshake, statues of liberty, Celtic crosses, and so on. The graves of twenty-one councillors who were also Freemasons have masonic references carved into their memorial stones.[38]

We pursue the argument through a variety of public buildings in Blackpool, starting with the Town Hall itself. The creation of a new borough council required a town hall, which served not only as the administrative centre of local government, but also as the architectural, artistic and ideological emblem of the new authority. Although the rhythms of masonic ritual centred on the Temple, their involvement in municipal politics, economy and culture might be such that masonic aesthetics would pervade the public buildings of the town, as in Blackpool. Architects such as Sir Horace Jones[39] and William Hill[40] imparted masonic characteristics to their town halls and other public buildings.

Blackpool Town Hall (1895–1900) is a distinctive case. Emerging effectively out of nothing, with no local precedent for such a building,

*Sculptural relief at the main entrance to Blackpool Town Hall: an allegorical representation of Justice and the goddess Athena, recurrent motifs in masonic symbolism. Justice, together with Prudence, Fortitude and Moderation, are the fundamental moral pillars of freemasonry*

it had to meet the expectations of a rapidly-developing town of a new kind, representing the popular tourist industry of northern England. In doing so, it responded to the strong masonic business and political influences in the town, following distinctive aesthetic parameters that reflected the hegemonic weight of local freemasonry at the time. It was constructed to the plans of Potts, Son & Hennings, between 1895 and 1900.[41] This practice was commissioned subsequently for the Blackpool Municipal Secondary School.[42]

The principal facade of the Town Hall, in an eclectic style, is three storeys high and has five symmetrical bay windows. The architects combined brick and local stone to create an interesting mix of colours. The main entrance, with its semi-circular stone arch, is flanked by a series of Tuscan pilasters, with accompanying grotesques in an Italian mannerist style. Contained in the spandrels between arch and pilasters, the allegory of Justice with her scales and the representation of the goddess Athena present a double masonic and institutional discourse. Both are recurrent symbolic elements in masonic buildings. An example is the set of sculptures on William Mangnall's Manchester lodge of 1863, probably by the

Freemason John Bell, which represent Prudence, Justice, Temperance and Charity.[43]

This entrance to the Town Hall is in axis with the extraordinary central bay window on the first floor, with its semicircular broken pediment in whose interior appears, appropriately, the sea god Poseidon. This window is flanked by stone Ionic columns. Within this axis the clock tower is an outstanding feature as the emblem of the building's identity, giving it the necessary monumental character in spite of its limited relative height. No contemporary coat of arms appears on the main facade, only on the frieze of the entrance on Corporation Street, with another one – the current version – closing off the Market Street corner. This could be due to controversy about the original civic coat of arms, which is discussed below. Perhaps for this reason, we find no coat of arms on the square downfall pipes and rainwater heads of the Town Hall, only the letter 'B' for Blackpool. The only reference to the coat of arms, apart from its presence on the lateral facade as mentioned above, is the word 'Progress' which forms part of the motto and is elegantly written on a scroll supported by an angel sitting in the stone vault of the retaining wall of the Mayor's Parlour.

*Interior of the Council Chamber, Blackpool Town Hall. The paintings on the walls illustrate the role of the Duchy and County of Lancaster in the making of the English nation. The formal furniture of the room, with the new Coat of Arms on display, reinforces the idea of Blackpool's historical roots and connections, as against the exclusive focus on progress and advancement on the older shield*

The most remarkable masonic elements in Blackpool Town Hall can be found in the side supports of the principal facade. On two stone supports displaying the Sun and Sea, the architects placed two semicircular pediments, divided in the same way as those above the central window with the Poseidon emblem. Here they introduced a very important masonic element: the sun in radiant splendour. It represents Hiram, constructor of the Temple of Jerusalem and father of freemasonry, and is symbolically connected with Osiris. The midday sun is a masonic symbol of alchemical gold, prosperity, intellect and higher understanding.[44]

The architects of Blackpool Town Hall were responsible for numerous industrial, public and institutional buildings across northern England,[45] such as Hind Street Technical College in Sunderland (1891–1900)[46] and the Cheshire Centenary Hall (1905–6).[47] Here they used similar stylistic approaches to those evident in Blackpool, but without the distinctive masonic elements, although Potts himself had worked with the masonic architect William Hill on Bolton Town Hall.[48] This reinforces the importance of local commissioning influences on the strongly marked masonic characteristics of this symbolic building: the masonic motifs must have been introduced at the behest of influential members of the local authority.

### The Masonic Hall, Adelaide Street

Freemasonry was already important in Blackpool when the borough charter was obtained in 1876. It was still gathering momentum in the expansive 1890s. Every masonic organization normally has its own premises for meetings and sociability, and in Britain there was a strong tendency from the early nineteenth century to bring together several lodges under the same roof. In Blackpool the Adelaide Street Masonic Hall was completed in 1899 for exactly this purpose. Such a project had been under discussion for a decade, as individual lodges were meeting in different places. In 1897 the Blackpool Masonic Hall Company Limited was established to construct and organize the new meeting place.[49]

The foundation stone-laying ceremony for a masonic temple was always a major event, and it was usual to invite a highly-placed senior member of the Order to officiate. Blackpool's Freemasons invited Lord Skelmersdale, Lord Chamberlain at Queen Victoria's court, and on 7 May 1898 he laid the first stone as part of a wider programme of masonic ceremonies in the town, which included another foundation stone ceremony for St Paul's Church, North Shore, and the holding of a Provincial Grand Lodge in Christ Church School, as discussed above. The new Masonic Hall was completed in 1899 and ceremonially opened on 23 September by the Earl of Lathom, another very senior Lancashire Freemason. Afterwards a provincial Grand Lodge was held under the banner of Clifton lodge, and His Lordship dedicated the new lodge room. Several mayors of provincial towns were present for a Masonic Congress that coincided with the event, and the mayors of Harrogate, Abingdon, and Bacup spoke at the ceremony.[50]

The Masonic Hall, designed by J. A. Nuttall, a Freemason and architect based in Blackpool at 29 Birley Street, contained various meeting rooms, offices and bars, but the core of it was the Temple. Its proportions, which conformed to the Golden Rule, and its symbolism were systematically masonic. The Temple was oriented from west to east, its sides aligned with the cardinal points of the compass, and the vault of heaven with its starry decoration covered the ceiling, with the twelve signs of the zodiac below it.[51] In the Blackpool building we see all the influences of John Flaxman's romantic classicism, with delicate white plasterwork on a blue background, where masonic symbols included the five-pointed star, the Bible, the square, the compass, and Pythagoras' Theorem. The rhythm of the rectangular room is imposed by the pillars which divide it in three parts; and the roof above the Master's Chair displays the signs of the zodiac, in the same way as Soane placed them in the Bank of England.

Nuttall enjoyed a sequence of commissions in Blackpool after the Masonic Hall, offering further hints about the close relationship between freemasonry, government, religion and business in the town. Some of his most important projects were the Congregational Church in Alexandra Road (1898–9); the Union Baptist Chapel Sunday School in Abingdon Street (1899); the municipal Fire Station in Albert Road (1900–1); and the Revoe Branch Library in Central Drive (1901), another commission from the local authority.[52]

### Freemasonry and the Church of England in Blackpool

The role of freemasonry in the Church of England was also very important in Blackpool. Freemasonry was very active within Anglicanism generally during this period. William H. Stacey, a Sheffield Mason, pointed out in 1893 that there could be no more important occasion for a Mason than the ceremony of laying the first stone of a religious building: 'The doctrines, rules and requirements of Freemasonry inculcate order, morality, social affection, beneficence, religion; therefore rejoice at the erection of those temples where the sublime truths and pure precepts of Holy Writ so eloquently enforce the spread and exercise of these virtues as essential to our happiness both in this world and that which is to come.'[53] In Blackpool these

Church of St Paul, Blackpool, by Garlick and Sykes, first stone laid in 1898, and now a health centre. The most important external masonic element is the tower. This is one of several Blackpool churches to have a close relationship with freemasonry, and its foundation stone ceremony immediately preceded that of the Masonic Hall

sentiments were expressed especially through the foundation of new Anglican churches, their decoration and furnishing. A good example is the laying of the foundation stone of St Paul's Church, as mentioned above.

The day in Blackpool began with the opening of a Provincial Grand Lodge in the school attached to Christ Church, another Anglican stronghold of freemasonry, attended by about 250 Freemasons. Christ Church was the work of James Medland Taylor, who designed several Victorian churches in northern England, including St Edmund at Falinge, Rochdale (1873), a cruciform church with masonic motifs pervading all its architecture and furnishings, donated by the Freemason Albert Hudson Royds.[54] After the Christ Church meeting a procession of Masons proceeded to the St Paul's site in all their pomp, with a large crowd of spectators lining the streets.[55] All the symbolic rhetoric of masonic banners and jewellery was unfolded in this highly-charged ceremonial, as the brethren marched in hierarchical order bearing offerings. The arrival of the Provincial Grand Master was announced by a flourish of trumpets, and the procession then entered the enclosure. The officiating brethren took the position in the east, west, north and south assigned to them by the Director of Ceremonies and his assistants, and deposited the vessels borne in the procession on the pedestal placed for their reception.

Amongst the clergymen present were Revd C. H. Wainwright (vicar of Christ Church); Revd T. Watson, curate-in-charge of St Paul's and himself a Freemason; Revd Job Edwards (St John's); Revd T. H. Ethell (All Saints); and Revd R. Lavers Kemp (curate of Christ Church), amounting to an impressive muster of Blackpool clergy. Bro. Revd Watson requested the Provincial Grand Master (Lord Skelmersdale) to lay the foundation stone, at the same time presenting him with a mallet, and thanked his fellow Masons for their kindly presence that day.[56] The Provincial Grand Chaplain offered a prayer, and the architect presented the plans of the church, which were inspected by the Provincial Grand Master. The singing of the national anthem concluded the proceedings at St Paul's, and the procession moved on to Adelaide Street to complete a very full day of masonic activity and public display.

Christ Church and St Paul's were not the only Anglican churches in Blackpool to have strong masonic links. When the original parish church of St John's was rebuilt and consecrated on 25 June 1878, the architects were Garlick, Park and Sykes, the same firm that designed St Paul's twenty years later, and the Freemason W. H. Cocker donated the three-light East window, while his fellow Mason councillor George Bonny supplied a reading-desk. St John's was the official church of the borough corporation, and although there was no masonic ceremony at the consecration, potentially masonic elements in its furnishings include the King David window and the Star of David motif in the tester above the pulpit. The stained-glass triptych in the south aisle features figures of Fortitude and Prudence flanking a central Christ, and the donor was the Freemason, waxworks proprietor and local councillor Elias Fletcher.[57]

Holy Trinity, South Shore, was also a strongly masonic parish church. Its vicar from 1881, Revd Sandys Bradshaw, was one of Blackpool's most prominent and active Freemasons. The foundation stone of the new late Victorian building (the parish had been founded in 1836) was laid in 1888 with full masonic honours. A second stone was laid by James Fish, the current mayor and a prominent local Freemason, and a paper listing the members of the building committee, the Masonic Committee, and those officials of the Borough of Blackpool who were present, was placed beneath it. Fittingly, two impressive windows in the south transept depict the dedication of Solomon's Temple and King David with the Ark of the Covenant, which are classic masonic themes.[58]

The foundation stone ceremonies for the new churches of All Saints (1904) and St Stephen's on the Cliffs (1911) also featured masonic processions along the lines of the St Paul's ceremony,[59] and the links between church and Freemasons in late Victorian and Edwardian Blackpool could hardly have been closer or more pervasive, reinforcing the business and political ties that connected freemasonry to the growth of the town and its businesses across a broad front. But even this is not the whole story.

## The coat of arms of Blackpool and the masonic identity of 'progress'

Freemasonry was so important to the fortunes of this pioneer popular resort that even Blackpool's original municipal coat of arms (or 'badge and seal', given its unofficial character) was adapted from that of the town's Clifton lodge, established in 1857. The town's official emblem was much discussed in the local press, and after a series of confrontations the coat of arms adopted in 1876 was replaced in 1899 by something more 'appropriate'.[60] In September 1876 the *Blackpool Gazette* had concluded that, 'The device which has been fixed upon as a coat of arms for our newly incorporated town is not inappropriate. On the ribbon surrounding the shield are the words "Corporation of Blackpool" and over all is a sea-bird, with outstretched wings, skimming over a ruffled sea. On the quarterings of the shield there are representations of a lifeboat, a bathing van, the Blackpool Pier and a locomotive engine. The motto underneath is the word "Advance."'[61] The 'sea-bird' in question looks more like a swallow than a seagull, and the whole production is crudely and ineptly drawn.[62]

'Advance' was abandoned almost immediately, to be replaced by 'Progress', which had been the motto of the Clifton lodge of 1857 since before the corporation received its charter. The 'locomotive engine' was replaced by a sailing vessel, and the changes returned the coat of arms to an even closer approximation to the existing emblem of the masonic lodge. The Clifton lodge was to provide Blackpool with eight of its mayors, including John Bickerstaffe, and its Master in 1860–1 was Dr John Cocker, father of the Dr W. H. Cocker who was the founder of the Winter Gardens and Aquarium, and the town's first mayor. Its banner still holds pride of place in the meeting room of the Masonic Hall in Adelaide Street.[63] The Blackpool lodge, which received its warrant in 1874, also adopted this motto, along with the same emblem, as the emblem on its ceremonial banner.[64]

'Progress' is an allegorical and symbolic word

*The original municipal 'coat of arms' of Blackpool, from an undated drawing preserved in Blackpool Central Library, representing the newly established corporation's identification with modernity. It refuses any allusion to nobility or lineage, preferring to present itself as an authentic symbol of 'Progress', the town's motto*

BLACKPOOL.

An arrangement of three representations of the town's pre-1899 'coat of arms', showing some variations. *Above left*: Shield and decorative surroundings on the eastern facade of the Town Hall, the only version of the 'coat of arms' to appear in stone on the exterior of the building. *Below left*: Shield and standard of Clifton Lodge, established in Blackpool in 1857. This is a reconstruction of 2003, based on the original. *Right*: Cast-iron pillar on Blackpool promenade railings, incorporating the original 'coat of arms'

frequently used in international freemasonry.[65] It is usually represented as the wheel of progress, or personified as Mercury, god of commerce. As a masonic idea it appears in numerous contemporary writings, in the same sense as in Blackpool.[66] The pursuit of intellectual, moral and economic progress was an objective of masonic lodges, so that they often named themselves after it. This was not always the case in England,[67] but many lodges in the nineteenth century took the name 'Progress', not only in Europe but also the US and Canada.

The word 'progress' was also current in Blackpool in a secular sense identified with industry, commerce and the local economy, although the (almost identical) emblems of Clifton lodge and of the town espoused limited versions of it, featuring a sailing boat alongside the first pier, a bathing machine, and a lifeboat. After living with this coat of arms for twenty years, the municipal corporation decided to accede to the mounting criticism and change it, taking the opportunity to reconcile it with the traditional authorities of British heraldry, to whom it had never been presented. The records of the

College of Arms indicate that, although Blackpool was permitted to use armorial bearings on its Common Seal when incorporated in 1876, it had made no official attempt to do so, and the first such petition was that of 1899. The College remained unaware of any attempt to use 'any Arms without authority' in the meantime.[68]

The proposal was discussed at length in the local press, and debated in full council.[69] The brothers John and Tom Bickerstaffe opposed the change vehemently in the council chamber, as did their fellow Freemason C. W. Callis; but Aldermen Heap and Grime argued for following normal practice elsewhere and going to the Heralds for approval of a more conventional design. Grime emphasized the ridicule that was increasingly attracted by the existing emblem, and the outspoken Councillor Kingsbury was wittily eloquent: the present coat of arms was 'the laughing stock of the Kingdom. It was a jumble of all sorts of things. There was a bathing van, the original pier, a thing supposed to be a lifeboat, and a Fleetwood sailing boat about to be wrecked on the shore. He wondered why the originators hadn't put a few beer tankards on.' The debate was widely reported, with much amusement. A Glasgow newspaper described the current coat of arms, in a parody of heraldic language, as 'A Pier couchant, a Lifeboat saltant in azure, a Bathing-Van vert, and a Fleetwood Sailing-Ship about to be wrecked sinister.' The only improvement could be a 'Landlady, rampant in ermine.'[70] The new coat of arms, a much more elaborate affair, was adopted in March 1899, but there was no time to incorporate it into the facade of the Town Hall building, because the work had been practically completed without it.[71]

Between 1876 and 1899, a period of unprecedented growth in Blackpool, the town's *de facto* coat of arms was based on that of its oldest masonic lodge. The movement to change it for something more 'respectable' and externally validated was successful only after the doubling in size of the council had diluted the influence of the older local elites who were drawn from the entertainment, building and drink interests, and strongly linked by freemasonry. Even then, Alderman John Bickerstaffe led fierce resistance to the proposed changes; and the motto 'Progress', which was itself masonic in origin, remained sacrosanct. It was, by this time, an established 'brand', and the label was good for business. But the symbolic significance of this episode should not be underestimated, despite the mirth from outside the town and the temptation to trivialize. These were important issues of local, and business, identity, especially when the locality was, effectively, itself a business.

18. http://www.masonichall.org.uk, accessed 20 Dec. 2008.
19. Walton, 'Social development of Blackpool', table 9.7 (p. 478) and p. 481.
20. Ibid., and *Blackpool Gazette*, 7 May 1898, 23 Sep. 1899; Blackpool Central Library, *Official handbook and souvenir to the masonic bazaar ... 23rd–26th September* (1903).
21. Walton, 'Social development of Blackpool', App. A (pp. 510–50) and pp. 483–8.
22. Walton, 'Social development of Blackpool', pp. 455–64, 480.
23. Ibid., pp. 453–5, 466–7.
24. Ibid., table 9.8 (p. 478).
25. Ibid., table 9.3 (pp. 466–7).
26. F. K. Pearson, 'The Douglas Head suspension bridge', *Journal of the Manx Museum*, 85 (1969), pp. 104–5; http://www.lynnpearson.co.uk/palaces3.pdf, accessed 21 Dec. 2008.
27. *Blackpool Gazette*, 12 July 1878, 21 Sep. 1891.
28. Walton, *Riding on Rainbows*, pp. 24–6, 34–6.
29. R. Ainsworth, *The Parkinson family of Lancashire* (Accrington, 1932); A. P. Baker, 'Sir Albert Lindsay Parkinson (1870–1936)', *Oxford Dictionary of National Biography*, 2004, http://www.oxforddnb.com/index101048091, accessed 5 Mar. 2009. We owe this reference to Mr Harold Monks, formerly of the Town Clerk's department, Blackpool, whose close and informed reading of the text has saved us from several errors.
30. *Official handbook [...]* (1903).
31. Walton, 'Social development of Blackpool', pp. 481–2; http://www.blackpool.gov.uk, accessed 21 Dec. 2008, for lists of mayors and freemen.
32. http://www.masonichall.org.uk, accessed 21 Dec. 2008; Walton, 'Social development of Blackpool', pp. 482–3.
33. Walton, 'Social development of Blackpool', pp. 474, 483–8.
34. Masonic symbolism is interpreted differently by speculative historical freemasonry and current practice. For an overview see James S. Curl, *The art and architecture of freemasonry* (London, 1993).
35. J. E. Cirlot, *Diccionario de Símbolos* (Madrid, 2004), p. 17.
36. R. W. Mackey, *El simbolismo francmasónico* (Madrid, 1929), p. 194.
37. K. Menué, *La Masonería* (Barcelona, 2004), p. 29.
38. The graves are located according to plans in the Archive of Layton cemetery and are, respectively, plots G 9.1., E 12. 7., T 2. 1., V 1. 15., A 16. 1., M 1. 7., B 4. 13., OO 1. 1., S 4. 1., J 6. 11., Y 2. 17., JJ 1. 15., E 13. 2., C 16. 2., K 1. 4., D 4.4, K 1. 51., K 3. 17., Q 11.6., E 12. 10 and A 15. 2. Our thanks to the Friends of Layton Cemetery.
39. S. Lee, ed., *Dictionary of national biography*, vol. 30 (Boston, MA; 2001), p. 111.
40. A. Scarth and C. A. Brian, *History of the Lodge of Fidelity* (Leeds, 1894).

41. *Blackpool Council Town Hall: a guide* (Blackpool, 2006), p. 1.
42. *Blackpool Gazette*, 4 Oct. 1904, and http://www.meliora.co.uk/oldbgs.htm, accessed 10 Jan. 2009.
43. T. Wyke, *Public sculpture of Greater Manchester* (Liverpool, 2005), p. 65.
44. J. C. Daza, *Diccionario de la Francmasonería* (Tres Cantos, 1997), pp. 353–4.
45. http://209.85.229.132/search?q=cache:KkGuGeV9IgwJ:services.salford.gov.uk/solar_documents/PLMB010408C.DOC+%22Potts,+Son+and+Hennings%22&hl=es&ct=clnk&cd=1&gl=es, accessed 9 Jan. 2009.
46. For more information on this building, which also has a Grade II listing, http://www.sunderland.gov.uk/apps/ListedBuildings/lbbuildingdetails.asp?Id=920-1/19/94&keyword=&Ownership=&Address3=&Grade=, accessed 10 Jan. 2009.
47. N. Pevsner and E. Hubbard, *Cheshire* (Harmondsworth, 1971), p. 342.
48. C. Cunningham, *Victorian and Edwardian town halls* (London, 1981).
49. http://www.masonichall.org.uk/Gazette%20News%2029%20April1.html, accessed 9 Jan. 2009.
50. http://www.masonichall.org.uk/New%20Masonic%20Hall.html, accessed 10 Jan. 2009.
51. B. Desantes and M. J. Frades Morera, *Atributos masónicos en el Archivo Histórico Nacional. Sección Guerra Civil* (Salamanca, 1993), p. 38.
52. Thanks to Ted Lightbown for this information.
53. W. H. Stacey, *History of the Royal Brunswick Lodge, 1793–1893* (Sheffield, 1893), p. 46.
54. N. Pevsner, *The buildings of England: North Lancashire* (Harmondsworth, 1969), p. 69.
55. http://www.masonichall.org.uk/St%20Paul's%20Church.html, accessed 10 Jan. 2009.
56. Ibid.
57. http://www.stjohnsblackpool.org.uk/history.htm, accessed 23 Jan. 2009; www.lancashirechurches.co.uk/blackpoolsj.htm, accessed 25 Jan. 2009; *Blackpool Gazette*, 28 June 1878.
58. http://www.htss.org.uk/articles.php, 'Holy Trinity and its Roots', accessed 23 Jan. 2009; http://www.holytrinityblackpool.org.uk/church.php, accessed 25 Jan. 2009; *Official handbook [...]* (1903).
59. http://www.masonichall.org.uk/Clifton.html, accessed 25 Jan. 2009.
60. The original coat of arms is kept in the Town Hall, where it is described as the 'Town Badge', a gift of the Cocker family, and the text suggests that it 'could not be described correctly in heraldic terms and was therefore never adopted as the Coat of Arms.' But it was actually used as the coat of arms, though without the sanction of the Heralds, until the present one was adopted in 1899. The Town Hall text also describes the bathing van as a bathing *hut*: http://www.blackpool.gov.uk/NR/

idonbgres/FACAD2E9-D407–4B8E–9E69–0F758096545B/0/aboutthe-TownHall.pdf, accessed 25 Jan. 2009.
61. *Blackpool Gazette*, 15 Sep. 1876.
62. Blackpool Central Library LP562(P) contains drawings of this 'coat of arms'.
63. http://www.masonichall.org.uk/Clifton.html, accessed 17 Dec. 2008.
64. http://www.masonichall.org.uk/Blackpool.html, accessed 23 Jan. 2009.
65. S. Hernández Guitérrez, *La estética masónica. Arte e Historia de los más afamados protagonistas de la Masonería internacional* (Tenerife, 1998), p. 116.
66. R. García Álvarez, *Catálogo del Gabinete de Historia Natural del Instituto de 2ª Enseñanza de la Provincia de Granada* (Granada, 1886).
67. J. Money, 'The masonic moment; or, ritual, replica, and credit: John Wilkes, the Macaroni Parson, and the making of the middle-class mind', *Journal of British Studies* 32 (1993), p. 387.
68. Windsor Herald of Arms to David Martín López, 20 Jan. 2009.
69. *Blackpool Times*, 3 July 1897, containing an official description of the new coat of arms.
70. *Blackpool Gazette*, 3 Jan. 1899; Blackpool Central Library LP562(P).
71. *Blackpool Gazette*, 3 Mar. 1899.

# Brewing in the North West, 1840–1914: sowing the seeds of service-sector management?

*Alistair Mutch*

Brewing has been relatively neglected in accounts of the industrial and economic development of the North West.[1] There is much justification for this, giving the epoch-shaping importance of cotton and engineering in the region. However, it might be just a little too easy to draw a contrast between the thrusting and dynamic textiles and engineering sectors and the sleepy conservatism of brewing. The latter is, to be sure, a sector with some profoundly conservative tendencies, as we will see, but part of the problem lies with how we define the field.[2] If we incorporate the distribution networks that accompanied the production of beer, then, especially if we explore the Liverpool experience, we can get more of a sense of innovation. In particular, the use of direct management of public houses in the city prefigured developments elsewhere. However, this is simply to raise another set of questions, which are: why did this innovation not spread more widely within the region and why did the region's brewers, including the major firms, ultimately fail to export their success to a national level? In order to answer these questions, we need first to consider the shape of the sector in the North West during the period. This then forms the backdrop for a sharper focus on differences between Liverpool and Manchester. This enables us to explore some key innovations but also suggests some reasons for why the region never developed the organizational 'clout' that developed around the major Birmingham brewers. However, before proceeding to these explorations, we need first to consider some questions of definition and evidence.

The boundaries of the area under consideration include the modern administrative county of Cheshire. This is in part because during the period, Warrington was both an important brewing centre and administratively within Lancashire's boundaries. It is also because of the relation of Stockport to Greater Manchester. The

|  |  | Common brewers | Licensed victuallers | Persons licensed to sell beer |
| --- | --- | --- | --- | --- |
| 1832 | Birmingham |  |  |  |
|  | Liverpool | 90 | 6 | 4 |
|  | Manchester | 24 | 50 | 25 |
| 1850 | Birmingham |  |  |  |
|  | Liverpool | 97 | 2 | 1 |
|  | Manchester | 55 | 28 | 18 |
| 1860 | Birmingham | 8 | 49 | 44 |
|  | Liverpool | 95 | 3 | 2 |
|  | Manchester | 70 | 18 | 2 |
| 1880 | Birmingham | 16 | 36 | 49 |
|  | Liverpool | 98 | 2 |  |
|  | Manchester | 93 | 4 | 3 |
| 1900 | Birmingham | 91 | 6 | 3 |
|  | Liverpool | 100 |  |  |
|  | Manchester | 100 |  |  |

Source: T. R. Gourvish and R. G. Wilson, *The British brewing industry, 1830–1980* (Cambridge, 1994), pp. 70–1.

**Table 1:** Percentage of brewers by category, 1832–1900

mention here of Warrington also points to a problem in 'locating' particular companies. The data which are drawn upon below place the important firm of Peter Walker & Son as a Cheshire firm, because their brewing operation was based in Warrington. However, the business was run from Duke Street in Liverpool and its pubs dominated the city's streets. The purpose of looking at the region as a whole is to identify some key features. As we will see, one of those features is that brewing activities were very different in parts of the region. As we know, much nineteenth-century business was intensely local in its focus and this was particularly true of brewing. Its prime product, beer, was a high-volume and low-value product whose distribution was therefore generally constrained by existing means of horse-drawn transport. Breweries, therefore, tended to be local affairs, sitting at the centre of local distribution outlets. The coming of rail, of course, meant some prospects for changing this and they were ones which were seized upon by Peter Walker & Son in particular. However, for many of the more remote areas there was little competition except where local zones of influence overlapped.

One caveat to this was the growing importance of bottled beer during the nineteenth century, especially the products of Burton on Trent. Burton possessed natural advantages in its gypsum-rich water which enabled it to produce bright and light ales which were widely popular. The development of the rail network meant that these products could be distributed on a national scale. The importance of some markets in the North West can be seen in the note in the directors' minutes for Allsopps in 1865, recording 'Reports from London & Liverpool as to the requirements in Ales this Season.'[3] However, companies such as Bass and Allsopps tended to work though agencies in the remoter areas and through other brewers in urban areas. It was not until 1891 that Allsopps bottled their own beer in Barrow, for example.[4] In addition, over the century the development of brewing science meant that other breweries were able to emulate the Burton product. It would be fair, though, to argue that the North West as a whole never developed products with a national appeal during this period (the development of brands such as Boddington's was a much later development). Rather it was more likely to be southern companies such as Whitbread with their greater orientation to the free trade who were more able to take advantage. So it is possible to argue that the prospects for expansion out of the North West were to some extent limited by product considerations.

Such a contention, however, requires that we also complete our examination of the background by considering the relation between brewers and the pubs which sold their beer.[5] Historically many licensed victuallers brewed on the premises for sale to customers, but the nineteenth century saw the triumph of the 'common brewer', that is, the brewing company supplying a range of outlets. Table 1 shows the extent and variability of this process by comparing the returns for Birmingham, Liverpool and Manchester. From these figures it is clear how advanced the process was in Liverpool and how, by the

*Andrew Barclay Walker, founder of Peter Walker & Son. Statue in Walker Art Gallery, Liverpool. Photo by author*

second half of the century, Manchester was starting to catch up. What is clearly visible is how different the practice was in Birmingham, where publican brewers maintained their status until the pivotal decade of the 1880s. What is also important in Manchester for much longer than Liverpool is the beer-seller brewing on the premises. In 1830 the Beer Act created a new class of licence by which a payment to the Excise secured a licence to brew beer which was enthusiastically taken up but with different results. In Liverpool such beer-houses provided a market for existing brewers, perhaps because of the poverty of the premises occupied which did not allow for brewing. By contrast many Manchester beer-sellers also brewed, although in nothing like the numbers found in Birmingham.

Another important relationship was between the growing ranks of the common brewers and the outlets they served. At the beginning of the century most public houses were 'free', that is, independent businesses either brewing their own beer or free to obtain it from a common brewer of their choice. Over the course of the century, for reasons explored well by Jennings,[6] many pubs came to be 'tied' to a particular brewery. In some parts of the country (notably London and Scotland) publicans were tied by means of loans secured on their property, but in most of the rest of the country, pubs came to be increasingly owned by breweries. The most common form of running such pubs was through tenancy, where a nominally independent tenant paid both a 'dry' rent (for the premises) and a 'wet' rent (by means of a premium of the wholesale price of beer). However, in some parts of the country, notably Liverpool and Birmingham, many pubs came to be under direct management, where a waged employee ran the pub. Liverpool was the source of this often-contested practice, and this is the key innovation which prefigures much later service-sector management practices.

Finally, a few words on the nature of the evidence are in order. Much of what follows rests on the experience of particular companies, notably that of Peter Walker & Son, because these are ones for whom we possess detailed historical accounts. The histories of many companies in the region are often a little sketchy, although this account draws on some of the best of these. In addition, the discussion draws on the tenacious work of members of the Brewery History Society (BHS) and other compilers of local gazetteers who assiduously trawl sources such as trade directories looking for evidence of brewery foundation and existence.[7] There are many problems with such evidence, not least because it is often difficult to determine just what constitutes the 'foundation' of many companies. Given that several have their origins in brewing at a pub, it can be difficult to establish just when this becomes brewing for wider consumption. The evidence which is presented, therefore, should be taken as indicative of broad trends. Given these caveats, the next section looks at some data on the distribution of brewing concerns in the North West and uses these to draw out some key themes.

## Brewing in the North West at the turn of the twentieth century

It is difficult to establish a point at which to take a snapshot of the universe of brewing companies, because of the degree of fluctuation and change in the key markets. However, an arbitrary census date of 1900 enables us to draw upon the work done by many volunteers and recorded in the BHS publication *A century of British brewers*.[8] This volume is organized by modern administrative counties and contains a wealth of detail. It is limited by the considerations noted above and is often sparse, in particular with regard to the numbers of pubs which a company controlled at any particular point. However, it enables us to isolate some numbers which indicate the broad contours of the field, as outlined in Table 2.

A noticeable feature is the large number of companies with over one hundred years of trading history in Cumbria. This points to the conservatism of trading and production patterns in rural areas, where breweries were tightly integrated with the agricultural economy. Jennings, for example, was founded in 1828 in the village of Lorton in the Lake District by a local farmer, John Jennings, whose father was a maltster. (The company remained independent until 2005, when it was taken over by Marstons.)[9] The company moved to Cockermouth in 1874 and the Cumbrian pattern is of long-established breweries at the heart of market towns. A list of such companies is in Appendix A; it is noticeable that of the list only Greenall Whitley and Duttons of Blackburn could really be considered as in the front rank of

Table 2: Breweries in the North West by county and date of formation

| Date of foundation | Cheshire | Cumbria | Lancashire | Greater Manchester | Merseyside | Total |
|---|---|---|---|---|---|---|
| Pre 1800 | 3 | 8 | 3 | 1 | 2 | 17 |
| 1801–1850 | 1 | 2 | 7 | 17 | 7 | 34 |
| 1851–1875 | 2 | 4 | 10 | 17 | 8 | 41 |
| 1876–1900 | 5 | 5 | 10 | 27 | 7 | 54 |
| Not given | 3 | 12 | 12 | 7 | 4 | 38 |
| Total | 14 | 31 | 42 | 69 | 28 | 184 |
| Pre-1800 % | 21.4 | 25.8 | 7.1 | 1.4 | 7.1 | 9.2 |

Source: data in N. Barber, *A century of British brewers, plus* (New Ash Green, 2005)

| Date of dissolution | Cheshire | Cumbria | Lancashire | Greater Manchester | Merseyside | Total |
|---|---|---|---|---|---|---|
| Pre 1914 | 3 | 4 | 10 | 15 | 6 | 38 (22.4%) |
| 1914–40 | 4 | 12 | 20 | 27 | 14 | 77 (45.3%) |
| 1940–70 | 4 | 8 | 7 | 21 | 6 | 46 (27.1%) |
| Post 1970 | 0 | 3 | 3 | 2 | 1 | 9 (5.3%) |
| Total | 11 | 27 | 40 | 65 | 27 | 170 |

*Source*: data in Barber, *A century*.

**Table 3:** Dissolution of breweries in the North West

companies. Much of the dynamism, that is, came from companies founded towards the middle of the nineteenth century, as with Peter Walker & Son and Robert Cain & Sons in Liverpool (both 1848), Threlfalls in Salford (1861), Frederic Robinson in Stockport (1838), and Wilsons of Manchester (1834).

The fate of the oldest-established company on the list, The Lion Brewery of Chester, alerts us to a trend towards consolidation which was already starting to become apparent. In 1902 the company was acquired by Bent's Brewery of Liverpool. It owned twenty pubs but traded mainly with 'hotels and private family concerns in the suburb'.[10] By contrast to this long-established family concern, Bents was publicly quoted in 1890, when it had 120 public houses. Its vice-chairman Archibald Salvidge was a significant figure in Liverpool politics.[11] The company is also interesting in that, although founded by John Bent in 1823, it later fell under the control of Edward Chevalier, a former customs official. It marked an early example of the loosening of family control, although most of the companies in the sector were firmly in the hands of the founding family and their descendants. Table 3 indicates when companies were dissolved or amalgamated and shows that, while there was some movement in the years before the First World War, it was really the inter-war years which saw the process accelerating. The process of amalgamation was, however, a continuous one but one which tended in this period to produce localized consolidation. In 1890, for example, William Clarkson, who had breweries in Liverpool and Burton and an estate of eighty pubs, offered his business to Peter Walker & Son:

> He would prefer that your Company should have the working of his properties rather than that they should pass into the hands of third parties … He is desirous of leaving the business entirely and he would feel more easy if that business which he has been so long

**Table 4:** Common brewers in Liverpool and Manchester

|  | Liverpool | Manchester |
|---|---|---|
| 1832 | 56 | 29 |
| 1841 | 74 | 84 |
| 1850 | 88 | 99 |
| 1860 | 73 | 118 |
| 1870 | 80 | 102 |
| 1880 | 70 | 94 |
| 1890 | 39 | 64 |
| 1900 | 28 | 39 |

*Source*: Gourvish and Wilson, *British brewing industry*, pp. 70–1.

> associated with and has built up with such care were in the hands of first class people such as your Company rather than left to be manipulated by other parties.[12]

This process led to considerable reduction in the number of brewers in both Liverpool and Manchester, as indicated in Table 4. A similar process is observed by Timmins in Lancashire:

> At St Helens, for example, Greenall's rebuilt their brewery in 1856–57, adding considerably to its capacity. Around ten years later they acquired and closed Speakman's Denton Green Brewery, giving them a virtual monopoly of brewing in the district. In Blackburn, too, three of the dozen or so breweries that operated in the town during this period closed, with the more successful, including Dutton's and Thwaites, extending capacity.[13]

The figures suggest a process of considerable dynamism at mid century, aided by relatively low barriers to entry. In 1849, for example, Joseph Holt, who had been working as a carter at Strangeways Brewery, began brewing behind a pub before moving to Ducie Bridge brewery in 1855.[14] What the century also saw was the emergence of particular patterns of operation of the distribution network. In Manchester, as in the rest of the region, the running of pubs was dominated by the tenanted tied house, but Liverpool developed a very different pattern.[15] It is to this contrast that we turn next.

barmen are drafted to the premises, where it is known the normal trade will for a certain period be doubled or even trebled.[20]

There was a powerful incentive, that is, to run the estate as a collective rather than as individual establishments, and direct management was ideal for this. However, this does not explain all, for elaborate pubs are to be found in Liverpool suburbs which in other towns would only grace the town centre. And, with a few exceptions, Manchester did not seem to develop a tradition of ostentatious city-centre pubs, certainly nothing like on the scale of Liverpool.[21] Economic factors also have their part to play, especially the tradition of casual dock employment. The structure of the Liverpool docks, strung out along the Mersey with no easy means of travel between them until the overhead railway late in the nineteenth century, meant that dockers lived close to the docks to be in the best position to obtain work. The enormous tidal range of the Mersey meant that access to the docks was irregular, not only conditioning the irregular working patterns of the dockers but also releasing vast numbers of sailors into the city at the same time.[22] Such customers, paid off at the end of a voyage, had substantial sums with which to consume, and tastes which often ran to spirits rather than beer. By contrast, Manchester and Salford had a more suburban and beer-centred pattern of consumption, in which local divisions were monitored closely in the pub:

> These divisions could be marked in many public houses, where workers other than craftsmen would be frozen or flatly ordered out of those rooms in which journeymen foregathered. Each part of the tavern had its status rating; indeed, 'he's only a tap-room man' stood as a common slur.[23]

In Liverpool, by contrast, there seems to have been much less attachment to particular pubs, something reflected in the common practice of naming pubs after the current manager rather than the traditional inn names. It would appear, too, that there was a far greater tradition of women drinking in Liverpool pubs than in Manchester (and indeed in other parts of the region). In a fictionalized account, the Liverpool journalist Hugh Shimmin notes of one pub:

> The vaults were long and narrow, but what space there was between the windows and the counter was well filled with men and women, chiefly the latter, in various stages of intoxication … At the far end of the vaults a small apartment was boxed off, with seats round the sides.[24]

In Liverpool most space inside pubs was given over to one long drinking compartment, with a fairly vestigial 'snug', in contrast to the smaller rooms into which other pubs were divided.[25]

Such factors suggest why full licences for the sale of spirits and wine as well as beer might be eagerly sought after in Liverpool. Full licences in their turn, especially on the scale needed to supply fluctuating demand, required considerable capital investment. All these were factors which might be thought to provide incentives towards the direct management of pubs, but they cannot explain all. For we need to understand why in Birmingham, a citadel of publican brewers until the later nineteenth century and, like Manchester, the home of the skilled engineering worker, direct pub management also took hold at the end of the century. And there are other dock cities, notably London, in which, as we will see, direct management never became established. We cannot provide an answer to all these paradoxes here. But they do suggest that two further factors, the nature of local regulation and the business strategies of key companies, had an important role to play.[26]

One clear difference between Manchester and Liverpool is that the licensing magistrates in the former set their faces firmly against the notion of the management of pubs. In their view (as with many other benches across the country) managers were not fit and proper persons as they had no vested (property) interest in the conduct of the pub. While there were arguments about the extent to which companies practiced deception by producing sham tenancy agreements to cover what were *de facto* managers, the official position remained one of opposition. By contrast the Liverpool bench was more divided, in turn reflecting the conflictual nature of politics in the town. Liverpool politics was characterized by a Liberal elite based on merchants confronting popular conservatism.[27] This matter was complicated by sectarian divides. Popular conservatism was tightly bound up with Protestantism, and was supported by the major brewers. The ranks of Irish Catholics who might also have been the natural allies of the Liberals were split by a religious and temperance orientation amongst traditional leaders and a pub-based nationalism which eventually won out.[28] This meant that licensing decisions were fraught with controversy.

The first wave of such controversy came to a head in the 'Free Licensing' movement of the 1860s.[29] Faced with pressure to convert beer-house licences into full licences, some magistrates began to advocate the dropping of the traditional test of the needs of the neighbourhood. Led by merchants such as Robertson Gladstone, with adherence to laissez-faire ideals (ideals which had been much to the fore in recent battles over control of the docks), this faction argued that the market would establish whether pubs were required or not. For a number of years in the 1860s control moved back and forth between competing factions, the result being the conversion of large numbers of beer-houses into full licences. Eventually the matter was settled by an act of parliament in 1869 which saw beer-houses returned to the control of the magistrates. The Liverpool bench responded by promptly closing as many as they could on grounds of structural inadequacy. This marked an epoch of tight control by the Liverpool bench, harried as they were by the attentions of temperance advocates.

The temperance movement acquired a militant edge in Liverpool, fuelled by Liberal opposition to the alliance between beer and conservatism. One result was that the magistrates, supported by the police, came to see that control of pubs was best done through, rather than against, the pub-owning companies. In this, house management, policed as it was by company inspectors, was a valuable ally. Temperance advocates protested against this alliance, but to no avail. By 1914,

> The Licensing Committee ... have never hesitated to express the opinion that where you have brewers in control of a house it is better for the management of the house to have a brewer's manager as licensee rather than a tied tenant.[30]

This was at considerable odds with the position in most other parts of the country where, with the exception of Birmingham, managers were tolerated at best and forbidden as a matter of course. The success of house management in Liverpool, therefore, owed much to the character of licensing regulation. But it also depended on the nature of the companies who controlled the city's pubs, most notably Peter Walker & Son.

Formed as a father and son partnership in the late 1840s, the company appeared to have started managing pubs in the following decade.[31] From the beginning, its operations were characterized by detailed record-keeping and the monitoring of activities. On this basis the company built up a significant estate. Its success was copied by others, notably Robert Cain & Sons, which also had most of its houses under management. These two companies came to dominate the pubs of Liverpool and ultimately were to merge after the First World War. However, what is instructive in the current context is to compare their practices with the response of other brewing companies in the region. A good opportunity to do this is presented by the minutes of evidence to the 'Peel Commission' on licensing in the 1890s. Evidence on behalf of Peter Walker & Son was given by the company secretary, Ernest Ellis, who proudly declared that 'the founders of my company are generally credited with being the originators of the [managerial] system'.[32] He produced a forthright defence of the system, pointing to its advantages in enabling control and discipline. The next witness was Thomas Down, managing director and secretary of Greenall Whitley, whom we remember brewed in Warrington alongside Peter Walker & Son. When asked his opinion of pub management, he responded 'I know nothing of the managerial system, but I believe the houses of Messrs. Walker in Warrington are as well conducted as they can be, and they are mostly under management'.[33] This statement points to the remarkable lack of channels for debate and comparison in an industry known for its traditionalism and secrecy. Another witness, James Groves of Groves and Whitnal, gives us a perspective from Salford when he observed that they employed no managers 'first of all, from a deliberate preference, and secondly, because a large number of our houses are beer-houses'.[34] This set of evidence nicely illustrates the differences in practice between the two cities and some contrasts with the situation elsewhere, which we consider in the next section.

## Success and failure in brewing in the North West

From this brief overview it should be clear that brewing in the north-west of England in the late nineteenth and early twentieth centuries was not a homogenous sector. In many parts of the region, brewing was part of a stable and traditional approach, tightly integrated with the rural economy and providing a familiar part of the landscape of market towns. In the more industrialized areas, most companies adhered to the common practice of supplying a dense network of local outlets, increasingly tied to take the products of the brewery. This practice lay at the heart of many successful organizations and some have managed to retain this approach throughout the period and into more recent times.[35] In this sense they may be considered a success, if not sharing the dynamism of the cotton and engineering sectors which employed so many of their drinkers. However, at the level of larger organizations, especially those based in the major urban centres such as Liverpool and Manchester, we might argue that ultimately there was the failure to move beyond their localized strength to expand into the rest of the country. We have seen that in some ways the region did not possess distinctive products with a broader appeal and that might have been one constraint on expansion. But we have also seen that the region, in the shape of Liverpool, was the birthplace of a distinctive 'managerial system' for running pubs which, in the direct management of public houses and the development of a distinctive built form of pub, prefigured many later developments. One remaining question, therefore, is why this practice failed to spread.

We have seen that regulatory responses were different in Manchester and Liverpool. This was in sharp contrast to the position in Birmingham, where the Birmingham brewers were at the centre of a powerful and unified trade association, the Birmingham and Midland Counties Wholesale Brewers' Association (BMCWBA). Surviving records only enable us to be tentative here, but something of the reach of the Association's activities can be gleaned from its surviving reports. In 1914, for example, it notes,

> As long ago as 1893 the Association took a leading part in the organisation of the great meeting in Bingley Hall which provided Mr Chamberlain with the opportunity for a masterly and eloquent statement in defence of the interests of the Wholesale and Retail Trade.[36]

This points to the importance of municipal management in the traditions of Birmingham, and the symbiotic relationship between good management of the locality and good management of the pub. While there were still bitter disagreements about the nature and pace of change, the general thrust was towards a common managerialism. This was in stark contrast to the position within Liverpool, and between Liverpool and Manchester. These tensions may have prevented the emergence of a body like the BMCWBA which, amongst other activities, was able to provide its members with common managerial agreements, ratified in advance with magistrates, and a register of barmen and managers.[37] These practices advanced the dramatic development of the fortunes of common brewers in the area and, in particular, the rise of Mitchells and Butlers who were to form the continuing heart of one of the major companies to emerge after the Second World War, Bass.

In their efforts to expand out of the North West, Peter Walker and Son had no such support. They faced local problems when seeking to bring their managerial system to towns such as Crewe. Here they faced the steely determination of the magistrates to resist such 'alien' practices. However, of more significance for the ultimate failure of the broader expansion plans of the company was their experience in London.[38] In 1911 Peter Walker and Son bought the De Beauvoir Arms in Hackney. This was part of a planned move into London which saw the purchase of stores and several other pubs. The De Beauvoir Arms was the test case which saw the company come up against not only the magistrates but also a powerfully organized Licensed Victuallers Association. The company had already attempted to win favour with such bodies by having their London agent host the annual dinner, but to no avail. They sought to have Percy Burford installed as manager, but the magistrates, in line with the common practice in London, refused to accept anything other than a tenant. They were being a little disingenuous here, as were the Licensed Victuallers, because there is evidence of multiple publicans putting managers into houses for which they formally held the licence, but the outcome was a check to the company's ambitions. This combined with divisions within the controlling family to see the company taken over after the First World War by the much smaller Liverpool firm of Robert Cain & Sons, to form Walker Cain. The pubs remained branded as Peter Walker & Son, but the power shifted to the Cain family. With that came a retreat to the Liverpool heartlands. While there was local expansion, the company eventually merged with Tetley of Leeds to form the short-lived Tetley Walker in 1960. This disappeared three years later into the giant Allied Breweries, a merger with Ansells and Ind Coope. In practice it was to be the latter company which provided much of the leadership of the new company.[39]

However, this lies much beyond our period. During the years up to 1914 brewing was a significant part of the North West's industrial landscape. In many places the sector was indeed a conservative and traditional one. But enough evidence has been presented here to show how elements of considerable dynamism were present. The heterogeneous nature of the region, however, together with other factors, meant that other centres, notably Birmingham, were to have more success with the formula devised in the North West.

**Appendix A: Breweries established in the eighteenth century and still in existence in 1900**

| Brewery | Location | Date founded | Age in 1900 |
| --- | --- | --- | --- |
| **Cheshire** | | | |
| Chester Lion | Chester | 1642 | 258 |
| Chester Northgate | Chester | 1760 | 140 |
| Lonsdale & Adshead | Macclesfield | 1790 | 110 |
| **Cumbria** | | | |
| Brampton Old Brewery | Brampton | 1785 | 115 |
| Carlisle Old Brewery | Carlisle | 1756 | 144 |
| Whitwell, Mark & Co | Kendal | 1757 | 143 |
| Maryport Brewery | Maryport | 1780 | 120 |
| Glasson's Penrith Breweries | Penrith | 1754 | 146 |

| Brewery | Location | Date founded | Age in 1900 |
|---|---|---|---|
| Hartley's Ulverston | Ulverston | 1755 | 145 |
| Henry Spencer | Whitehaven | 1790 | 110 |
| Workington Brewery | Workington | 1795 | 105 |
| **Lancashire** | | | |
| Dutton's Blackburn Brewery | Blackburn | 1799 | 101 |
| Massey's Burnley Brewery | Burnley | 1750 | 150 |
| Yates & Jackson | Lancaster | 1669 | 231 |
| **Greater Manchester** | | | |
| Boddingtons | Manchester | 1778 | 122 |
| **Merseyside** | | | |
| Higson's Brewery | Liverpool | 1780 | 120 |
| Burton, Bell | Liverpool | 1880 | 20 |
| Greenall Whitley | St Helens | 1762 | 138 |

*Source*: extracted from data in Barber, *A century*.

## Notes

1. J. Walton, *Lancashire: a social history, 1558–1939* (Manchester, 1988); G. Timmins, *Made in Lancashire: a history of regional industrialisation* (Manchester, 1998).
2. T. R. Gourvish and R. G. Wilson, *The British brewing industry, 1830–1980* (Cambridge, 1994); A. Mutch, *Strategic and organizational change: from production to retailing in UK brewing, 1950–1990* (London, 2006).
3. Directors minute book 1865–1887, National Museum of Brewing (NMB), Burton; Allsopps 1a, 14 Dec. 1865.
4. Directors' minute book 1890–1893, NMB, Burton; Allsopps 2, 18 Dec. 1891.
5. P. Mathias, *The brewing industry in England, 1700–1830* (Cambridge, 1959); P. Jennings, *The local: a history of the English pub* (Stroud, 2007).
6. Jennings, *The local*.
7. J. Barge, *A gazetter of Liverpool breweries* (Swinton, 1987).
8. N. Barber, *A century of British brewers, plus* (New Ash Green, 2005).
9. [Jennings Brewery], 'History', http://www.jenningsbrewery.co.uk/history/, accessed 13 Dec. 2009.
10. K. H. Hawkins and C. L. Pass, *The brewing industry: a study in industrial organisation and public policy* (London, 1979), p. 29.
11. S. Salvidge, *Salvidge of Liverpool: behind the political scene, 1890–1928* (London, 1934).
12. Miller Pech Hughes & Co, to Ernest Ellis, 28 Nov. 1890, Liverpool

Record Office (LRO). Peter Walker & Son, PWK/1/8, loose private letters.
13. Timmins, *Made in Lancashire*, pp. 200–1.
14. M. Dunn, *Local brew: traditional breweries and their ales* (London, 1986), p. 187.
15. A. Mutch, 'Manchester and Liverpool public houses compared, 1840–1914', *Manchester Region History Review*, 16 (2003), pp. 22–9.
16. N. Richardson, *A history of Wilson's brewery, 1834–1984* (Swinton, 1983), p. 5.
17. R. Roberts, *The classic slum* (Manchester, 1971), p. 6.
18. Mass-Observation, *The pub and the people* (London, 1970), p. 21.
19. G. Brandwood, A. Davison and M. Slaughter, *Licensed to sell: the history and heritage of the public house* (London, 2004), p. 77.
20. [Anon], 'Advance of the managerial system', *Brewers' Journal*, 15 Oct. 1921, pp. 417–18.
21. Mutch, 'Manchester and Liverpool'.
22. T. Lane, *Liverpool: gateway of empire* (London, 1987).
23. Roberts, *Classic slum*, p. 6.
24. J. K. Walton and A. Wilcox, *Low life and moral improvement in mid Victorian England: Liverpool through the journalism of Hugh Shimmin* (Leicester, 1991), p. 169.
25. A. Mutch, 'The design of Liverpool pubs in the nineteenth century', *Brewery History*, 127 (2008), pp. 2–26.
26. A. Mutch, 'Shaping the public house 1850–1950: business strategies, state regulation and social history', *Cultural and Social History*, 1 (2004), pp. 179–200.
27. P. J. Waller, *Democracy and sectarianism: a political and social history of Liverpool, 1868–1939* (Liverpool, 1981).
28. J. Belchem, *Merseypride* (Liverpool, 2000).
29. A. Mutch, 'Magistrates and public house managers, 1840–1914: another case of Liverpool exceptionalism?', *Northern History*, 40 (2003), pp. 325–42.
30. 'Tied tenant controversy', *Liverpool Daily Post*, 5 May 1914, in 347 JUS 1/7/2, Newscuttings on licensing 1909–1915, LRO.
31. A. Mutch, 'Public houses as multiple retailing: Peter Walker & Son 1846–1914', *Business History*, 48 (2006), pp. 1–19.
32. *Royal Commission on Licensing*, Peel Commission (1898), C–8693, 1898, XXXVI, Third volume of evidence, p. 391.
33. Ibid., p. 409.
34. Ibid., p. 376.
35. N. Hyde, *Brewing was a way of life* (Hale, 1999); L. Pearson, *The history of Robinson's brewery* (Altrincham, 1997).
36. BMCWBA Reports of the Birmingham and Midland Counties Wholesale Brewers' Association, NMB (1914), p. 8.

37. BMCWBA Reports of the Birmingham and Midland Counties Wholesale Brewers' Association, NMB (1912), pp. 19, 36.
38. Mutch, 'Public houses as multiple retailing'.
39. Mutch, *Strategic and organizational change*.

# 'An absorbing epic'? The development of toy-manufacturing in the North West, c1851–1931

Ken Brown

In the early 1920s the author of what purported to be the first serious book in English on the development of commercial toy-making asserted that the emergence of the sector as 'one of the standing industries of Great Britain' was the direct result of what he euphemistically termed the recent 'continental upheaval'.[1] A decade or so later, a London journalist was equally confident in reiterating that the country's toy industry could 'be said to date from about the beginning of 1915'.[2] Sir William Crawford agreed, referring to the post-war success of the nascent British industry as 'one of the absorbing epics of modern business'.[3]

It is unlikely that many contemporaries would have echoed this somewhat exaggerated rhetoric since the hyperbole reflected less a reality than Crawford's professional background in advertising and the fact that his agency held a major contract with Meccano Ltd, then one of the country's leading toy manufacturers. Nevertheless, that the First World War had in effect created this new young industry in Britain was – and long remained – a widely shared perception. It rested, however, on two misconceptions.

The first was a failure to recognize the extent to which an indigenous industry had developed prior to 1914. In official censuses of occupations and industrial output, the major industries on which British prosperity had grown from the early nineteenth century naturally tended to overshadow smaller scale, more widely dispersed, manufacturing activities. Consequently, as one economist put it in 1900, the latter were 'hardly taken into account' in contemporary accounts of Britain's economic development.[4] Yet as another nineteenth-century writer observed, such manufactories produced a variety of foodstuffs, textiles, and household items which were in constant everyday demand. Objects such as these, he concluded, 'which we all require to use ... cannot in any way be considered unimportant', a conclusion which has been supported, particularly in recent years, by the findings of economic historians who have explored and increasingly stressed the enduring significance of small-scale activity in the world's most advanced economies.[5]

In the case of children's toys there was a further, specific reason for contemporaries' failure to appreciate the extent of indigenous development before 1914. By that date Germany was the world's leading producer, a position secured in the 1890s, largely through aggressive marketing which allowed three-quarters of total output to be exported.[6] Along with the US, Britain was a major destination for German toys drawn in by a domestic demand which was rising as a consequence of higher rising real incomes, generally low unemployment, falling family size, and the extension of schooling, together with changes in attitudes towards childhood and children. By 1913 Germany supplied about 80 per cent of Britain's total toy imports. Yet precisely these same forces of demand were simultaneously fostering significant developments in Britain's own manufacturing capacity, even though official records show that total toy imports worth £1.45m in 1913 were almost six times larger than the £265,000 of domestically produced toys recorded in the 1907 census of production.[7] In fact, however, as I have shown at length elsewhere, this latter figure represented a massive under-estimation, but by virtue of the fact that it carried the official, statistical imprimatur of the Board of Trade, it served to reinforce the widespread perception that Britain had little toy-manufacturing of its own before 1914.[8] While German merchants and German-based agents were certainly prominent in developing the distribution side of the trade in Britain, E. E. Williams was quite wrong to claim in the 1890s that the playthings of British children were to a large and ever increasing extent manufactured in Germany.[9] However, his claims appeared all too plausible to a British public and press increasingly paranoid about the long-term strategic threat thought to be posed by the rapid and spectacular expansion of the German economy and state. Nor did it much concern his temperamentally receptive readership that Williams was equally inaccurate in implying that the German industry benefited from operating with modern technology and better organization, a claim which completely overlooked the fact that German toy-making, like its British equivalent, was still predominantly small scale and essentially hand-based. Germany's occupational census of 1907, for instance, showed that a third of those employed in industry and handicrafts (*Industrie und Handwerke*) worked in firms with fewer than five employees.[10]

Second, the notion that no significant British industry existed prior to 1914 gained additional credence from the activities of the Board of Trade itself during the First World War. It may appear somewhat

Liverpool capturing German trade, *Liverpool Express*, c1910

paradoxical that even as the country engaged in what was to prove its bloodiest and costliest international conflict to date, an innocent and unwarlike activity such as toy-making should have prospered. Yet its growth was inherent in the very nature of a war which for the first time in British experience developed a sustained, systematic and comprehensive economic dimension. As early as September 1914 the Board of Trade organized an exhibition of products, including toys, which it believed could be manufactured in Britain in the enforced absence of German competition. As a further incentive, emergency legislation was used to scrap many extant German patents. The following year the Board held a meeting for industrialists engaged in such industries. What happened at this meeting subsequently became a source of contention after the war when British toy-manufacturers, faced with renewed German competition, promptly demanded tariff protection in line with the pledges which, they claimed, had been made by Board of Trade officials at the 1915 meeting. No written evidence of any such promises exists, and one importer told a 1922 Board of Trade inquiry that the government had given no commitment to restrict imports; rather, he said, the notion had been 'fostered'.[11] However, the manufacturers themselves were unanimous that verbal assurances were given and indeed effectively reaffirmed in Lloyd George's later declaration that 'new industries have been set up and we are not going to drop them after the war'.[12] Certainly if no such promises had been made, it is difficult to understand why so many existing toy businesses expanded in the early years of the war, or why so many new entrepreneurs should have been attracted into the trade. But whatever was said in 1915, it is clear that as part of the manufacturing lobby's ultimately unsuccessful struggle to secure an import tariff after the war, it was tactically convenient to emphasize that the *de facto* protection bestowed by the war had effectively created an indigenous industry, where virtually nothing had existed prior to 1914. In this way, post-war political manoeuvrings acted to reinforce the popular misunderstanding about the chronology of toy-making's development in Britain.

Developments in the North West contributed significantly to this interpretation of the industry's emergence because toy-manufacturing in the region appears to have sprung into existence virtually overnight and as a specific response to the opportunities afforded by the outbreak of the First World War. Within a year or so of the Board of Trade meeting in 1915, for example, local journalists were proclaiming proudly that no other city had adopted the trade to anything like the same extent as Liverpool.[13] Estimates in the trade press suggested that this 'city of toys' had between 2,500 and 3,000 people engaged in toy-making by 1916.[14] In the same year toy interests in Manchester joined with their Liverpool counterparts to establish one of the first regional branches of the new Incorporated Association of British Toy Manufacturers and Wholesalers Ltd, set up by the trade to exploit the opportunities created by the war. Altogether, almost a half of the new organization's 111 members were based in Lancashire.[15] Shortly after the armistice came into effect in November 1918, a trade journalist predicted a rosy future for the British toy-manufacturer, claiming, that 'in a very little time now the markets of the whole world will be open to him and the demands from overseas will dwarf into insignificance the business he had been doing during the past four years'. More specifically, he went on to suggest that in the North West prospects were so promising that even the armaments giant, Vickers, was said to be considering toy-making as an alternative activity for its extended workforce.[16] An official guide for overseas toy-buyers, published in 1919, identified Lancashire as Britain's second main toy-making centre after London, stressing in particular the importance of Liverpool.[17] In the same year a similar list, based on a 1918 survey conducted by the Ministry of Labour, coupled Liverpool with Manchester as two of the trade's main cities.[18] W. H. Nicholls, himself engaged in the local trade and thus unconstrained by any official reticence, verged on the ecstatic in claiming that over the last three years the regional industry had 'leapt into prominence', its foundation laid in Liverpool, now 'the most important toy making centre in the country' with over twenty manufacturers providing employment for more than 4,000 individuals. 'Great enterprise has been shown', he enthused, 'and in no place has this exceeded the united effort of the members of the toy-trade in Liverpool.'[19]

This somewhat heady rhetoric was in marked contrast to the total absence of any official recognition of a regional toy industry before 1914. Lancashire's pivotal role in the industrial revolution resulted in a predictable emphasis on cotton, shipbuilding, coal, iron, steel, and engineering, all of which reached their peak in the decades before 1914; such was their physical presence and their dominance in official records and statistics that smaller-scale activities tended to get overlooked by contemporaries. Even under the single heading of 'miscellaneous', which lumped together the work of the thousands engaged in small-scale and often scattered manufactures such as beer, biscuits, jam, matches, tobacco and billiard tables, the editors of the 1908 *Victoria county history of Lancashire* apparently saw no justification for including any mention of toy-making.[20] The industry fared no better in a survey of Lancashire manufacturing published on behalf of the county's Chambers of Commerce in 1912. The editors referred to the 'numerous and varied ... enterprises' to be found in Manchester that were not based on textiles, but toys found no place even in a list which included corsets, elastic bands, and candle wicks.[21] It was the same with respect to Liverpool which, while dominated by shipping, was also home to numerous minor industries whose very existence 'is scarcely suspected by the visitor and hardly realised by the residents'.[22] Once again, however, toys were not mentioned. This was entirely consistent with the 1911 occupational census which, whilst noting an increase in the numbers employed nationally in the manufacture of fishing-tackle, games, and toys, identified London and Worcestershire as the main centres of activity in Britain.[23]

Interestingly, however, unlike some of his less careful contemporaries, W. H. Nicholls was one of the few to acknowledge that the wartime growth of the toy industry in the North West rested on foundations that had been laid much earlier in the previous century. What follows in the rest of this essay charts that earlier development, shows that expansion between 1914 and the ending of the post-war boom in 1921 was merely temporary, and suggests that the industry's wartime prosperity was more apparent than real, in the longer term primarily benefiting only those enterprises already well established before the war began.

In tracing the emergence of the regional industry before 1914, considerable care has to be exercised in the interpretation of the major sources, occupational censuses and trade directories. Indeed, such are their limitations that the structure and dimensions of the industry can be outlined only in the very broadest terms and for the most part with little statistical reliability. It has long been acknowledged that occupational classification was imprecise and variable and data collection too random to confer much credibility on figures of occupational structure before the beginning of the twentieth century, especially in the case of small-scale industries with relatively few workers. Furthermore, in the case of toy-manufacturing, interpretation of the data is further complicated by semantic considerations, as the meaning of the word 'toy' evolved over time. Although by the mid nineteenth century the term was widely an increase in the number of toy businesses is readily apparent in Table 3. With the growth of regional prosperity, distributors could be found in most urban centres by the 1860s and some appeared even earlier. Sassi's in Wigan, for example, dated from the 1830s, although its staff were evidently missed from the 1851 census. According to one account of its removal to new premises in 1926, a visit there had long been counted by local children 'as one of the supreme joys of existence'.[24] Bury and Oldham had fourteen and five toy businesses respectively in 1853. As Liverpool's largest wholesale enterprise, Riley and Co. could trace its origins back to the 1840s, while its main local competitor, G. E. Garnett & Sons, was only a decade or so younger. Much of the stock sold through such outlets was acquired from Manchester which from the 1860s was the location for the annual toy fairs established by German manufacturers and agents and through which much of the upsurge of German toy exports to Britain was channelled. By 1913 over a fifth of Manchester-based fancy-goods importers were German.[25]

|  | Liverpool |  |  | Manchester |  |  |
|---|---|---|---|---|---|---|
|  | 1853 | 1870 | 1900 | 1850 | 1876 | 1901 |
| Toy Dealers | 30 | 37 | 37 | 30 | 48 | 65 |
| Fancy Warehouses | 28 | 38 | 132 | 6 | 137 | 44 |
| Toy/Fancy Goods Importer |  | 7 | 17 |  |  | 60 |

Sources: *Commercial directory and shippers' guide to Liverpool* (1870); *Gore's Liverpool directory* (1853); *Gore's directory of Liverpool and Birkenhead* (1900); *Slater's directory of Manchester and Salford* (1876; 1901).

**Table 3:** North West businesses engaged in toys and related trades, 1850–1901

But indigenous manufacturing had also been developing in the North West since the middle of the nineteenth century. As early as 1836, for example, the Collinson family in Liverpool began to make rocking horses of so fine a quality that Queen Victoria is said to have purchased one in 1851. Also in Liverpool, George Richardson was advertising himself as a manufacturer and dealer in mechanical toys and boats in the 1860s.[26] A few years earlier, William Lindop had begun production of indoor games in Manchester. With easy access to a heavily populated hinterland, manufacturing in both cities benefited from the rising domestic demand for children's toys which gained particular momentum over the last two decades of the century. Ready access to textile wastage from the cotton industry encouraged firms such as Nunn and Smeed, for example, to enter the soft-toy market, while at the turn of the century Messrs Gray and Nicholls extended its existing line of soft toys by becoming one of the first British firms to produce the popular new teddy bear. Indeed, this firm's product diversification at this time was so marked that it prompted one observer to suggest later that it produced 'probably … the greatest variety of toys turned out by any one firm'.[27] The growing use of rubber also found an echo in the toy market. In 1895 the New Eccles Rubber Works opened in Manchester with an initial output target of 70,000 rubber balls a week, rather more ambitious than a similar establishment launched in the same year in Liverpool by R. B. Donkin.

Slightly earlier Liverpool saw the establishment, respectively in 1888 and 1893, of Baby Carriages Ltd, producers of large wooden toys, including prams for dolls, and Usher and Co., rocking-horse- and dolls' pram-makers. Both firms were able to access timber very easily, reflecting the important role played by Liverpool since the early nineteenth century as a major national centre for timber imports. By 1912 there were over 200 importers and more than fifty saw mills operating in the city.[28] Of particular importance were Irvin and Sellers and the Liverpool Timber Company, both specializing in the supply of the birch dowels and three-ply timber widely used in the trade. The opening of the Ship Canal led some Liverpool importers to establish facilities in Manchester where storage facilities for timber were cheaper. By 1914 the city boasted a number of wooden-toy-makers, the largest of which was J. and T. Thorp, employing almost 900 workers.

Even more significant, however, was the growth of a tin-toy sector. The Manchester firm of Wallwork, for instance, began to make tin-floor trains as a sideline in the 1880s, but it was Liverpool which led the way in this sector, benefiting in part at least from the ready availability of tin offcuts from the tobacco industry. Merseyside was home to a number of major tobacco firms, including Gallahers and Ogdens, together with three component firms of the Imperial Tobacco Company of Great Britain and Ireland – Hignett Brothers and Co., William Clarke and Son Ltd, and Richmond Cavendish Co. Ltd. Framus, a metal construction toy made by Gray and Nicholls, for example, was manufactured from waste tin acquired from Wills and Sons. Paton Calvert and Co., manufacturers since 1887 of a variety of tin-plate objects, expanded into metal-toy production with its Happynak range from 1908. In the same year and notwithstanding some initial doubts about the market appeal of his new metal construction toy, patented as Meccano in 1901, Frank Hornby established Meccano Ltd. His confidence was well founded, for in 1914 he was able to move his new company into a purpose built factory in Binns Road, covering some 216,000 square feet and housing a workforce about 1,000-strong.[29]

By that date Meccano construction sets were said to have the largest world wide sales of any single toy before 1914, reflecting the early establishment of company offices in Europe and the success of the product in the American market, where sales rose from $7,000 to $114,000 between 1909 and 1912. In this respect, of course, Hornby benefited from the well established facilities, services and expertise associated with Liverpool's docks, which serviced more of Britain's exports than any other port. A corollary of this was that employment opportunities in the city focussed around the docks and their associated trades, portering and carrying, warehousing, financial services such as underwriting and insurance, and the corn and cotton exchanges. It is true that by 1914 the city's industrial hinterland did incorporate heavy industries such as shipbuilding and milling in Birkenhead, glass-making in St Helens and chemicals in Widnes, but it has been suggested that Liverpool made a positive virtue out of the fact that it had little heavy manufacturing of its own.[30] In this context there was comparatively little industrial work for females. Women, however, were ideally suited for the light assembly and finishing processes associated with particular sectors of the toy industry. Female labour was also well suited to soft-toy making, much of which was carried out at home and could thus be combined with family responsibilities. Women were also widely employed by tin-toy makers such as Meccano where by 1914 forty male toolmakers worked in the plating department alongside 'several hundred girls'.[31] For those who employed women, whether in the home or the factory, there was the added and considerable benefit that female labour was cheap, Hornby telling one government inquiry that prior to 1914 he employed girls for between five and six shillings a week.[32] Other manufacturers, particularly those in London, certainly

Hornby Locomotive 3435.
J.Gamble

regarded pre-war wage rates in the Liverpool toy industry as being extraordinarily low.[33]

Yet it remained the case in 1914 that the north-western toy industry was still more concentrated in Manchester than in Liverpool. Of fifty-nine north-western enterprises listed in what purported to be the first ever comprehensive list of manufacturers and wholesalers, published in 1913, thirty-six were located in Manchester and ten in Liverpool, with the remaining thirteen shared between other local towns.[34] Seven years and one Great War later, however, a second survey revealed a significantly different picture. By that date some 120 local enterprises were to be found in the North West and if Manchester still dominated with fifty, this represented a growth rate significantly smaller than that of Liverpool which now had thirty-five.[35] As suggested above, contemporaries wasted no time in trumpeting the 'emergence' of Liverpool as the leading toy centre, not only regionally but also nationally. But the war's primary impact on manufacturing in Liverpool and Manchester was catalytic rather than creative, boosting what already existed rather than creating an entirely new sector, although it did also provide an impetus for some entrepreneurs to begin the manufacture of playthings previously supplied, in the main, by German companies. Most prominent amongst these in Liverpool were two new soft-toy producers, Sloan and Co. and J. P. Millar. In Manchester, the newcomers included tin-toy makers J. G. Brenner and Co. Ltd and the Acme Toy Company. By and large, however, such enterprises remained small, certainly in comparison with some of the well established pre-war firms. More commonly, the absence of German competition encouraged existing manufacturers to extend their product ranges. Ultimately this was to see Frank Hornby emerge as the world's leading producer of model-train sets, even though his initial venture in this direction, a clockwork railway engine exhibited at the British Industries Fair in 1915, was not universally acclaimed and he was unable to pursue production because within a year or so his Binns Road factory was commandeered for war work. Also in 1915, another Liverpool company, Whiteley Tansley, which had originally made press tools for German toy-makers, began to produce its own range of toys. In a different sector of the industry, Dolls Supplies Ltd added soft toys to its existing range of dolls. Gray and Nicholls also extended their already extensive product lines, ending the war with a catalogue of 150 different items.[36] Finally, there were a number of distributors who responded to the declining requirement for their services by diversifying into manufacturing in their own right. These included the importers, Nunn and Smeed, who began making jointed dolls in 1914, and toy factors Hawksley & Co., a firm which first manufactured a range of war-related toys, including wooden forts and battleships, before diversifying into soft toys, games, and stone building blocks. J. C. Plimpton was another enterprise which prior to the war had been primarily engaged in importing American toys to Britain but which now entered large-scale production on its own account, turning out wooden toys such as playhouses.

However, it was not long before war-induced shortages began to impact adversely on these activities. As far as labour was concerned, the initial rush of volunteers to the colours affected primarily those sectors of the toy-trade that were particularly reliant on male workers, mainly the heavy wooden-toy producers. In Manchester, Thorp suffered particularly badly in this respect since its workforce was almost entirely male: so, too did J. C. Plimpton and Usher and Co. in Liverpool, with both firms reporting scarcities of skilled male workers.[37] Toy-sectors with predominantly female labour forces were better placed, at least in the early stages of the war: indeed, the diversion of men to the military had the effect of driving more women into the labour market. In the longer run, however, labour supply to the industry became a major problem as the introduction of national conscription systematically weeded men out of the labour force, and the steady expansion of better paid work in munitions and other industries eventually acted as a check on the supply of female labour to the toy-makers.

By the middle of the war, the rising price and diminishing supply of raw material were also affecting toy-manufacturers with varying degrees of severity. Within a month or two of the start of the war the price of strawboard, widely used in the industry for packaging, rose by some 75 per cent, while the North West's wooden-toy sector was also hit by a 60 per cent increase in the cost of planking in the first six months of the conflict. Even the price of the plush required by soft-toy makers doubled between the autumns of 1915 and 1916. As import restrictions and controls on usage for non-essential purposes were progressively extended, so accumulated stocks were exhausted. Timber supplies to toy-makers effectively dried up, for example, much to the annoyance of one of their number who complained that only a member of a British government could be such a fool as to allow the import of golf-club shafts whilst banning the import of timber dowels on which toy-makers depended.[38] As for metals, lead prices shot up between 40 and 60 per cent by October 1914 while tin prices tripled between 1914 and 1916.[39] Major users like Meccano had taken good care to buy up as much in advance as was legitimately possible, thereby safeguarding to some extent against rising prices, but in 1917 all metal supplies were controlled for the exclusive use of strategic industries.

In one sense, this did not matter too much, for by that time increasing proportions of workers in the largest firms had been diverted to war production. However, this throws up yet a further caveat on the notion that the Great War was the prime mover in the emergence of a north-western toy industry centred in Liverpool. Whilst it is true that employment in the toy industry did expand in the way highlighted by contemporaries, two things must be emphasized. First, six firms in the city, Meccano (1,200 employees in 1915), Whiteley Tansley (over 600 at its peak), Nunn and Smeed (200 at the end of the war), Gray Nichols (250 employees in 1919), Hawksley and Co. (400) and Paton Calvert and Co. (unknown but the firm had 400 employees in 1901) accounted for about three-quarters of the 4,000 said to be engaged in the industry.[40] Second, from 1916 onwards toy-makers were increasingly required to devote their resources to war work rather than toy-production and the expansion of the labour force, therefore, did not necessarily reflect any increase in the scale of toy-manufacturing. By 1918, for example, half of the Whiteley Tansley workforce was producing war-related goods. At the Paton Calvert and Co. factory in Binns Road, Happynak toys gave way in the middle of the war to military products for the forces, including boot polish, gas-mask parts and fuse cases. On the other side of Binns Road, the requisitioning by the government of his factory effectively curtailed Frank Hornby's capacity for toy production and well over 40 per cent of his company's total sales by the end of the war were generated by war work rather than toys.[41] Furthermore, a growing proportion of his toy revenue came from repairs and sales of accumulated stocks.

Finally, it is worth noting that as soon as peace returned and the immediate post-war boom worked itself out, much of the war-induced change in the local toy industry, especially in Liverpool, simply disappeared. With it also vanished official recognition of the North West region as a leading toy centre. It will be recalled that both Liverpool and Manchester were identified as national hubs in 1919 but a Ministry of Labour survey eight years later indicated that London and the Midlands had regained their positions as the main centres, accounting respectively for over a half and a fifth of the country's toy-manufacturing concerns. The four north-western counties between them contained just forty-six manufacturers, reflecting the relative decline of the industry once imports recovered.[42] Indeed, it had been in anticipation of just such a post-war contraction that many north-western manufacturers had demanded, while the war was still in progress, guarantees that tariff protection would be provided. The more percipient demanded a total ban on all imports, conscious perhaps of the potential threat from relative newcomers like Japan, whose toy exports tripled in value between 1914 and 1916 and then tripled again by 1920 to ¥21,000,000.[43] But the main fear was the prospect of revived German competition. Liverpool members of the Incorporated Association were debating this as early as September 1916 and had proposed a five-year ban on imports from the country's present enemies once peace was restored. The Manchester branch returned to the same theme in 1917 and led the protests against German imports after the war was over, urging buyers and wholesalers to buy no German goods for two years. North-western firms Whiteley Tansley, Paton Calvert, Nunn and Smeed, and Meccano, all appeared as witnesses on behalf of the manufacturers when the Board of Trade considered the case for protection under the auspices of the 1921 Safeguarding of Industries Act. Ultimately, however, the case was rejected as it was not supported by wholesalers, importers or retailers, all of whom argued that, with a few exceptions, British manufacturers could not compete in terms of price, quality, or service. The unsuccessful outcome was made even more galling for the manufacturers who could only watch in envy as their American counterparts launched a similar campaign and successfully persuaded the Senate Finance Committee to pass the Fordney-McCumber tariff bill doubling the previous tariff on toys to 70 per cent.[44]

One indirect outcome of the manufacturers' failure to secure protection was a partial resurgence in the fortunes of the Manchester toy-fair, as the return of peace saw an upturn in the international toy trade to the benefit of importers and wholesalers. But Manchester never regained its status as the sole focus of the nation's toy trade. Major domestic manufacturers tended to follow the example set by Frank Hornby, shunning Manchester in favour of London which effectively became the more important focal point of the industry in the post-war years. A second and more significant consequence of the failure to secure protection was a spate of failures among manufacturers, exactly as had been anticipated. However, most of the casualties occurred among firms which took up toy-making during the war itself, just as the wholesalers and importers had predicted to the Board of Trade inquiry. In the Manchester-Liverpool region, for example, Montague and Sons went out of business in 1921, Leonard and Francis followed suit in 1922 as did the Manchester tin-toy makers, J. G. Brenner and Co. in 1923, and Tribe and Astin in 1925. Whiteley Tansley, which had produced £93,000 of toys in 1920 with a workforce of some 300, may have survived but only by dint of abandoning toy-making altogether in 1921 by which time its labour force was down to fifty-four. Employment at Nunn and Smeed contracted similarly, falling from 260 in 1920 to fewer than twelve in 1922 and while this firm also survived, it did so only by giving up manufacture and reverting to its original import business. Interestingly, both firms had been established well before the war. So too, had the manufacturer Gray Nicholls, which, while it survived the conflict, subsequently fell victim to the Great Depression in 1930.

Its demise left Liverpool with only one manufacturer of any significance, Meccano. Frank Hornby's company weathered the post-war depression by reducing its labour force from 1,454 in 1921 to 453 by early 1922, before being transported to new heights of national and international prominence on the back of highly successful product innovation in the form of Gauge 0 train sets and die-cast Dinky model vehicles. Meccano, of course, was a pre-war foundation: that it survived as the lone flagship of toy-making in the North West after 1918 confirms that the significant development of the industry in the North West preceded the Great War, and that much of the expansion encouraged by the war was temporary. North-western toy making was, in other words, more of a blip than 'an absorbing epic'.

## Notes

1. W. T. Makinson, *Toy manufacture* (London, n.d.), p. 1. Although the book itself is undated, the British Library accession date is given as 6 June 1921.
2. *Morning Post*, 14 Dec. 1931.
3. *Toy Trader* (Jan. 1930), p. 2.
4. P. Kropotkin, 'The small industries of Britain', *Nineteenth Century*, 48 (1900), p. 270.
5. G. C. Bartley, 'Toys', in G. P. Bevan, ed., *British manufacturing industries* (London, 1876), p. 200. For examples of work on the importance of small-scale manufacturing see C. Sabel and J. Zeitlin, 'Historical alternatives to mass production: politics, markets and technology in nineteenth-century industrialization', *Past and Present*, 108 (1985), pp. 133–76; M. Berg, 'Factories, workshops and industrial organisation', in R. Floud and D. McCloskey, eds., *Economic history of Britain since 1700*, vol 1: 1700–1860 (3 vols., Cambridge, 1994), pp. 123–50; G. Herrigel, *Industrial constructions: the sources of German industrial power* (Cambridge, 1996); P. Scranton, *Endless novelty* (Princeton, 1997); P. Hudson, 'Industrial organisation and structure', in R. Floud and P. Johnson, eds., *Cambridge economic history of modern Britain*, vol. 1 (3 vols., Cambridge, 2004), pp. 28–56.
6. G. Cross and G. Smits, 'Japan, the US and the globalization of children's consumer culture', *Journal of Social History*, 39 (2005), pp. 873–90.
7. Kenneth D. Brown, *The British toy business: a history since 1700* (London, 1996), pp. 46, 65. In the same year America imported some $10,000,000-worth of German toys. See M. Tanimoto, 'From peasant economy

to urban agglomeration: the transformation of labour intensive industrialization in modern industrial Japan', http://www.e.u-tokyo.ac.jp/cirje/research/dp/2007/2007cf516.pdf, accessed 17 Dec. 2009.
8. Brown, *British toy business*, pp. 65–78.
9. E. E. Williams, *Made in Germany* (London, 1896), p. 110.
10. D. Geary, 'The European working classes in the late nineteenth and early twentieth centuries', in H. Kaeble, ed., *The European way* (Oxford, 2004), p. 122. See also W. Egle, 'The progress of mass production and the German small-scale industries', *Political Economy*, 46 (1938), pp. 376–95; D. Hamlin, 'Flexible specialisation and the German toy industry, 1870–1914', *Social History*, 29 (2004), pp. 30–46. For contemporary descriptions of the German toy industry, see 'How Germany makes toys', *Playthings* (Feb. 1908), pp. 49–54; 'The toy industry of Germany', *Scientific American*, 10 Dec. 1904.
11. PRO BT 55/80/88. Minutes of Proceedings before the Committee Appointed under the Safeguarding of Industries Act 1921 to Consider Complaints with Respect to Toys, 6 Feb. 1922, p. 127.
12. Quoted later in *Toyshop and Fancy Goods Journal* (Oct. 1918), p. 147.
13. *Liverpool Post and Daily Mercury*, 26 Aug. 1916.
14. *Toy and Fancy Goods Trader* (Aug. 1916), p. 28.
15. Guildhall Library MS 17688. Toy and Fancy Goods Federation Minutes, 1 June 1916.
16. *Toy and Fancy Goods Trader* (Dec. 1918), p. 54.
17. *Overseas buyers' guide to British toys and fancy goods* (1919).
18. PRO LAB 2/482. *The Toy Trade. Summary Report on the Present Position* (1919).
19. W. H. Nicholls, 'Toymaking', in [Liverpool Chamber of Commerce], *Liverpool: its trade and commerce* (Liverpool, 1920), p. 100.
20. W. Farrer and J. Brownbill, eds., *Victoria history of the county of Lancaster* (London, 1908), p. 408.
21. R. S. Attwood and J. Child, eds., *The Lancashire year book of industries and commerce* (Manchester, 1912), p. 151.
22. Ibid., p. 183.
23. Census of England and Wales, 1911. *British Parliamentary Papers*, 78 (1913), p. 399.
24. *Toy Trader* (June 1926), p. 57.
25. *Slater's Manchester and Salford trades directory and professional directory for 1913* (Manchester, 1913).
26. *Routledge Magazine for Boys* (Sep. 1868), p. 576.
27. *Toy and Fancy Goods Trader* (Aug. 1916), p. 50.
28. Attwood and Child, eds., *Lancashire year book*, p. 183.
29. In the absence of any extant figures for employment, this is a calculation based on the size of the firm's wage bill. For the pre-war development of the company see Kenneth D. Brown, *Factory of dreams: a history of*

*Meccano Ltd* (Lancaster, 2007), pp. 27–40.
30. H. B. McCartney, *Citizen soldiers: the Liverpool territorials in the First World War* (Cambridge, 2005), p. 9.
31. *Toy and Fancy Goods Trader* (3 May 1915).
32. PRO BT 55/80/88. Minutes of Proceedings before the Committee Appointed under the Safeguarding of Industries Act 1921 to Consider Complaints with Respect to Toys, 6 Feb. 1922, p. 57.
33. Guildhall Library MSS 16778. Meeting of the Employers' Side of the Trade Board, 3 Aug. 1922.
34. R. B. Tattersall, ed., *Directory of manufacturers and wholesalers of toys and fancy goods* (1913).
35. H. R. Simmons, ed., *Games and toy trade directory for 1920* (1920).
36. *Overseas buyers' guide*, p. 58.
37. *Toy and Fancy Goods Trader* (Aug. 1916), pp. 44, 50.
38. Ibid. (June 1916), p. 2.
39. Ibid. (July 1916), p. 4.
40. The figure for Meccano is derived from the reference given in support of Roland Hornby's application for an army commission and quoted in J. Gamble, *Frank Hornby: notes and pictures* (Nottingham, 2001), p. 68. Figures for Whiteley Tansley and Nunn and Smeed were given in evidence to the Board of Trade inquiry: See PRO BT 55/80/88. Minutes of Proceedings before the Committee Appointed under the Safeguarding of Industries Act 1921 to Consider Complaints with Respect to Toys, 6 Feb. 1922, p. 36; 17 Feb. 1922, p. 88. The figure for Gray and Nichols is from *Overseas buyers' guide*, p. 58, and that for Hawksley and Co. is from *Toy and Fancy Goods Trader* (Aug. 1916), p. 62. That Paton Calvert had 400 employees in 1901 and expanded during the War is suggested by M. Fawdry, *British tin toys* (London, 1990), p. 96.
41. Merseyside Maritime Museum, Meccano Archives, B/ME/B/2.
42. PRO LAB 2/1142/TB135/23/1926. Ministry of Labour Information Relating to the Toy Manufacturing Trade (1927).
43. Tanimoto, 'From peasant economy'. Celluloid toys were Japan's 13th-most important export between 1914 and 1918. Production in Tokyo alone went up to ¥1,920,000 in 1918 from ¥300,000 in 1914.
44. M. Formanek-Brunell, *Made to play house: dolls and the commercialization of American girlhood, 1830–1930* (Baltimore, MD; 1998), p. 148.

merchants, each underwriting part of a ship and its cargo for a single journey with a defined route, became the predominant form of marine insurance, at least while English law prevented the formation of any stock companies that would breach the privileges of the two London corporations.

The expansion of Liverpool shipping was closely related to the transatlantic trade in slaves and slave-produced commodities, notably cotton and sugar. The port became the primary location for the UK's raw cotton imports and re-exports, which grew from 1.6m lbs in 1730 to 60.4m by 1800.[9] By 1730 Liverpool merchants were regularly outfitting and insuring slave ships for the African coast and the journey on to the Americas. By mid century the town had seized the lead in the trade from Bristol and London. Between 1780 and the abolition of the trade in 1807, Liverpool merchants financed three-quarters of all British slaving voyages.[10] Abolition, however, did not have a noticeable impact on the amount of marine insurance taken there.[11] Indeed, there is evidence to suggest that the insurance capacity of underwriters in Liverpool was increasing, as they were able to take slices of larger or more difficult marine risks not fully covered by underwriters at Lloyds or by the two London insurance corporations. The *Scaleby Castle*, for instance, travelling from Bombay to London in 1801, was insured for £148,100, mostly in London, but £20,000 of this was insured in Liverpool and Manchester.[12] Moreover, the establishment of the Liverpool Underwriters' Association in 1802 helped reduce the port's dependence on London underwriting and reflected the expanding local market for the insurance of all types of transatlantic trade.

**Eighteenth-century fire insurance**

Towards the end of the eighteenth century, the business communities of Liverpool and Manchester grew rapidly in size, wealth and confidence as traders in slaves, cotton, sugar and other plantation crops, and the rising ranks of textile merchant-manufacturers, diversified their activities into banking, canal, insurance and property ventures, and moved into positions of dominance in municipal government and civic life.[13] Business diversification occurred not only into marine insurance, as a close offshoot of overseas trade, but also into fire insurance. Before the 1770s all fire insurance in the region was imported from London. The Royal Exchange Assurance had agents operating out of Liverpool and Lancaster in the 1730s.[14] The Sun Fire office had a continuous sales representation in Manchester and Liverpool from 1730, and agencies in Lancaster from 1735 and in the Preston district from 1759. Despite these sales outlets, fire insurance remained heavily skewed towards southern England until the final two decades of the eighteenth century. As late as 1781, the Sun received eighteen times more premium income per inhabitant in London than in Lancashire. By the end of the century, however, this ratio had fallen to five as agency business in Manchester and Liverpool exploded. Sun's average annual premiums from the North West rose from just £295 in 1740 to nearly £11,000 by 1799.[15]

The Sun Fire Office was almost the only fire insurer operating in the North West before 1770. This near monopoly, however, was rudely interrupted by two new local offices, the first such business ventures in the region. In 1771 the Manchester Bank and Insurance Office was established as an offshoot of the town's first private bank.[16] It appointed agents in places like Salford and Stockport and had some initial impact on the Sun's local business. However, by the end of the decade that impact had worn off. With the cotton boom attracting capital and people to Manchester, the Sun's local agency premiums increased eightfold between 1783 and 1793. When the banking arm of the Manchester firm foundered in the financial crisis of 1788, its insurance business was offered to the Phoenix Fire Office of London, which had only been established six years earlier and was expanding rapidly in the North West.[17]

The second insurance venture in the North West was the Liverpool Fire Office, founded by eight local merchants in 1776 with a nominal capital of £80,000.[18] The initial success of this venture owed much to the powerful social and business connections of its owners. Of the seventeen men who were proprietors of Liverpool Fire Office during its eighteen-year existence, all but one, an attorney, were merchants, and eleven were shipowners. They included some of the largest slave traders operating out of the port, such as Thomas Earle, John and Thomas Tarleton, and three members of the wealthy merchant-banking family of Heywood. They drew bills on each other, sold shares in ships, bought each other's property, invested together, in ones and twos, in a range of ventures, including a cloth mill, a coffee house and a sugar refinery. They also signed petitions and memorials to parliament for various causes, and were prominent in local government. The Fire Office furnished four mayors of Liverpool, and, in the year of the company's foundation, eight of the forty-four members of the parish committee.[19]

The close interlocking of business interests among the Liverpool Fire Office proprietors is one example of the power of mercantile and manufacturing elites collectively diversifying into the service sector of their regional economies towards the end of the eighteenth century. The new company appointed some two dozen agents in 'most of the principal towns' of Cheshire, Lancashire, Derbyshire, Staffordshire,

Leicestershire, Yorkshire and as far north as Edinburgh, and in 1788 it competed vigorously with the London offices for the business of the Manchester Insurance Office while the latter was being transferred to the Phoenix.[20] The Sun's annual income from Liverpool fell from £1,200 in 1775 to a low of £650 by the mid 1780s. As in Manchester, however, premiums did recover, so that the impact of the Liverpool Fire Office during the final years of its operations was much reduced. The main effect of the competition seems to have been to delay the take-off in the growth of Sun's local insurances, so that the Liverpool agency lagged behind its counterpart in Manchester in profiting from the cotton boom. In the winter of 1794/5, when many of the partners' trading activities were struggling, the Liverpool Fire Office fell into the hands of the Phoenix Fire Office. The acquisition gave the Phoenix at least £1.2m of local insurances and considerably strengthened its position in the Liverpool market.[21]

There was one further effort to establish a fire-insurance company in Liverpool when a group of merchants, including John Gladstone, founded the St George Office in 1801. The St George, however, was soon fatally wounded by a huge fire among the Goree warehouses in Liverpool in the following year. Its £3.5m of insurances were acquired in 1805 by another new London office, the Imperial.[22] Thus, after more than three decades of trying, fire insurance in the North West reverted back to its position before 1771, of relying entirely on underwriting imported from outside the region, mainly from London. Why did these efforts end in failure? First, fire insurance was unlikely to succeed when run by small private partnerships. The Manchester bankers did not have the underwriting expertise or the deep pockets of their rivals among the London insurance companies. The first Liverpool fire office had more partners than the Manchester firm, but still not enough to raise the capital required to underwrite widely enough outside the region and avoid dangerous local concentrations of risk, while the St George was snuffed out in its infancy by a huge urban fire disaster. Given the limited underwriting capacity of these small offices, they eventually found it hard to compete with the large London offices doing business on a national scale. Fire insurance risks were not discrete like ships – the contiguity of insured property to other hazards became a major issue for underwriters in Britain's towns at the end of the eighteenth century – and they were not short-term like sea voyages. Fire-insurance policies were usually issued for seven-year terms, or, alternatively, for one-year terms that were annually renewable. Moreover, commercial and industrial risks became more complex with technological developments at the end of the eighteenth century, and this created more novel problems than anything faced by contemporary marine underwriters. To that extent, therefore, Adam Smith was correct in asserting that fire insurance was best suited, not to individuals or small partnerships, but to joint-stock enterprise. Success in wresting the business in the North West from the control of London insurers had to await the large stock companies of the nineteenth century, beginning with the Manchester Fire and Life Assurance Company and the Liverpool Fire and Life Office. The latter, in particular, was to form one of the pillars of the North West's towering position in global insurance markets from the middle of the nineteenth century onwards.

## Fire and general insurance in the nineteenth and twentieth centuries: the rise of the multinationals

The Manchester Fire & Life Assurance Company, founded in 1824 with a nominal capital of £2m in 20,000 shares and nearly 1,000 shareholders, was the first insurance company in the north-west of England that proved durable and successful over the long term.[23] The new company was promoted by members of the merchant-manufacturing oligarchy that dominated Manchester. At least forty-six of the first sixty-six directors were involved in some branch of cotton manufacture or distribution.[24] Some could boast family connections within the group that stretched back decades. They shared investments in many local infrastructural developments such as the Manchester gas works and the Manchester-Leeds railway. Eleven insurance directors had family or business connections with local banking. Collectively, the insurers were also prominent in the public life of Manchester, being heavily represented on the committees of municipal government, and on the governing bodies of a wide range of cultural and philanthropic institutions. Its deep capital base, regional sales focus, and the commercial and industrial expertise of its managing directors, quickly gave the Manchester Fire & Life Assurance a major role in the UK insurance market. Between 1825 and 1850 it was consistently the third-largest provincial fire insurance office.[25] In 1843 it had 123 agencies, mostly in the north and midlands of England, and in many Lancashire cotton towns it challenged the market share of the biggest London insurers.[26] Its weaker life-assurance department was sold off in 1846, but the fire business continued to grow. By 1899, the renamed Manchester Assurance Company, with premiums of £927,000, was the eighth-largest fire insurer in the UK.[27]

The Manchester insurer found it hard, however, to loosen the early stranglehold of the London offices over the property insurance market in Liverpool. That market continued to expand rapidly, notwithstanding the end of the slave trade, as Liverpool's economy

Manchester Assurance Co., fire-assurance policy, 1855

moved further into trades such as grain, timber, meat and palm oil, as well as cotton and sugar. Between 1810 and 1850 imports of raw cotton increased five-fold, and imports of American wheat rose from 8,000 tons to 75,000 tons. On Merseyside, capital investment in dock construction soared.[28] In one year alone (1848), five shipping basins were opened along the north shore of the Mersey. A further four were opened in the next four years. The Huskisson Dock, opened for the timber trade in 1852, set a new standard in dock construction. The Canada Dock, opened in 1859, was even larger. By 1850 Liverpool's shipping tonnage, 3.26m, approached that of London (3.29m). During the second half of the nineteenth century the tonnage of shipping using Liverpool further increased by a factor of four, while the city's population increased to 746,000 by 1911.[29]

The unrelenting pace of development in Liverpool made insurance there increasingly difficult for London-based offices as they tried to maintain high-premium rates in face of persistent losses on warehouse and dockside risks. In 1836 a new insurance office was launched in Liverpool by a group of investors led by George Holt, a leading Unitarian banker and cotton broker. Its first secretary (manager) was a fellow Unitarian, Swinton Boult, a twenty-eight-year old Liverpudlian who had been working in the city as the agent for the London Assurance Company.[30] After a difficult first few years, during which Boult had to defend the new company against disgruntled shareholders and take-over attempts by London rivals, the Liverpool Fire & Life began to grow rapidly. Sums insured rose from £4.7m in 1840 to £8.7m in 1850. During the 1840s Boult fought hard to improve Liverpool's water supply and fire-fighting facilities. In 1845 the Liverpool Fire Prevention Act was passed, following an inquiry led by Boult into the causes of local fires. In the following year he organized the Liverpool Fire Salvage Association to promote better warehouse-construction and fire-prevention methods. He also negotiated with London offices a common tariff for warehouses and mills in Liverpool and Manchester, and a uniform policy form (which had been another point of competition). Growth was further promoted through a series of acquisitions – ten companies in Britain and abroad were taken over in twenty-five years. In 1847 the purchase of the London, Dublin & Edinburgh Insurance Company led to the Liverpool office establishing a second board in London and changing its title to the Liverpool & London Insurance Company.

The initial success of the Liverpool Fire & Life rested on growth in an improved local market, followed by expansion throughout the UK. But this was only the prelude to what might be called the Liverpool export revolution in UK insurance. In 1846 the Liverpool office resolved to establish agencies overseas for the first time. Between 1848 and 1850 agents were appointed in New York, Newfoundland and Hamburg, all places familiar to Liverpool merchants. The New York appointment was probably the first insurance agency to be established in the city by a UK company since the Phoenix Fire Office was forced out by a hostile New York state legislature in 1814.[31] In 1851 the Liverpool & London set up a local board of directors in New York to supervise its US operations, and also appointed further agents in Philadelphia, Charleston and New Orleans. In 1853 Boult set off for Australia, travelling westwards across the US, establishing agencies on the way in Cleveland and San Francisco. New boards were also established in Melbourne and Sydney, and agents appointed in Bombay and Calcutta. By 1859 further agencies had been founded in Portugal, Valparaiso, Manila, Natal, Cuba and Jamaica. In Australia, the Australasian Life Insurance Company was acquired, which proved a highly profitable investment – some policies of this office were still on the books in the 1920s.[32] Liverpool & London also purchased the Canadian business of the Globe Insurance Company of London, and set up a local board at Montreal. This pattern of expansion through acquisitions, agencies and local boards was repeated in the UK domestic market. Within a decade, therefore, the Liverpool & London had hugely extended its business across the UK and abroad. Its fire-premium income rose from £54,000 in 1851 to £436,000 by 1862, and the need for additional capital to underpin the massive growth had become urgent. This resulted in the acquisition of the Globe Insurance Company of London in 1864, which led to another change of title for the office to the Liverpool, London & Globe (hereafter LLG). By 1867, with a premium income of £836,000, the LLG had become the largest fire-insurance company in the world. This was a staggering achievement, but it was not the only insurance behemoth to appear in the north-west of England during the mid Victorian years.

In March 1845, partly in response to what were perceived as continued oppressive premium rates for fire insurance in the city, a group of Liverpool merchants and ship-owners founded the Royal Insurance Company for fire and life insurance, with a capital of £2m.[33] Among the promoters were Charles Turner, chair of the Liverpool Dock Board; T. B. Horsfall, son of a wealthy merchant, who became mayor in 1847–8 and Tory MP for Liverpool (1853–68); John Bramley Moore, another Tory mayor and chair of the Dock Board; and the cotton merchants Edmund Molyneaux and George Wainwright. The company was launched during the upswing of the railway mania, and three-quarters of the share issue was bought up within a few weeks. The company quickly opened an office in London, and recruited Percy Dove from the Royal Exchange Assurance to be its manager. Benefiting from the improved construction and fire-prevention methods in Liverpool, the early years of the Royal were prosperous. By 1849 only 32 per cent of the £154,132 premiums earned had been paid out in claims.[34] The company also turned overseas, appointing agents in Calcutta, Bombay, Batavia, Demerara, Manila, Singapore and New Brunswick by the end of 1846. By 1851, agencies in Chile,

Liverpool, London & Globe fire-insurance policy, 1879

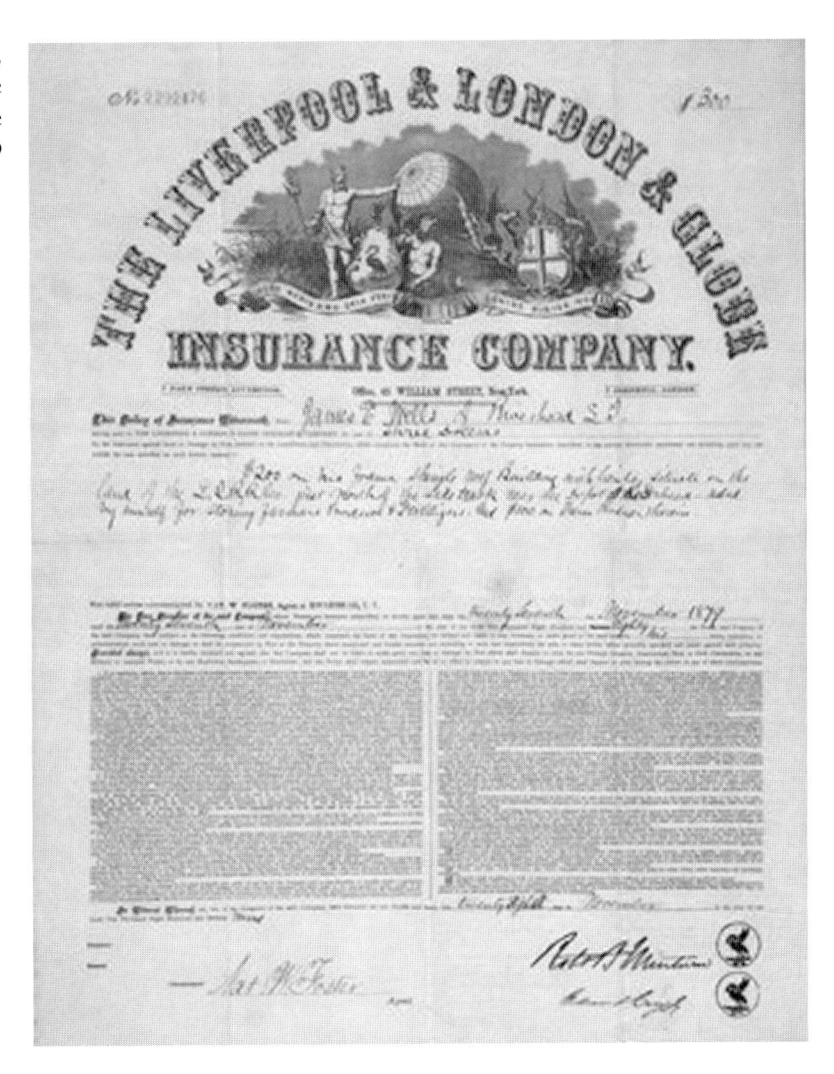

Peru, Surabaya, Barbados, Gothenburg, Newfoundland, Montreal and Sydney had been added. In 1851 Dove visited Canada and the US, appointing agents in New York, Savannah, Charleston, Baltimore and Philadelphia.

In 1852–3 further agents were appointed in Boston, Cincinnati, Louisville, Mobile, New Orleans and San Francisco. The Royal's foreign premium income rose from £8,196 in 1850, earned from eleven agencies, to an annual average of £594,067 by 1871–5, earned from more than ninety agencies. By the latter date, the Royal, like the LLG, had left the older generation of London insurance exporters far behind in terms of both size and entrepreneurship. Clive Trebilcock, who has analyzed this first phase of the Royal's overseas expansion, has argued that its success was due to direct selling through deep as well

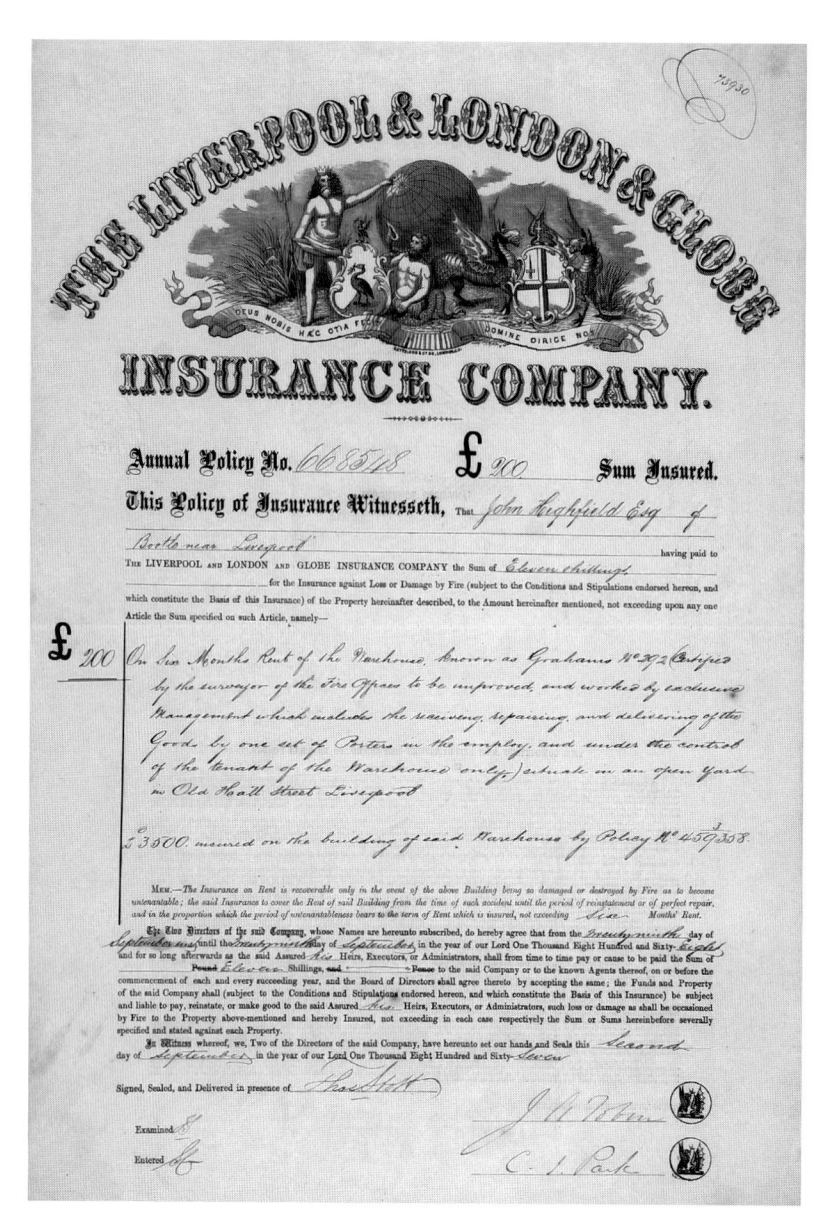

A policy issued by the Liverpool, London & Globe Insurance Company, 2 September 1867, insuring for £200 the risk of loss of six months rent on a warehouse in Old Hall Street, Liverpool, in the event of fire damage. The building itself was also insured by the same company for £3,500. Insurance against the loss of rental income was a relatively new product at this time, it had been almost unheard of in the previous century. Courtesy of Hersh Stern

as extensive networks of overseas agents and an early commitment to the rapidly growing US market. By comparison, older London offices such as the Phoenix were far more hesitant about appointing agents in unfamiliar areas of the American frontier and relied far more on taking US risks that had been reinsured by other US and British offices.[35]

The decades that followed the American Civil War witnessed an explosive growth in US industrialization and urbanization, and the nation's insurance markets. Dozens of foreign fire- and marine-insurance companies rushed to American shores, but they faced stiff competition, not only from the large native offices, but also from the Liverpool companies that were already well established there. The great fires in 1871 and 1872 that devastated Chicago and Boston respectively cost the LLG and the Royal huge sums in claims.[36] By settling with claimants quickly and often in full, however, they emerged with their reputations enhanced among Americans looking for a better quality of insurance protection than many of the smaller US offices had been able to provide.

By 1901 the two biggest UK insurers, the LLG and the Royal, had long been the two biggest foreign insurance companies operating in the US. Their US premiums in that year, at $5.50m and $4.06m respectively, were several multiples of their nearest rivals. The Royal and the LLG, however, did not stand alone in the North West as home-grown insurance multinationals. Three other offices were particularly notable. The Lancashire Insurance Company, established in Manchester in 1852, had grown to a medium-sized office by 1869, with net fire-insurance premiums of £92,516. In 1872 the company established a US branch office in New York, and general agencies in Chicago, Cincinnati, Charleston, Houston, and San Francisco. By 1881 its net fire premiums had risen to £556,984, with the US generating about one-third of this.[37] By 1890, the Lancashire was ranked sixth among foreign fire insurers in the US.[38] The Queen Insurance Company was launched in Liverpool in 1857 and quickly extended its business through the UK, North America and Australia. By 1881 its net fire-premium income was £599,138, about 42 per cent of which came from the US.[39] In 1890, on the eve of its acquisition by the Royal, it was ranked eighth among foreign fire insurers in the US with premiums of $1.58m. Finally, there was the London & Lancashire Fire Insurance Company, established in 1861 with twin boards in Liverpool and London. It too expanded its sales network quickly throughout the UK and overseas – it had over 500 agencies by 1865 – but a crisis of rising expenses and heavy losses led to a *coup d'état* in 1867 by a group of Liverpool shareholders, as a result of which the management of the company was transferred entirely to Liverpool.[40] The London & Lancashire then embarked on a phase of rapid growth overseas and at home, much of which was achieved through the acquisition of local offices. By 1900 the London & Lancashire was ranked fifth among foreign fire insurers operating in the US, and seventh among fire insurers in the UK. In 1934 it was still the eighth-largest foreign insurer in the US with premiums of $3.4m.[41] Despite important changes in the composition of its business during the twentieth century – notably the rise of accident and liability insurance to comprise over half of group premiums by 1959 – the organizational structure of the company and its geographical distribution of business remained largely intact. Whereas the US had accounted for 41 per cent of premiums in 1882, it accounted for over half the group's £37m premium income in 1960.[42]

Royal Insurance building, 201 Sansome St, San Francisco, built 1907

As noted below, the established rank order of UK insurance companies was affected by the wave of company acquisitions during the first two decades of the twentieth century and the emergence of giant composite groups underwriting multiple lines of insurance. The biggest Liverpool offices, however, consolidated their position. The Queen and the Lancashire were absorbed by the Royal in 1890 and 1901 respectively. The success of these acquisitions encouraged the Royal in 1919 to seek a fusion with the LLG. The resulting conglomerate boasted a total premium income from all lines of nearly £16m.[43] Together as a group they remained at or near the top of the ranking order for much of the twentieth century, a remarkable testimony to first-starter advantages and the goodwill and social capital accumulated from decades of reputation-building and underwriting competence. In 1937, the Royal led the table of foreign insurers in the US with $8.89m in fire, casualty and marine premiums, while the LLG was second with $8.71m.[44] The global distribution of their business also remained fairly constant. An early commitment to overseas insurances determined the structure of the company's business well into the twentieth century. 66 per cent of LLG's net fire premiums in 1906 were generated in the US, and just 14 per cent in the UK. The figures for 1928 were 59 per cent and 15 per cent.[45] In 1961, amidst a renewed frenzy of take-over activity in British insurance, the Royal acquired the business of the last of its nineteenth-century Liverpool rivals, the London & Lancashire. The enlarged group became the largest in the UK and the third-largest UK insurer in the US. During the 1970s and 1980s, like many of its larger competitors, the Royal diversified into reinsurance, asset management and property services, and also bought up stakes in other major foreign insurers. Several of these ventures came to grief in the recession of the early 1990s, when share and property prices fell and insurance claims rose. In 1996 the Royal finally merged with its oldest London rival, the Sun Alliance, having already begun to combine underwriting operations with the Sun in Australia during the 1980s. On its 150th anniversary the giant multinational comprised over 120 subsidiary and associated companies, operating in eighty-six countries with almost 23,000 staff.[46]

## Liverpool marine insurance in the nineteenth century

In 1824 the monopoly of the two London marine insurance corporations was repealed, but depressed premium rates and profits meant that the handful of new marine insurance companies struggled, and the London market retained its command over UK maritime insurance. The first serious inroads to Lloyd's share of the ocean-marine market were made by the new London and Liverpool companies of the 1860s, attracted by the huge transfer of American marine business to Britain during the American Civil War.[47]

In 1860 the Liverpool Underwriters' Association consisted of eleven syndicates with nearly 300 private underwriters. The structure of marine-underwriting in the city, however, was to change dramatically in the next twenty years. Private underwriting partnerships began to launch joint-stock companies that heralded the end of Lloyd's-type syndicates in the city. The first of these companies was the Thames & Mersey, launched in 1860 with a nominal capital of £2m. Its 100,000 shares were distributed in the ratio of 45:30:25 to investors in London, Liverpool and Manchester respectively, but within a few decades the great majority of shares found their way back to the North West. The company operated local boards in the three cities, each with discretionary underwriting powers. The first overseas agents were appointed in 1870 in India, the Far East and Australia, and in the US from 1876. Early underwriting was remarkably profitable, with net losses incurred in only three years out of twenty-one. By 1877 the Thames & Mersey was Britain's largest marine-insurance company with a premium income of £310,000.[48] Another company, the British & Foreign, was established in Liverpool in 1863 with a capital of £1m. Its annual premium income in its first twelve years averaged nearly £300,000. By the 1890s it was the largest marine insurance office in Liverpool. A third company, the Union Marine, was also founded in 1863 by a group of Liverpool shipowners and merchants. It too benefited from the huge transfer of American marine business to the UK. By the early 1870s it had established agencies in several UK ports and also in India, China, Singapore and the Philippines. Its first US agency was opened in San Francisco in 1873 to capture some of the business insuring the Californian grain trade. In 1875 the company entered Canada, and concluded an agreement with the Western Assurance of Toronto. By 1911, the Union Marine had become Britain's largest marine insurer, with a net premium income of £472,000 and 115 agencies around the world.[49]

By the 1870s there were several dozen stock companies underwriting marine insurance, together accounting for perhaps 40 per cent of the UK market, and Liverpool rivalled London as a world centre for the industry. In 1877 five of the nine largest UK marine-insurance companies were based in Liverpool. Their combined premiums were over £1m, which amounted to 62 per cent of the company sector in UK marine insurance.[50] On the eve of the First World War, many felt that Liverpool had overtaken the capital. 'Marine underwriters at the Mersey port', claimed the *Financial Times* in 1911, 'are inclined to patronise their confreres in London, and recently there has been a tendency to regard the northern city as the true home of marine insurance'.[51] The rivalry between the capital city and the great northern port, however, was not exhaustive. Some Liverpool offices continued the tradition set by eighteenth-century Liverpool underwriters of developing profitable links with their London counterparts. The Union Marine, for instance, in 1867 entered into an arrangement with the Ocean Marine of London (established in 1859) under which each office in its own city would act as agent for the other, which helped both to share risks.[52]

As the specialist Liverpool marine insurers attained the peak of their powers, the ground began to change under their feet. From the 1890s through to the early 1920s the British insurance industry embarked on a massive merger wave in which large fire-insurance companies constructed huge multi-line composite offices to sell all types of property, casualty, liability and life insurance. The attraction of the general accident insurance market, which grew from less than £2m in premiums in 1895 to nearly £17m by 1914, was one factor behind the corporate mergers and fusions.[53] Other factors included the desire to remain competitive and keep a customer base by extending the range of insurance cover on offer. As Lloyds underwriters began to diversify into non-marine insurance, single-line companies, selling only fire or marine or life insurance, perceived themselves at a disadvantage in a more demanding market.[54] Within a few years, almost the entire ranks of the Victorian marine-insurance companies, including all the great Liverpool offices, disappeared into one of these composite groups. The Union Marine was absorbed by the Phoenix of London in 1911.[55] The Standard Marine became a subsidiary of the London and Lancashire in 1907. The British & Foreign Marine was swallowed up by the Royal in 1909. The Thames & Mersey was acquired by the LLG in 1911, which itself fused with the Royal in 1919. The Royal, having absorbed or allied itself with so many companies, emerged after 1920 as the one Liverpool insurance giant of global dimensions.

## Other branches of insurance

The region's construction, textile and engineering industries spawned a number of ventures in new insurance lines which can only be briefly mentioned here: they were mostly of regional or, at best, national, rather than global, significance. Probably the most distinctive was boiler insurance which became a speciality of Manchester. In 1854 the Manchester Steam Users' Association was formed, following growing concern about the number of fatal boiler explosions in textile mills and other industrial plants. The main movers were the engineers Sir William Fairburn and Sir Joseph Whitworth, and the cotton-spinner Henry Houldsworth. The association aimed to conduct experiments on boilers and engines and investigate explosions to improve safety. It also offered a boiler inspection service but Fairburn and his colleagues resisted venturing into boiler insurance. Five years later a breakaway group of shareholders formed the Steam Boiler Assurance Company in Manchester selling both inspections and insurance of boilers, engineering and power plant. Agencies were established throughout the UK, although the opportunity to extend operations to Europe was rejected. As the market grew rapidly – by 1870 it was estimated that there were up to 110,000 industrial boilers in use in the UK – a flurry of other boiler insurance companies followed in Manchester and in other industrial areas.[56] The companies forced their policy-holders to conduct regular inspections as a condition of their insurance, and this helped reduce the incidence of fatal boiler explosions in the UK after 1875 and improve the standard of boiler construction. From the 1880s the biggest Manchester boiler insurance companies also began to extend their business into the insurance of steam and gas engines, lifts and cranes, and later, electrical plants, and into new lines such as employer's liability, personal accident and motor-car insurance. During the first decades of the twentieth century, most of them were absorbed into composite insurance groups. The British Engine Boiler Insurance Company, which had been launched in Manchester in 1878, became allied with the Royal in 1912. The Steam Boiler Assurance Company, which had been renamed the Vulcan Boiler and General Insurance in 1896, was acquired by the London Assurance in 1920. The business of these companies, however, continued to be largely confined to the UK. The Vulcan, for instance, having rejected proposals to underwrite boiler insurance in India and the US in the 1890s, waited until 1951 before extending its operations overseas, and even then it adopted a cautious approach, initially insuring only boilers of British construction.[57]

Other insurance lines that appeared in the second half of the nineteenth century were less specific to the North West. The region's first plate-glass insurance companies, for example, were established in Manchester and Liverpool in 1863 and 1866 respectively.[58] There were general accident and employers' liability companies from the 1880s and 1890s, some specializing in the cotton industry.[59] There were several industrial and ordinary life assurance companies, beginning with the British Industry Life Assurance Company, founded in Liverpool in 1852 and acquired by the Prudential in 1860. And there were local fire-insurance companies for particular categories of property, such as the Co-operative Insurance Society founded in Rochdale in 1867 for the insurance of co-operative property against fires and accidents, and the Primitive Methodist Insurance and the Wesleyan Methodist Trust Assurance companies, established in Manchester in 1866 and 1871 respectively, to insure connexional property.[60]

Finally, there was the Provincial Fire Insurance Company, established in Bolton in 1903 by the Scott family, who had made their wealth in the cotton trade. The Provincial operated outside the Fire Offices Committee's tariff system, discounting the tariff rates but underwriting cautiously through local agents in Bolton, friends and business connections in the Lancashire and Midlands textile districts, and through brokers in Manchester and London.[61] It accepted foreign fire risks at an early stage, mostly via brokers or reinsurance treaties with foreign companies. The company's first overseas branches were set up in Canada and South Africa in 1910 and 1915 respectively, both supported by the Lloyd's broker firm Willis Faber. Between 1907 and 1918 the Provincial commenced general and personal accident, employers' liability, marine and motor insurance. The latter became the great engine of inter-war growth for the company. Its motor-premium income rose from £26,000 in 1920 to £699,000 by 1938.[62] Although the Provincial also underwrote motor insurance in Canada and South Africa, its main strengths lay in the UK. Its foreign fire account, while widely spread, continued to rely on business from brokers or reinsurance from other companies. Branch development and direct underwriting outside South Africa and Canada remained negligible. The company remained too small to afford the costs of an extensive agency system overseas.[63] The Provincial remained an example of the success that could be achieved by a medium-sized, non-tariff family firm exploiting the entry opportunities available in an oligopolistic market consisting of a small number of giant tariff companies. Although an extraordinarily interesting company, the Provincial never became a global giant. In none of the above areas of general-accident or life insurance did the North West achieve the kind of world stature that it did in fire and marine insurance during the nineteenth and twentieth centuries.

## Conclusions and speculations

The rise of the North West after 1850 as an international emporium for fire and marine insurance emphasizes the diversity of the regional economy, even at the height of its industrial powers. We cannot yet fully explain this dramatic rise. All the region's insurance giants still await a comprehensive academic analysis, and their records are difficult to access or their whereabouts unknown.[64] The above survey, however, does throw up a few clues. First, we might speculate that Liverpool's terrible record for dockside and warehouse fires between the 1790s and 1840s, and the concentration of warehouse and mill fires in Manchester and the cotton towns of south-east Lancashire during the same period, helped fortify local underwriters for the later experience of underwriting hazards in rapidly growing and combustible property insurance markets in the US and elsewhere overseas. Second, while the success of its marine insurance companies in the later nineteenth century was clearly linked to the growth of Liverpool's overseas trade, it perhaps also owed something to the long heritage of private marine underwriting during the eighteenth century which had centred on the trade in slaves and colonial products. Other clues relate to the importance of networks, reputation, and entrepreneurial and technical ability. As Anderson has pointed out, the long-term success of marine underwriting in Liverpool depended not only on adequate capitalization and participation in the London market, but also on a secure share of the local market and the proven underwriting ability of the personnel involved.[65] The ship-owning/slave-trading/insurance groups in eighteenth-century Liverpool worked through the mechanisms of mutual trust and social capital

|  | Royal Exchange | Royal | London & Lancashire |
|---|---|---|---|
| Percy M. Dove (1804–68) | Clerk (1821–) Asst. actuary | **Actuary** (1845–68) | |
| Charles G. Fothergill | | Asst Secretary (1861–8) Sub-manager (1868–74) | **Manager** (1874–99) |
| John McLaren (1827–93) | | Asst Secretary (1856–8) Sub-manager (1858–68) **Manager** (1868–93) | London manager (1850s) |
| Charles Alcock | | Asst Secretary (1885–92) Sub-manager (1893) **Manager** (1893–1911) | |
| John M. Dove (son of Percy Dove) | | Clerk (1863–5) Asst secretary (1865–73) | |
| Digby Johnson | | Clerk (1862–73) Asst Secretary (1873–7) Sub-manager (1877–93) | |
| William P. Clirehugh | | | **Manager** (1862–7) |

Source: *Post Magazine and Insurance Monitor* 29 June 1895; Francis, *London and Lancashire*, appendix

**Table 1:** The career paths of managers of north-west insurance companies

built up amongst their members over many years.[66] The same was true of the promoters and investors in the region's fire and marine insurance companies during the late eighteenth and nineteenth centuries. Business networks in the North West provided a solid foundation for the collective investments of their members as they diversified out of trade and manufacturing into insurance, banking and other activities. Individuals in these networks, the Earles and Tarletons in eighteenth-century Liverpool, the Woods and Birleys in early-nineteenth century Manchester, brought into insurance an entrepreneurial and financial acumen developed in their core businesses. They already knew how to launch ventures, generate credit, raise capital, develop competitive strategies and balance books. What they lacked was the specific expertise in underwriting. This was supplied, it seems, by the construction of a durable conveyor belt of insurance talent moving within the North West, and between the North West and London during the course of the nineteenth century. The capacity of the big insurance offices in Manchester and Liverpool to draw upon prior underwriting expertise may have often been critical to their success. As Table 1 shows, the managers of the Lancashire (1893), the LLG (1876) and the London and

| Hercules Fire | London | LLG | Lancashire | Queen |
|---|---|---|---|---|

Clerk (1842–9)

      employed
      (1865–85)

            Sub-manager
            (1873–6)
            **Manager** (1876–)

                        **Manager** (1893–)

                                        **Manager** (to 1862)

Lancashire (1874) had all been previously employed and trained by the Royal. The first actuary of the Royal (Dove, 1845) had trained with the Royal Exchange Assurance of London. The Royal's second manager (McLaren, 1868) had been employed by the London and Lancashire. Its third manager (Alcock, 1893) had previously worked at the London Assurance. Thus the London-Liverpool business axis, which had been first established in the days of the slave trade, was operating vigorously in the Victorian era to sustain personal insurance connections between the two cities, and to help develop the Lancashire port as a global insurance emporium.

## Notes

1. Revisionists include William D. Rubinstein, *Capitalism, culture and decline in Britain, 1750–1990* (London, 1993); Peter Scott, *The triumph of the south* (Aldershot, 2007). On the Lancashire cotton industry, see Seymour Shapiro, *Capital and the cotton industry in the industrial revolution* (Ithaca, 1967); Douglas A. Farnie, *The English cotton industry and the world market, 1815–1896* (Oxford, 1979); Roger Lloyd-Jones and M. J. Lewis, *Manchester and the age of the factory* (Manchester, 1988).

2. Harold E. Raynes, *A history of British insurance* (London, 1948), pp. 65–7.
3. Sheryllyne Haggerty, *The British-Atlantic trading community, 1760–1810: men, women and the distribution of goods* (Leiden, 2006), p. 43.
4. I am grateful to my colleague David Richardson for advice on these points.
5. *Lloyd's List was* first published in 1734, but it had antecedents in a weekly newspaper commenced by Edward Lloyd in 1692: John J. McCusker, 'The early history of "Lloyd's List"', *Historical Research*, 64 (1991), pp. 427–31.
6. Kingston estimates, from stamp duty on policies, that the two corporations together averaged 6 per cent of the London market between 1800 and 1823. We have no comparable figures for the eighteenth century, but their market share is unlikely to have been much higher: Christopher Kingston, 'Marine insurance in Britain and America, 1720–1844: a comparative institutional analysis', *Journal of Economic History*, 67 (2007), pp. 379–409.
7. Calculated from Liverpool Record Office, Ms 942 Hol 10, Holt and Gregson Papers, pp. 361, 363, 415–17.
8. Ralph Davis, 'Seamen's sixpences: an index of commercial activity, 1697–1828', *Economica*, 23 (1956), pp. 328–43, at Table II. My thanks to David Richardson for drawing my attention to this work.
9. Brian R. Mitchell, *British historical statistics* (Cambridge, 1988).
10. David Richardson, 'The British empire and the Atlantic slave trade, 1660–1807', in P. J. Marshall, ed., *The Oxford history of the British empire: the eighteenth century*, vol. 2 (Oxford, 1998), pp. 440–64. On the factors accounting for Liverpool's pre-eminence in the slave trade after 1750, see Paul E. Lovejoy and David Richardson, 'African agency and the Liverpool slave trade', in David Richardson, Suzanne Schwarz and Anthony Tibbles, eds., *Liverpool and transatlantic slavery* (Liverpool, 2007), pp. 43–65.
11. The insurance of slaves was finally made illegal in Britain by acts of parliament in 1806 and 1811, though some underwriters continued to insure slavers sailing under foreign flags.
12. Raynes, *History of British insurance*, p. 178.
13. Robin Pearson and David Richardson, 'Business networking in the industrial revolution', *Economic History Review*, 2nd ser., 54 (2001), pp. 657–79.
14. Barry Supple, *The Royal Exchange Assurance: a history of British insurance, 1720–1970* (Cambridge, 1970), p. 98.
15. Robin Pearson, *Insuring the industrial revolution: fire insurance in Great Britain, 1700–1850* (Aldershot, 2004), pp. 107–11 and Table 3.3.
16. Ibid., pp. 126–7.
17. Clive Trebilcock, *Phoenix Assurance and the development of British insurance*, vol. 1: 1782–1870 (2 vols; Cambridge, 1985), pp. 361–2.

18. *Prescott's Manchester Journal*, 8 Feb. 1777. On this office, see Pearson, *Insuring the industrial revolution*, p. 131; Pearson and Richardson, 'Business networking'.
19. Calculations from the list of mayors in Thomas Baines, *History of the commerce and town of Liverpool* (London, 1852); and from H. Peet, ed., *Liverpool vestry books, 1681–1834*, vol. 1 (1912).
20. *Leeds Mercury*, 1 Apr. 1777; *Manchester Mercury*, 24 June, 1 July, 8 July 1788.
21. Trebilcock, *Phoenix Assurance*, vol. 1, pp. 361–2, Table 8.4 (p. 495).
22. Pearson, *Insuring the industrial revolution*, p. 157.
23. It survived for eighty years, being acquired by the Atlas Assurance Company of London in 1904.
24. The following is based on Robin Pearson, 'Collective diversification: Manchester cotton merchants and the insurance business in the early nineteenth century', *Business History Review*, 65 (1991), pp. 379–414.
25. Pearson, *Insuring the industrial revolution*, Table 5.3.
26. For an analysis, see Robin Pearson, 'Taking risks and containing competition: diversification and oligopoly in the fire insurance markets of the north of England in the early nineteenth century', *Economic History Review*, 2nd ser., 46 (1993), pp. 39–64.
27. Oliver M. Westall, *The Provincial Insurance Company, 1903–38: family, markets and competitive growth* (Manchester, 1992), p. 26.
28. A. G. Kenwood, 'Fixed capital formation on Merseyside, 1800–1913', *Economic History Review*, 31 (1978), pp. 214–37, at Appendix A, Table III.
29. Henry Rees, *British ports and shipping* (London, 1958), pp. 35–6; [Anon,] *Centennial story: the Union Marine and General Insurance Company Limited, 1863–1963* (Liverpool, 1963), p. 11; P. J. Waller, *Town, city and nation: England, 1850–1914* (Oxford, 1983), p. 9.
30. Robin Pearson, 'Swinton Boult (1808–76)', in Colin Matthew, ed., *The Oxford dictionary of national biography* (Oxford, 2004).
31. Trebilcock, *Phoenix Assurance*, vol. 1, p. 201.
32. Liverpool Record Office, Royal Insurance archives, 368.ROY, J. C. Rimmer, *Notes for a history of Liverpool, London & Globe* (typescript, 1923), p. 6a.
33. The following, unless otherwise stated, draws on Clive Trebilcock, 'The City, entrepreneurship and insurance: two pioneers in invisible exports – the Phoenix Fire Office and the Royal of Liverpool, 1800–90', in Neil McKendrick and R. B. Outhwaite, eds., *Business life and public policy: essays in honour of D. C. Coleman* (Cambridge, 1986), pp. 137–72.
34. *Post Magazine and Insurance Monitor*, 29 June 1895.
35. Trebilcock, 'City, entrepreneurship and insurance'.
36. The LLG paid out £654,000 in Chicago and £280,000 after the Boston fire. No dividend was paid in 1872 as a result, which cost Swinton Boult his job. Hugh Cockerell, 'Swinton Boult', in David J. Jeremy, ed.,

*Dictionary of business biography*, vol. 1 (London, 1984), pp. 396–8. The Royal lost just £20,000 at Chicago, but paid out £187,879 in Boston: *Post Magazine and Insurance Monitor*, 29 June 1895.
37. The ratio is estimated from 1882 data in *Insurance Times* (1883), p. 420.
38. Clive Trebilcock, *Phoenix Assurance and the development of British insurance*, vol. 2, 1870–1984 (2 vols; Cambridge, 1998), Table 3.6 (p. 253).
39. The ratio is estimated from 1882 data in *Insurance Times* (1883), p. 420.
40. E. V. Francis, *London and Lancashire history: the history of the London and Lancashire Company Limited* (London, 1962), pp. 9–23.
41. Trebilcock, *Phoenix Assurance*, vol. 2, Table 3.6 (p. 253); Table 9.8 (p. 705).
42. Calculated from *Insurance Times* (1883), p. 420; Francis, *London and Lancashire*, p. 115.
43. Peter Pugh, *Absolute integrity: the story of Royal Insurance, 1845–1995* (Cambridge, 1995), p. 152.
44. Raynes, *History of British insurance*, p. 273.
45. Liverpool Record Office, Royal Insurance archives, 368.ROY, LL&G, Net Fire Results by region 1923–8; *Progress of the company during the ten years, 1907–1916 inclusive* (typescript, n.d., probably 1923).
46. Pugh, *Absolute integrity*, p. 281. In 2008 the Royal Sun Alliance changed its name to RSA. By this time its global business had extended to 130 countries: www.rsagroup.com/rsa/aboutus, accessed 14 Jan. 2009.
47. A few marine insurance companies had been formed in Liverpool in the 1830s, but none survived more than a few years: B. L. Anderson, 'Institutional investment before the First World War: the Union Marine Insurance Company, 1897–1915', in Sheila Marriner, ed., *Business and businessmen: studies in business, economic and accounting history* (Liverpool, 1978), pp. 37–79, at p. 41.
48. Ibid., p. 40.
49. Trebilcock, *Phoenix Assurance*, vol. 2, pp. 355–6.
50. Calculated from [Anon,] *Thames and Mersey Marine Insurance Company Limited, 1860–1960* (Liverpool, 1960), p. 40.
51. Cited by Trebilcock, *Phoenix Assurance*, vol. 2, p. 354.
52. Raynes, *History of British insurance*, pp. 321–2.
53. Westall, *Provincial Insurance Company*, p. 36.
54. Raynes, *History of British insurance* pp. 387–8.
55. On this takeover, see Trebilcock, *Phoenix Assurance*, vol. 2, pp. 343–57.
56. W. H. Chaloner, *Vulcan: the history of one hundred years of engineering and insurance, 1859–1959* (Manchester, 1959), p. 4.
57. Ibid., p. 64.
58. Respectively, the Guardian Plate Glass Insurance Company and the Liverpool Plate Glass Insurance Company: H. A. L. Cockerell and Edwin Green, *The British insurance business: a guide to its history and records* (Sheffield, 1994).

59. For example, the Bleachers and Dyers Mutual Indemnity Company and the Cotton Trade Insurance Association, both established in 1898 in Manchester and Blackburn respectively.
60. See the references to these companies in Cockerell and Green, *British insurance business*.
61. The company moved its head office to Kendal in 1919, largely for social and family rather than business reasons. The following is based on Westall, *Provincial Insurance Company*.
62. Ibid., p. 209.
63. Ibid., pp. 301–7.
64. Trebilcock, 'City, entrepreneurship and insurance'; and Anderson, 'Institutional investment', provide partial, but serious, analyses of Liverpool fire and marine offices. Francis, *London and Lancashire*, is limited but still useful. Pugh, *Absolute integrity*, the in-house history of the Royal, is totally inadequate.
65. Anderson, 'Institutional investment', p. 41.
66. Robin Pearson and David Richardson, 'Social capital, institutional innovation and Atlantic trade before 1800', *Business History*, 50 (2008), pp. 765–80.

# Lancashire's highway men: the business community and road improvements during the industrial revolution

*Rosine Hart and Geoff Timmins*

The development of Lancashire's turnpike road network during the industrial revolution period brought fundamental improvements in both the methods of constructing roads and the routes that roads took. As far as the former is concerned, differences in maintenance costs fostered a growing preference for laying paving rather than broken stones, especially where heavy traffic flows were experienced. As to the latter, the construction of new inter-town roads and the realignment of existing ones, which often involved substantial excavation work, created much easier and more even gradients, as well as wider carriageways and gentler bends.[1] The advances achieved played a crucial part in generating, and coping with, the massively increased traffic flows arising from unprecedentedly high rates of economic growth, allowing swifter and more frequent transport services to operate and extending the range of destinations between which direct services were available.

Given the economic environment in which they operated, local businessmen in general benefited considerably from Lancashire's road improvements, but especially those engaged in cotton-textile production, by far the biggest amongst the county's industries. In part, this is because they needed to make regular journeys to meet suppliers and customers, especially in Manchester. Thus, by the mid 1820s, no fewer that 1,200 of them, mainly cotton-spinners and manufacturers, were visiting the city on one or more of the three market days (Tuesday, Thursday and Saturday).[2] Also entering into the account is the dispersed nature of production within the cotton textile industry, which necessitated large and growing quantities of yarn and cloth being moved by road from one site to another as each stage of production was completed. The dependence of the weaving branch of the industry on domestic production added further to this traffic, particularly in collecting from, and delivering to, rurally-based handloom weavers. Only to a limited extent could waterways meet these transport needs, with navigable stretches of rivers being situated outside the main textile production zone and canals serving only part of it.

Since Lancashire's business community benefited considerably from road improvements, what contributions, financial and otherwise, did its members make towards developing the county's turnpike road network? That merchants and manufacturers were involved in making loan subscriptions to help with the costs of establishing turnpike trusts has been demonstrated for various parts of Britain, including Lancashire. For example, as subscription lists reveal, most of the initial capital required by the Oldham to Ripponden (Yorkshire) trust in 1795 was advanced by clothiers, woollen manufacturers, cotton manufactures and merchants from Halifax, Manchester, Oldham and Saddleworth. It is also known that businessmen were active in lending further sums to turnpike trusts beyond their initial subscriptions. (William Albert has drawn the distinction between initial subscribers and secondary investors, though, as he also demonstrates, the two were by no means mutually exclusive.) Lancashire examples cited include John Smith, a plumber and glazier of Preston, who advanced £2,000 to the Preston-Wigan (North of Yarrow) Trust in 1823, and a further £500 in 1826.[3]

Recent research has revealed further instances of how local businessmen, many of whom are named in the lengthy lists of trustees appearing in turnpike acts of parliament, were involved in financing Lancashire's turnpike roads. The purpose of this article is partly to report these instances, thereby creating a fuller picture of the circumstances in which businessmen, acting either individually or with others, provided initial and secondary funding for turnpike road development. In so doing, the notion is considered that, with regard to making loans to turnpike trusts, businessmen had greater initial, rather than subsequent, interest. New evidence concerning the role of businessmen in promoting and administering turnpike trusts is also considered. This is an area largely neglected by historians, though Albert has noted the roles professional men in particular could play as turnpike-trust clerks and treasurers.[4] The indications from the Lancashire evidence are that, whether or not they funded turnpike roads, many businessmen were prepared to bring their professional experience and expertise to bear in helping to ensure that the affairs of turnpike trusts were efficiently managed.

## Initial and secondary lending

Establishing turnpike roads, either along existing or new routes, required some form of financial provision to meet the costs incurred before any toll income was generated. These costs mainly arose from obtaining private acts of parliament; undertaking essential construction work, including the erection of toll-houses, gates, boundary walls and fences; route surveying and mapping; demolition of buildings; and making any necessary purchases of land. Plainly, the expenditure involved and the time taken to implement toll charges would vary considerably, much depending on the situation in which the promoters and trustees found themselves and the degree of ambition they had. Even so, the amounts required might be substantial, with multiple, and sometimes sizeable, loans being required.

Some insights into these matters can be obtained from the records of the Prescot to Liverpool road. This was the second road in Lancashire to be turnpiked, its promoters being keen to facilitate the conveyance of coal from Prescot to Liverpool in winter as well as in summer. An act of parliament to permit toll collection along the road was obtained in April 1726, but it was not until February of the following year that those using the road began to pay tolls. In the interim, expenditure was being incurred and to meet their outstanding bills, the trustees raised a £500 loan in September 1726. The loan was secured on the anticipated toll income. The costs of obtaining the act of parliament for the road, which amounted to just over £360, had first call on this income, the remainder being used mainly to pay for the construction of toll-houses and gates. With toll income still lacking and expenditure still being incurred, it was deemed necessary to raise the amount of the loan to £1,000 in January 1727.[5] How far the business fraternity was involved in providing these loans is unclear, though, given the importance of the road in transporting coal, they are likely to have played a part.

Clearer evidence of businessmen making early loans to turnpike trustees can be found in relation to other Lancashire roads. In the case of the Rochdale to Bury road (via Bamford), for which a turnpike act was secured in 1797, four local cotton manufacturers were each listed as lending sums of £52 10s to the trustees in October 1798, seemingly the minimum amount they could advance. It may be that other businessmen who cannot be identified as such were amongst the subscribers – the designations of esquire and gentlemen are given in a number of instances – but men from other occupations, including several yeomen, a clergyman and a surgeon, predominated.[6] Businessmen were also well represented amongst early investors in the Clitheroe to Whalley and Blackburn turnpike trust, for which an act was obtained in 1821. Loans totalling £1,150 were subscribed in July 1823, £550 of which was advanced by cotton manufacturers, cotton-spinners, calico printers and merchants. Amongst them were Jeremiah Garnett, partner in a substantial cotton spinning and weaving enterprise at Low Moor, Clitheroe, who made a £200 loan along with Thomas Colbeck, a Leeds merchant, and two members of his business partner's family, namely John Horsfall of Halifax, cotton-spinner and Thomas Horsfall, a merchant from Benholme in Yorkshire. A loan of £100 was also made by James Thompson, John Chippendale, James Burton and William Thompson, partners in a calico printing and merchanting enterprise based at Primrose Mill, Clitheroe.[7]

Taking a national perspective, William Albert has remarked that the landed interests were the major providers of loans to turnpike trusts, but merchants, manufacturers, tradesmen and others came to assume a more prominent role as secondary investors than they had as initial subscribers.[8] The paucity of records makes this proposition hard to test in relation to Lancashire's turnpike trusts. Lancashire's landed proprietors certainly continued as secondary investors, but in such a highly industrialized county, it might be anticipated that merchants, manufacturers and tradesmen did indeed come to play the greater role. However, that this was so is by no means certain, with the position anyway being somewhat clouded by successful industrialists, such as Henry Sudell, textile manufacturer and merchant of Blackburn, buying land to create their own country estates.[9]

The example of the secondary loan made by John Smith, plumber and glazier, to the trustees of the Preston to Wigan road has already been noted and other such loans made by businessmen to turnpike trustees certainly occurred, as in the case of the Bury, Haslingden, Blackburn and Whalley road, for which the first act was obtained in 1789. The trustees of this road opened an early subscription list, with 25 per cent of the sums promised to them being due in May 1790. They were helped by toll income becoming available from the summer of the following year, but this was insufficient to meet their needs. At their meeting of 1 September 1791, they discussed whether to place a newspaper advertisement for a loan of £1,000, secured on toll income. The bulk of this sizeable sum was probably needed to pay for constructing new sections of the road, since the same meeting authorized the payment of over £261 to John Metcalfe and his partners and lesser sums to others. In December 1791, however, four of the road's trustees, namely Joseph Feilden, Richard Cardwell, John Fowden Hindle and Bertie Markland, all prominent local businessmen or landowners, offered to lend the trust £1,500 at 5 per cent interest.[10] Yet this loan soon proved inadequate and by the following March, another £2,000 was needed, half of it to repay a temporary loan

This system enabled trustees to pass on the risks and costs of toll collection to others and gave them an accurate figure for the amount of toll income that would be available to them during the coming year. Problems did arise, however, as in July 1831, when the Prestwich, Bury and Radcliffe trustees did not let the tolls because they deemed the bidding to be inadequate.[15]

The system of letting tolls gave further opportunity for people from various walks of life, including businessmen, to make financial contributions to the development of turnpike trusts. Firstly, they might bid for the right to collect tolls, seeking to realize a profit by generating more from tolls than they paid for the right to collect them. Secondly, in line with the requirements of the 1773 Act, they might provide surety for bidders in case they proved unable to meet their obligations, thereby safeguarding the interests of trustees.

In some of Lancashire's turnpike trust records, the names of those bidding for tolls are given, along with those providing surety for them. However, the occupations of both groups may be lacking. This is so in the case of the Preston to Blackburn road via Salmesbury (Preston New Road) for which an act of parliament was obtained in 1824. Taking the period from October 1827 to March 1832, the trustees' minutes give the names of seven individuals who were bidders, and nine who were giving surety.[16] Scrutiny of the Blackburn, Preston and Chorley sections of Baines's 1824/5 trade directory, as well as those of the surrounding rural districts, reveals entries that may refer to four of these individuals. In two instances, however, more that one person has the same name. Thus a William Ward is listed in the Blackburn entries as a farrier and in the Chorley entries as an innkeeper and wholesale brewer, whilst there are two John Haworths at Blackburn, one an attorney and another a carrier. Both gave surety. The two names receiving only a single mention in the directory are John Hindle and William Tootell. The former may have been John Fowden Hindle, barrister and JP of Gillibrand Hall, Chorley, who, as noted above, had lent money to the Bury, Haslingden, Blackburn and Whalley turnpike road. The latter, also Chorley based, was a watch- and clock-maker.[17]

Such scant evidence at least raises the possibility that Lancashire's businessmen might have had an interest in facilitating the toll-letting system, but, fortunately, some of Lancashire's turnpike trust records provide much firmer evidence. This is now being investigated in detail and a full analysis has yet to be completed. Some of the early findings can be used to illustrate the type of insights it provides, however. Thus, in the case of the Prestwich, Bury and Radcliffe turnpike road, the trustees' minute books record the names and occupations of both bidders and those providing surety, along with where they lived. The earliest entries date from June 1830 and they show that publican Edmund Partington of Birch, near Bury, was the highest bidder for the year's tolls at Hardy's Gate, Lane End and that he offered William Butterworth, a farmer and carrier of Marland Mill near Rochdale, as surety for his bid of £90. At the same meeting John Ramsbottom of Cheetham (north Manchester) secured the Besses o' th' Barn tolls with a much larger bid of £1,725, suggesting that this was a far busier toll-gate. Ramsbottom, who gave his occupation as toll-bar keeper, named two sureties for this higher figure, coach-proprietor John Greenway of Pendleton and shopkeeper Richard Kay of Strangeways, Cheetham (Manchester).[18]

When the tolls were re-advertised two years later, Norman Lowe of Regent Road Bridge, Salford, who described himself as lessee of tolls, was declared successful at Blackley Wells gate. He provided William Eckersley, a Salford butcher, and William Ambler of Hulme, in Winwick parish, a fellow lessee of tolls, as guarantors for his offer of £1,020. Bidders also included James Nuttall, a Haslingden shopkeeper, who secured the tolls at Blackford Brow for £840. He was perhaps unknown to the trustees, for he provided five sureties, all from Haslingden. They were fellow shopkeepers James Ashworth, James Hindle and Robert Whitaker, common brewer Jacob Coupe and Henry Holden, a gentleman. Henry Eastwood, a Burnley farmer, secured Stone Pale toll-gate, offering £2,160 for the year's takings. His bid was supported by John Spencer, innkeeper of the Thorn Inn, Burnley, and Eli Pickles, a miller from nearby Altham. The successful bid for Hardy's Gate, Lane Ends, by James Kirk, a potter from Grimshaw Park, Blackburn, realized £120. His guarantors were publicans John Ratcliffe of Ewood Bridge and John Haworth of Edenfield, together with toll-collector Robert Arrowsmith of Daub Hall near Bolton.[19]

Further evidence that can be cited to illustrate the toll-bidding system concerns the Skipton to Colne turnpike road. Details of nine contracts for toll collection on the road made between 1824 and 1834 have survived. Occupational descriptions are fuller for bidders than for guarantors, but Thomas Inman, a toll-taker from near Gargrave, bid successfully in 1824, as did Joseph Wood of Colne, a toll-keeper and -taker in 1834. Additionally, a consortium outbid the rest at the three auctions held between 1830 and 1832. Members of it were Thomas Whitaker of Colne, a gentleman; Henry Eastwood of Burnley, a butcher; Eli Pickles of Altham, a corn-dealer; John Spencer of Burnley, an innkeeper; and John Butterworth of Burnley, an agent. Amongst the guarantors were a hostler and a toll-taker from Skipton, along with a bar-keeper from nearby Kildwick; a toll-farmer and a butcher from Hunslet, Leeds and a machine-maker from Holbeck, also near Leeds; a cotton-spinner and a yeoman from Colne; and a toll-taker and keeper from near Kendal.[20]

A key point to emerge from this evidence is that businessmen in a varied range of occupations, sometimes operating in association with others, were represented amongst both the bidders and those standing as surety for them. Several, including the innkeeper, the publicans, the carrier, the ostler and the coach proprietor may have been involved because they had a direct interest in road improvement from a business point of view. The farmers amongst them may also fall into this category, especially if they were supplying milk and other perishable products to urban consumers. Noteworthy, too, is the strong representation of individuals with a professional interest in toll collection, whose varied designations include toll-keeper, toll-collector and lessee of tolls. As has been noted elsewhere, enterprising toll-keepers themselves became businessmen, seeking to take advantage of the speculative opportunities that their occupation could offer.[21] Precisely what the distinction was between a toll-collector and a lessee of tolls is unclear, though the implication is that the latter did not operate as a toll-house keeper at all, but relied entirely on others to act in that capacity.

What also arises from the evidence presented is that the toll auctions drew interest from local bidders, but also those operating over a wider compass. Thus the successful bidders for the Prestwich, Bury and Radcliffe road came from various parts of east Lancashire, namely Burnley, Blackburn, Haslingden, Bury, Rochdale, Salford and Manchester. The indications are that, more generally, toll-bidders may have operated on a sub-regional level, with some of them, especially the lessees of tolls, bidding for the right to levy tolls at several bars. In doing so, they may have had to draw on quite a wide range of people to act as surety for them, though, in the examples cited, reliance seems generally to have been on local contacts.

**Promotion and management**

Teasing out only the financial input of local businessmen in creating and developing Lancashire's turnpike road network is to overlook the importance of their wider contribution. Also noteworthy are the role they played in securing turnpike acts, and the management functions they undertook as turnpike trustees. Both their standing in local communities and their business expertise were valued and utilized for these purposes, with the contributions of the more influential amongst them no doubt being particularly sought.

Many businessmen are named amongst the lengthy lists of trustees given in turnpike acts and those who are well known can be identified easily enough, even though occupational detail is often lacking. For example, no fewer than seven Peels were trustees of the Bury, Haslingden, Blackburn and Whalley turnpike road in 1781. They included five sons of Robert 'Parsley' Peel, being Robert (later Sir Robert Peel), then of Chamber Hall, Bury, William Peel of Church, Jonathan Peel of Accrington, who was a calico printer at nearby Church Bank, Lawrence Peel, a merchant of Ardwick, Manchester, Joseph Peel, a London merchant, along with John Peel, a merchant of Burton on Trent. In 1810 Sir Robert Peel was also a trustee of the road from Blackburn through Burnley and Colne to Addingham in Yorkshire. His brother Jonathan, and Jonathan's son Robert, were also trustees of the new Blackburn to Preston road, the construction of which commenced in 1824.[22]

This kind of involvement by members of the business community in turnpike trusteeships was repeated across Lancashire's road network and could extend to several turnpike trusts. Thus, leading handloom-weaving manufacturer and landowner Henry Sudell, who was Blackburn-based, featured on four lists of trustees of Blackburn's road network. The roads concerned were the south-eastern road to Haslingden and Bury, the north-eastern route to Addingham in Yorkshire, and the westbound old and new roads to Walton-le-Dale and Preston. The Boardman family provide another example. Former tanner Robert Boardman senior was a member of Blackburn's Tontine committee and his sons William, a draper, James and Robert junior, were both textile manufacturers, albeit not in partnership. The Boardmans acted as trustees for three of Blackburn's turnpikes, and the younger Robert Boardman was particularly active in the management of Preston New Road.[23]

The extent to which Lancashire's businessmen became turnpike trustees should not be exaggerated, however. Even a cursory glance at the numbers of business concerns recorded in contemporary trade directories reveals that those named in turnpike acts comprised only a small fraction of the local businessmen who might be expected to have an interest in improving the roads they used. Consider, for example, the case of the cotton-spinners and manufacturers at Colne and Barrowford in north-east Lancashire. It might be anticipated that they would have had a strong interest in acting as trustees for the turnpike road that connected Colne to the turnpike road between Clitheroe and Skipton. The act for this road was obtained in 1824 and comparison of the trustees it names with cotton firms listed in Baines's 1824/5 directory shows a varying situation. Thus, at Colne, it seems likely that all four firms described as cotton-spinners and manufacturers were represented amongst the trustees, whereas this was the case with only two of the nineteen concerns listed as specialist cotton manufacturers. At Barrowford, where all six cotton concerns were spinners and manufacturers, only one is represented in the trustees list. Nor did the trustees include the proprietors of the three coaching inns at Colne.[24]

Eric Pawson has argued that it is not possible to ascertain from the turnpike promoters' lists precisely who the instigators of road improvements were.[25] And the same point might be made with regard to lists of turnpike trustees. However, that some businessmen were involved in several turnpike ventures gives an indication of those who were amongst the most active participants. And further insights into this matter can be obtained by considering the varied and quite demanding roles that such people played in administering turnpike trusts.

Once given legal sanction, turnpike trusts established committees drawn from the trustees to administer their affairs. Again, businessmen were amongst those who played a prominent role, attending meetings, taking part in discussions and contributing to the decision-making process. For instance, three Blackburn businessmen William Throp, a cotton-spinner, John Threlfall, an ironmonger, James Cowban, a grocer and tea-dealer, James Cunliffe, a banker, and John Fleming, a cotton merchant, regularly attended committee meetings of the Preston New Road turnpike trust during the mid 1820s, sometimes taking the chair.[26] Similarly, textile entrepreneurs Richard Cardwell and Richard Birley, also of Blackburn, were often present at the meetings of the Bury, Haslingden, Blackburn and Whalley turnpike trust between 1790 and 1805, as well as those of the Blackburn to Preston (Old) Road.[27]

Besides offering general advice as turnpike-trust committee members, businessmen were also called on to undertake specific tasks. An example is the route survey undertaken in 1791 on behalf of the trustees of the Preston to Blackburn Road via Walton-le-Dale. The seven-man committee appointed to this task included Richard Cardwell, Richard Birley and their partner John Hornby, along with Joseph Feilden and Henry Feilden, all Blackburn entrepreneurs. They were to survey the entire eleven miles of the road with the intention of purchasing extra land to widen it.[28] Another example of business interests being involved in route surveying concerns the Liverpool to Prescot road. By 1753, this road had been extended to Warrington and Ashton in Makerfield, and a renewal act was envisaged to extend the term of its existence. To effect this development, a general survey was undertaken. It was conducted by subcommittees of prominent local trustees for each of the three main sections of the road. Members included Liverpool merchant Thomas Seel; the prominent coal-mine owner Sarah Clayton; Jonathan Case of Redhassles, a colliery proprietor and Sarah Clayton's nephew; and another colliery proprietor Legh Master, who was lord of the manor of New Hall in Ashton.[29] The presence of Mrs Clayton is of particular interest because, although women were legally prohibited from becoming turnpike trustees, they frequently became involved in other ways with the finance of local roads, mainly by lending money on the security of the tolls, as was noted earlier. In this instance, her status as lady of the manor and major coal owner overrode any gender barrier.[30]

Other tasks undertaken by businessmen in their capacity as turnpike trustees made more direct use of their professional expertise. Negotiating contracts is a case in point and can be exemplified by the trustees of the Preston Old Road turnpike appointing Richard Cardwell, a Blackburn merchant, to conduct contract negotiations with fellow trustee Thomas Brewer over arrangements to extract roadstone from Brewer's quarry at Shadsworth, near Blackburn in 1793.[31] No details of the resulting contract have been found, but the outcome was evidently to the satisfaction of all parties, as later references are made to the use of the quarry. To take another example, calico-printer Jonathan Peel, Sir Robert's brother, undertook contractual negotiations on behalf of the Bury, Haslingden, Blackburn and Whalley trust on several occasions. At a meeting on 7 May 1795, the trustees deputed him to contract with anyone interested in repairing that part of the road within the township of Old Accrington. Peel's authority to conduct negotiations contrasts with the lesser power of surveyor John Mason, who was merely required to provide a certificate for satisfactory completion of the work, rather than contract for work to be done.[32]

Other managerial responsibilities undertaken by turnpike-trustee businessmen included inspection of contractors' work. For example, Jonathan Peel formed part of a subcommittee to which surveying duties on the Bury, Haslingden, Blackburn and Whalley road were delegated in 1797. This group found it necessary to exchange harsh words with John Thorp, who was thought to have neglected his duties as repairer of the road in Bury. Thorp's excuses for the state of the road were deemed to be unacceptable, as the trustees had provided 300 cartloads of stone to improve the surface. Rather than make use of this material, Thorp had simply abandoned it to become overgrown with grass at the roadside.[33] Businessmen like Peel had the necessary personal authority to deal with contractors who were perceived to be misusing the trust's resources, though what remedial action was taken in this case is unknown.

Businessmen were also involved with auditing turnpike trust accounts. In 1794 Blackburn textile entrepreneurs Richard Cardwell, Richard Birley, James de la Pryme and Bertie Markland were members of a five-man subcommittee appointed by managing trustees of the Blackburn and Burscough Bridge (Walton-le-Dale) road to check the treasurer's accounts. Cardwell and Markland, along with cotton entrepreneur John Hornby, were also among five auditors who approved the road's accounts for 1797.[34] A similar role was undertaken by manufacturer trustees of the Doffcocker turnpike near Bolton, where brothers John and Thomas Ridgway, who ran a major bleaching enterprise, were among those approving accounts between 1780 and 1800.[35]

A final and no doubt unusual way in which businessmen contributed actively to Lancashire's turnpike trust management can be noted. By the summer of 1826, the economy was depressed and the trustees of the new turnpike road between Preston and Blackburn found that their reserves were exhausted, whilst only part of the road had been completed. Led by Blackburn businessmen Robert Boardman, James Cowban and William Hindle, they nonetheless continued to press for completion of the road, on the grounds that an adequate level of toll income could not otherwise be achieved and that the £10,000 treasury loan the trustees had secured still needed repayment. A plan was drawn up to complete the remaining section of the road, which led into Preston from a new wooden bridge across the Ribble. The projected cost of so doing was £3,300, a sum that was deemed to be unacceptably high and at a trustees' meeting in March 1829, one of their number, handloom-manufacturer and commission-broker John Fleming announced that he would contract for completion of the road. Fleming, who was regarded as one of Blackburn's leading citizens, evidently had great confidence in his purchasing and man-management skills. The trustees accepted his estimate of £1,795 – a saving of almost 50 per cent on the original estimate – having received promises of £2,000 to complete the task. Fleming further saved the £120 cost of resurfacing the Preston section of the road, stating that an acceptable standard had already been achieved. He also waived his personal entitlement to £263 15s 4d for services rendered, prompting his fellow trustees to record their thanks for his 'very handsome and liberal conduct'.[36]

## Conclusion

In Lancashire, as elsewhere in Britain, businessmen played their part in helping to develop turnpike roads. They were involved in providing both initial and secondary loans to trustees, as well as in bidding for tolls and standing as surety for successful bidders. Additionally, they were active in promoting turnpike trusts and in undertaking various tasks relating to trust management. That many of them had much to gain from road improvements no doubt helps to explain their involvement, though the opportunities trusteeships offered to meet with fellow businessmen, and notions of public duty, may also have entered into the account.

Given the limitations of the available evidence, however, the extent of their involvement is difficult to gauge. Certainly they were often concerned with promoting turnpike trusts, their names commonly appearing in the lists of trustees given in turnpike acts. Yet these lists contain the names of highly selective groups of local businessmen, some of whom appear in more than one list. Those engaged in textile production frequently appear amongst them, though whether or not they did so proportionately is unclear. Further detailed work on these lists will shed more light on the matter, especially where evidence to compare with that in the lists can be obtained from contemporary trade directories.

In terms of financial considerations, the indications are that, contrary to William Albert's quite reasonable expectations, Lancashire's businessmen may not have played a more prominent role as secondary investors than they did as initial subscribers. In part, the explanation may lie in the reluctance of businessmen to tie up capital for lengthy periods that could be used for more productive purposes. Equally, given the marked expansion of the Lancashire economy during the late eighteenth and early nineteenth centuries, trustees appear to have been able to obtain loans from a varied range of those who had prospered, including well-to-do retired people seeking investment outlets that were relatively safe and that could be expected to yield a good return.

As to the more general involvement of businessmen in the affairs of turnpike trusts, the evidence suggests that a varied range of functions were undertaken, seemingly on an unpaid basis. In some cases, as with negotiating contracts and auditing accounts, businessmen were plainly drawing on their professional expertise to facilitate the work of turnpike trustees. But they also helped out in more general ways, including being regularly involved in meetings of trustees and carrying out road surveying. Whether, as a rule, they were more willing to give their time to trust activities than become financially involved with trusts is a moot point. However, the range of their activities in turnpike trust development certainly merits closer investigation in other parts of the country and may well lead to a fundamental reappraisal of the roles they played.

## Notes

1. For details, See G. Timmins, 'Techniques of easing road gradients during the industrial revolution: a case-study of textile Lancashire',

*Industrial Archaeology Review*, 25 (2003), pp. 97–117: G. Timmins, 'Paving the way: advances in road-building techniques in Lancashire, 1770–1870', *Journal of Transport History*, 26 (2005), pp. 19–40; G. Timmins, 'Coping with road traffic in expanding urban areas: Manchester and its environs during the industrial revolution', in D. Broomhead and T. Wyke, eds., *Moving Manchester: aspects of the history of transport in the city and region since 1700* (Manchester, 2005), pp. 69–90.
2. They are listed in E. Baines, *History, directory, and gazetteer of the County Palatine of Lancaster*, vol. 2 (1825; Liverpool, 1968), pp. 378–92.
3. W. Albert, *The turnpike road system in England, 1663–1840* (Cambridge, 1972), pp. 110–11.
4. Albert, *Road system*, pp. 72–81.
5. F. A. Bailey, 'The minutes of the trustees of the turnpike roads from Liverpool to Prescot, St. Helens, Warrington and Ashton in Makerfield, 1726–89, part 1', *Transactions of the Historic Society of Lancashire and Cheshire*, 88 (1936), pp. 159, 169, 188.
6. Lancashire Record Office (hereafter LRO), Rochdale-Bamford-Bury Turnpike Trust, Toll Mortgages, TTH/4–25.
7. LRO, Clitheroe-Whalley-Blackburn Turnpike Trust, Mortgage Book, 1823–1871, TTB2. The Low Moor enterprise is discussed in O. Ashmore, 'Low Moor, Clitheroe: a nineteenth-century factory community', *Transactions of the Lancashire and Cheshire Antiquarian Society*, 73/4 (1966), pp. 124–52.
8. Albert, *Road system*, p. 110.
9. For details of Sudell, see J. G. Timmins, 'Sudell, Henry (1763/4–1856)', *Oxford Dictionary of National Biography* (Oxford, 2004).
10. For details of these men, see W. A. Abram, *A history of Blackburn, town and parish* (Blackburn, 1877), pp. 391, 397–8, 401, 758; G. Miller, *Blackburn: the evolution of a cotton town* (Blackburn, 1951), pp. 399–403.
11. LRO, Bury-Haslingden-Blackburn-Whalley Turnpike Trust, Minute Book, 1789–1803, TTA1.
12. LRO, Clitheroe-Whalley-Blackburn Turnpike Trust, Mortgage Book, 1823–1871, TTB2, 20 May 1830 and 1 Oct. 1831.
13. LRO, Clitheroe-Whalley-Blackburn Turnpike Trust, Mortgage Book, 1823–1871, TTB2, 15 Oct. 1833.
14. Albert, *Road system*, pp. 85–7.
15. Bury Library, Prestwich-Bury-Radcliffe Turnpike Trust, Minute Book, 1829–57, 22 July 1831, APT 2744.
16. LRO, Blackburn-Preston (New Road) Turnpike Trust, Minute Book, TTJ 7.
17. Baines, *History*, vol. 1, pp. 515, 518, 523, 603, 605, 607.
18. Bury Library, Prestwich-Bury-Radcliffe Turnpike Trust, Minutes Book, 1829–57, 18 June 1830, APT 2744.
19. Bury Library, Prestwich-Bury-Radcliffe Turnpike Trust, Minute Book,

1829–57, 25 July 1832, APT 2744; [Pigot & Co.,] *New commercial directory* (London, 1828).

20. LRO, Skipton-Colne Turnpike Trust, Toll Contracts, TTI28/2–10, 4 Jan. 1824; 18 Dec. 1830; 24 Dec. 1831; 24 Nov. 1832; and 20 Dec. 1834.
21. E. Pawson, *Transport and economy: the turnpike roads of eighteenth-century Britain* (London, 1977), p. 210; S. and B. Webb, *English local government: the story of the king's highway* (1903; London, 1963), p. 138.
22. Bury Library, Bury-Haslingden-Blackburn-Whalley Turnpike Trust, Trustee List, 1789, A39.1 (P) ROA; LRO, Blackburn-Addingham and Cocking End Turnpike Act, 1810, TTI6; LRO, Blackburn-Preston Turnpike Act, 1824, TTJ6.
23. Bury Library, Bury-Haslingden-Blackburn-Whalley Turnpike Trust, Trustee List, 1789, A39.1 (P) ROA; LRO, Blackburn-Addingham and Cocking End Turnpike Act, 1810, and Trustee List, 1827–37, TTI6 and DDBd57/1/5/2; LRO, Blackburn-Preston Turnpike Act 1824, TTJ6; Harris Library, Preston, Blackburn-Walton-le-Dale Act 1793, N14GRE.
24. Colne Library, Colne to Clitheroe and Skipton Road Turnpike Act, 1824, LN14/GRE; Baines, *History*, vol. 1, pp. 622, 624, 638.
25. Pawson, *Transport and economy*, p. 82.
26. LRO, Blackburn-Preston (New Road) Turnpike Trust, Minute Book, TTJ 7.
27. LRO, Bury-Haslingden-Blackburn-Whalley Turnpike Trust, Minute Book, TTA1; Blackburn-Walton-le-Dale Turnpike Trust Minute Book, TTE1.
28. LRO, Blackburn-Walton-le-Dale Turnpike Trust, Minute Book, 10 Oct. 1792, 19 Nov. 1792, TTE1.
29. F. A. Bailey, 'The minutes of the trustees of the turnpike roads from Liverpool to Prescot, St. Helens, Warrington and Ashton in Makerfield, 1726–89, part 2', *Transactions of the Historic Society of Lancashire and Cheshire*, 89 (1937), p. 42.
30. For details of Sarah Clayton and Jonathan Case, see T. C. Barker and J. R. Harris, *A Merseyside town in the industrial revolution: St Helens, 1750–1900* (London, 1959), pp. 24–30.
31. LRO, Bury-Haslingden-Blackburn-Whalley Turnpike Trust, Minute Book, 11 May 1792, 10 Sep. 1793, TTA1.
32. LRO, Bury-Haslingden-Blackburn-Whalley Turnpike Trust, Minute Book, 19 Jan. 1797, TTA1.
33. LRO, Bury-Haslingden-Blackburn-Whalley Turnpike Trust, Minute Book, 26 Aug. and 21 Sep. 1797, TTA1.
34. LRO, Blackburn-Walton-le-Dale Turnpike Trust, Account Book, TTE3.
35. LRO, Doffcocker Turnpike Trust Accounts, 1779–1819, DDPi 10/5.
36. LRO, Blackburn-Preston Turnpike Trust, Minute Book, Mar. 1829, Mar. and Apr. 1830, Apr. 1832, TTJ7.

# Straws in the wind: the local and regional roots of an occupational disease epidemic

*Geoffrey Tweedale*

Each year, the Health and Safety Executive (HSE) – the government department charged with industrial health and safety – updates its statistics on industrial accidents and diseases. Like most official bodies, it often presents a favourable picture of government achievements and improving industrial hygiene. No amount of spin, however, can hide the worsening statistics for asbestos-related diseases (ARDs).[1] In 1968 (when numbers were first logged), deaths from the asbestos cancer mesothelioma were 153; the latest statistics for 2007 show 2,156 casualties (see Figure 1). However, the picture is far worse. That figure needs supplementing by deaths due to asbestos-related lung cancer (believed to be one asbestos-related lung cancer death per mesothelioma) and those due to asbestos-related fibrosis of the lungs (asbestosis). The HSE believes that total asbestos-related deaths are about 4,000 each year – though others say that the figure is much higher. Certainly, that total is rising each year and no one knows when it will peak. The best scenario is that the number will begin to decline in another five or six years, but even then it will be decades before asbestos morbidity and mortality disappear.

Asbestos remains a staple of press reporting. In March 2009, the *Daily Mirror* ran a feature over several days.[2] The reportage had been partly triggered by a study that highlighted the grim news that 'an entire generation of carpenters [one in ten born in the 1940s] has been blighted by asbestos cancer' and would die of mesothelioma or lung cancer.[3] This identified the 1970s and 1980s as key decades when workers were negligently exposed. What is so shocking is that the lethal nature of asbestos had been reported by the Factory Inspectorate (the HSE's predecessor) as long ago as 1900. So these statistics raise a huge question: how has the present situation been allowed to develop? Scientists have expressed puzzlement. According to one leading epidemiologist: 'Historically it is incomprehensible

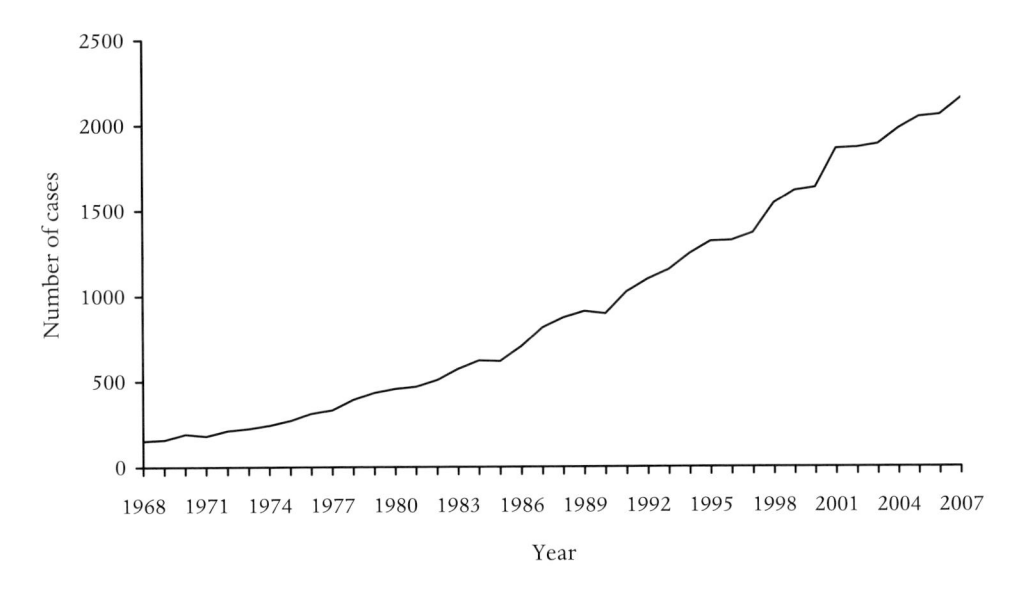

**Figure 1:** Death certificates recording mesothelioma in the UK, 1968–2007

that this has happened. That Britain should have made this extraordinary industrial error seems hard to understand'.[4]

Whatever the reason for current deaths, the North West remains at the centre of events. It contains some of the worst 'hot spots' for mesothelioma and asbestos-related lung cancer in the UK. This is partly due to the past use of asbestos in the North West's shipbuilding and engineering industries. Moreover, the North West was home to the country's biggest asbestos company. This was Turner & Newall (T&N), based in Rochdale. Between the 1920s and the 1970s, T&N dominated the asbestos industry in Britain and accounted at peak for some 60 per cent of the country's asbestos production.[5] The workforce grew from about 5,000 in 1924 to over 35,000 world-wide by 1970. The company became a 'universal provider' of asbestos products, through a string of UK subsidiaries, with the headquarters at Turner Brothers Asbestos (TBA) in Rochdale. Not only was T&N a giant in the UK, but it was also a major multinational, second only in sales to the American Johns-Manville company. In 2000, I documented the occupational health history of T&N, using legal-discovery documents from the US. However, new material comes into the public domain each year. This article will shed more light on those key decades – the 1960s, 1970s, and early 1980s – when mesothelioma was 'discovered' and attempts were made by the government to regulate the industry. It argues that the present situation, far from being hard to understand, is the logical result of actions fostered at a local level. These actions ensured that asbestos manufacture could continue untrammelled in the North West and elsewhere.

**The Brooks case**

Asbestos fibres scar the lungs and cause asbestosis. They can also trigger lung cancers. Mesothelioma – now the most frequently publicized ARD – is a cancer of the lining of the chest (pleura) or the abdomen (peritoneum). It is an aggressive, painful disease that usually causes death within months (even though the disease may not develop for thirty years or more after exposure). The only known cause is asbestos and in the majority of mesotheliomas evidence of past asbestos exposure can be found.[6] Disturbingly, it can result from relatively trivial exposure (days or months, rather than years) and many individuals who have developed the disease have never worked in the asbestos industry. Working in an ancillary occupation that used asbestos (such as lagging or construction work) can be enough. Mesothelioma was given world-wide publicity in the early 1960s after South African research linked the cancer with exposure (both occupational and non-occupational) to asbestos.[7] In 1964, the disease was publicized at an international conference in New York, which ensured that 'there was little reason to doubt that asbestos was a cause of mesothelioma'.[8] Occupational health physicians and pathologists then began the hunt for further mesothelioma cases by combing company files, hospital records, the past medical literature, and contemporary case-histories.

As long ago as the 1930s, two TBA asbestos textile workers in Rochdale – William Pennington and Edmund Pilling – had died from asbestos-related pleural cancers. By 1960, T&N had several mesotheliomas on the books, though the company's official recognition of the disease only began in 1964. It involved Frank Brooks, a long-serving TBA employee who had been born in 1907 and joined the company when he left school as a fifteen-year-old in 1922. Brooks's first job was in the card room and the work was dusty. He left after only a year, but returned to TBA for a much longer stint between 1929 and 1964. During this period he worked in the rubber and warehouse departments. Here he was also exposed to asbestos dust, but government regulations made an important distinction between this job and asbestos textile work. The latter was designated a *scheduled* occupation after 1931, which meant that it was subject to government safety checks. Sick workers could also be compensated. Many other jobs, such as warehouse work, were not scheduled and were deemed so safe that no protection or compensation was offered. Brooks had spent only sixteen months in the scheduled textile areas.

By 1961, Brooks had problems in swallowing and in March 1964 was admitted to Birch Hill Hospital in Rochdale, suffering from breathlessness. It was caused by a pleural effusion (fluid on the lung) and he was sent home. By May, however, the same symptoms had returned and Brooks was again admitted to hospital. Acute breathlessness and heart failure developed and Brooks was found to have an unspecified pleural tumour. He died on 2 December 1964, aged fifty-seven.

Brooks had the classic signs of mesothelioma. The post-mortem showed that the right lung was encased in thick tumour tissue.[9] The tumour was pleural and his lungs were filled with asbestos fibres, though he did not have asbestosis. Samples were sent for analysis to the government doctors (the Pneumoconiosis Medical Panel, or PMP). Meanwhile, an inquest was organized in Rochdale. The coroner was the father of the Birch Hill pathologist Dr Coupe, who had conducted the post-mortem. Coupe, the coroner, was therefore well aware of the significance of the post-mortem findings and the link between asbestos and pleural tumours. He could have delayed proceedings until the tumour was analyzed, but he declined to do so on the grounds that it would hold up the funeral. Far from raising any industrial hygiene concerns, he expressed full confidence in TBA and told the inquest that 'further investigations were in the hands of Dr Knox [the company physician] and certain expert colleagues, and that any obligations which the company felt they should honour as a result of such findings would be duly carried out'.[10]

By January 1965, the government had confirmed that Brooks's tumour was a mesothelioma. The company had confirmed it, too, though the way in which it did so is illuminating. TBA would only accept a case of mesothelioma if it was confirmed by a hand-picked panel of seven experts, two of whom were American. This usually caused delays and, as one company physician later remarked to the present author, total unanimity was not always possible (in which case the mesothelioma was not accepted).[11] As the reports trickled in from the Brooks's case, Dr John Knox stated that it 'does not prove anything', though he grudgingly admitted that it was a 'straw in the wind'.[12] Knox had been first told in 1958 by a South African pathologist (who visited TBA) that asbestos might cause mesothelioma, but Knox later explained: 'I did not accept the hypothesis readily. From a position of frank disbelief I gradually accepted a position of qualified acceptance'.[13] Knox failed to re-examine the company's medical files and showed no inclination to look at the experience of other companies in the T&N group. Instead, in the early 1960s he helped prepare public-relations leaflets for the workforce and the media that would help T&N conduct a damage-limitation exercise against mesothelioma.

However, the PMP physician involved in the Brooks's case was Dr Hilton Lewinsohn, who was soon to replace Knox at TBA. Lewinsohn would later list Brooks as TBA's first proven mesothelioma (with

William Pennington also acknowledged as TBA's first historical casualty in 1936). Faced with the proof of Brooks's cause of death (which confirmed published medical research on mesothelioma), TBA made no effort to inform Frank Brooks's widow, Dora, even though it would have been easy to do so. She had worked at TBA for nearly thirty years. Dora was eventually awarded a paltry £300 state death benefit – the maximum allowance – for her husband's death. This would be supplemented by an equally modest *ex gratia* from the company. TBA never accepted in official communications that Brooks had died of mesothelioma; and never retained a copy of Brooks's death certificate. As a result, no negative publicity appeared and Brooks's mesothelioma effectively disappeared into the company files. The diagnosis had no impact on the open verdict, because the coroner was under no obligation to close it. Dora Brooks did not launch a legal claim.

**Effacing the evidence**

What happened in the Brooks's case looks like a cover-up, though the process was more subtle than that phrase implies. It was never hatched by one individual or even by TBA alone, but was part of a social and legal mechanism which effaced and filtered out damaging news. That mechanism can be seen operating in other spheres besides asbestos. The inadequacy of the coroner's system and inquest procedures has been highlighted in accounts of other north-west tragedies, such as the career of Harold Shipman.[14] In asbestos, the mechanism certainly did not involve Brooks alone. If that was so, then his death would lose its significance. For decades many other industrial disease deaths had slipped through the official net and had fallen victim to the same process. It was a process in which doctors, coroners, and government medical officers played a role, often at a local level.

Jack Myers was a TBA spinner who died in a Rochdale hospital in 1971 from lung cancer. His death certificate, however, stated cause of death as 'cerebral thrombosis'. There was no post-mortem, but TBA and the PMP obtained specimens of the lung and agreed that the cancer was linked with asbestosis. Neither TBA nor the PMP told the widow.[15] Emma Marshall, a part-time office cleaner at TBA, had died of mesothelioma in 1972. The coroner signed off her death as due to 'natural causes', with no suggestion of an 'industrial disease'. Yet her post-mortem report in the TBA archive, dated 21 March 1972, shows that the cause of death was a 'malignant mesothelioma'. Her lungs were filled with asbestos fibres, even though she had not worked in a 'scheduled area'. Margaret Priestley was another TBA worker. She had been certified by the government as 70 per cent disabled by asbestosis and was receiving state compensation. When she died in 1977, aged sixty-nine, the coroner immediately certified the cause of death as first, 'bronchopneumonia', and second, as 'diffuse interstitial fibrosis of both lungs'.[16] The certificate was signed off before the coroner had waited for the obligatory post-mortem report on an asbestosis death. Two weeks after the death certificate was issued, the PMP reported a 'death due to asbestosis'.

In 1977, TBA worker Arthur Sutcliffe had died in Rochdale, aged sixty-five. His death certificate, in TBA's files, stated that his death was due to a heart attack and lung cancer. The attached correspondence, however, shows a more complex situation. TBA had somehow obtained (possibly from the widow) copies of all relevant correspondence, including letters from Rochdale Area Health Authority and the local hospital. The documents show that Sutcliffe's post-mortem gave the cause of death as lung cancer due to asbestosis. The hospital consultant had immediately alerted Rochdale Health Authority, because he felt that someone 'should be able to put a claim for compensation'.[17] However, the coroner did not call an inquest and the PMP made no attempt to confirm the findings (the widow, hardly surprisingly, had made no legal claim). When she did so, she enlisted the support of Cyril Smith, Rochdale's MP. Smith contacted the local health authority, which surprisingly (after the prompting it had received from the hospital pathologist) merely told Smith that the cause of death 'was clearly stated on the death certificate given to Mrs Sutcliffe at the time of her husband's death'. While they watched this scenario play out, TBA's personnel manager privately disputed the post-mortem findings and wrote to a colleague: 'Attached are some photocopies from our files ... [It is] perhaps unwise to let C. Smith know they are in our possession'.[18]

In June 1978, Robert Maitland, a senior foreman in TBA's carding and spinning department, had died aged seventy-one. He had been retired for over a decade, incapacitated by asbestosis, for which he received a state pension. After a post-mortem, the coroner gave the cause of death as heart failure, fibrosis of the lungs, and lung cancer.[19] But there was no mention of asbestos, asbestosis, or industrial disease (soon confirmed by the PMP). Again, no attempt was made to inform the widow of the final verdict, which would have dramatically altered the legal circumstances of any claim.

In 1980, coroners were instructed by the government to defer their conclusions until after the PMP had reported. But this made little impact initially. In 1981, TBA worker Teddy Wellings was judged by the coroner to have died from ordinary causes (heart disease and bronchitis). This appeared on the death certificate and the family's request for an inquest was refused. The PMP verdict, however, was 'cancer of the lung and asbestosis'. Because government compensation was geared towards the 'scheduled areas' and 'official' cases of disease, some families never had the luxury of either a post-mortem or inquest. For example, in October 1982 Rochdale's radical magazine *RAP* [*Rochdale's Alternative Paper*] documented details of the death of Phyllis Heywood (1907–1977), who in the 1920s and 1930s had been a worker in the unscheduled proofed goods section at TBA.[20] She had died of mesothelioma, but there had been neither a post-mortem nor an inquest. It is a comment on the rigorousness of TBA's follow up that the company knew nothing about it. A TBA manager informed a director, after seeing details of the case reported: 'This is a new meso case for our records'.[21]

Events in Rochdale were not unique. In other towns and districts around the UK where T&N had subsidiaries, local officialdom and vested interests served to blunt the recognition of the scale of ARDs and the extent of individual suffering. The T&N archive is replete with examples of workers from around the country who died of horrific asbestos cancers yet had neither post-mortem, nor inquest, nor even the full facts recorded on their death certificates.[22] This had profound implications. As the *New Statesman* underlined: 'spouses and relatives have been prevented from gaining compensation and the statistics on the true levels of death from asbestos cancer and disease are significantly reduced'.[23] This was particularly so because death certificates were relied upon by epidemiologists and the government to track the extent of ARDs.

### The role of Sir Cyril Smith

While the adverse health impact of asbestos was being effaced and diluted at local level, the use of asbestos was able to continue nationally. On the national scene, the leading asbestos companies such as T&N conducted a rearguard action against government regulation. This loomed in the shape of a major parliamentary enquiry, the Simpson Committee, which began its deliberations in 1976. T&N escaped relatively unscathed from Simpson. The government wanted to ban crocidolite (blue asbestos), but the industry had pre-empted that by voluntarily withdrawing it. Simpson recommended tightening dust controls on the use of white asbestos (chrysotile), with tighter controls for brown asbestos (amosite). But neither product was to be banned. T&N was a major user of chrysotile and though it was winding down its use of amosite, that latter was still used and marketed by T&N at the start of the 1980s. Crocidolite and amosite could also still be imported in products such as asbestos-cement sheets. Crucially, the Simpson Committee had only produced *recommendations*. No timetable had been set for the implementation of these measures, which allowed the industry leeway to defend asbestos and conduct a staged withdrawal.

This defence was fought at both national and local level. In Rochdale, TBA was a major job-provider (with over 3,000 workers) and could still count on significant worker loyalty. Rochdale was not quite a company town – it had many engineering and textile firms – but TBA wielded crucial support among local politicians. The key figure in the 1970s and early 1980s was (Sir) Cyril Smith (b. 1928), who was Rochdale's Liberal member of parliament after 1972. Smith's impressive girth and man-of-the-people persona had made him a national figure. But he was even more dominant locally, where many individuals beat a path to his door in Emma Street. Amongst these were some of Smith's constituents, who had been damaged by asbestos. These included – as we have seen – Mrs Arthur Sutcliffe. Smith's help may have been critical in her winning an initial legal appeal for compensation.

TBA was wary of Smith. But as government regulation began to tighten, any distrust (on either side) apparently soon vanished. By the summer of 1981, Smith was discussing with TBA several proposed European Economic Community (EEC) directives about asbestos safety standards. These directives were to be discussed in parliament within months. Smith initially served as a useful intermediary between the company and leading political figures. He arranged an invitation to the factory for David Waddington, the government Minister of Employment. He also arranged a private meeting between the unions and Waddington. The minister had been suitably impressed and later wrote a fulsome letter to the company praising 'how much effort had gone into [the visit] – not least into the admirable lunch! … I was very impressed by the effort and investment TBA have put into identifying and controlling the dangers from asbestos: it was only when I saw them at first hand that I realised the cost and sophistication of the equipment involved'.[24] The HSE had also been invited on the factory tour and its representative was similarly effusive. 'Dear Sid', wrote a member of the HSE's Hazardous Substances Division to TBA's personnel manager Sidney Marks, 'I must add my personal thanks once again for a most interesting and enjoyable day … [and] for continuing in such a patient way to add to my education. Please convey my appreciation to *all* concerned with the arrangements which went with enviable smoothness'.[25]

The visit enabled Smith to portray himself as the local fixer. 'I am delighted to have been totally involved', he proclaimed in his Rochdale newspaper column, 'for I want to see Turner's thrive and I want them to continue to provide employment for my constituents'.[26]

It was an involvement Smith and TBA intended to continue. Within a fortnight of the Waddington visit, Smith wrote to Marks:

> I understand that the debate on Asbestos will be on Friday, 23 October. [¶] Could you please, within the next eight weeks, let me have the speech you would like to make (were you able to!), in that Debate? In particular, points of disagreement with EEC documentation, points to urge, etc. [¶] Perhaps you could send this to me at 14 Emma Street, Rochdale, as the House is now in Recess. I will then read it and telephone you to discuss it.[27]

Taking up the invitation, TBA managers prepared a draft of several pages for Smith to use. Copies from the company files show that considerable care was taken in its preparation. On 11 August 1981, a final copy of the draft, headed 'suggested speech', was forwarded to Smith.[28]

The draft was largely composed of the ideas and defences of asbestos that had been formulated over several years by T&N and its public relations advisers (who were kept up to date with Smith's involvement). The pillars of those defences were: asbestos was indispensable; substitute materials (such as glass fibre) were potentially as dangerous; the public were not at risk; dust-control measures within industry were adequate; workers' smoking habits were partly responsible; and regulation would damage the economy.[29] Above all, TBA's strategy aimed at avoiding the substitution of asbestos by other products, or, even worse, the banning of asbestos.

Feeding into this strategy were TBA's anxieties over the projected EEC directives. These directives had highlighted tensions between UK asbestos firms and their European counterparts – especially between T&N and the leading continental asbestos-cement conglomerate Eternit. Not surprisingly, Eternit had influence in Europe, as T&N did in the UK. Eternit mixed crocidolite into its cement and, even though the medical consensus was that blue asbestos was the major cause of mesothelioma, Eternit argued for its continued use. The UK government was on the point of a statutory (not simply voluntary) ban on crocidolite, but the EEC directives would allow certain exemptions, such as its use in asbestos-cement pipes (a sure sign of Eternit's influence). This, T&N argued, would be advantageous to European companies, in a situation in which UK firms had voluntarily withdrawn crocidolite. On the one hand, while it loosened regulation in one direction, the EEC intended to tighten it slightly in another. Dust-control limits were to be tightened beyond current UK standards.

T&N opposed these EEC directives and this was the main burden of Smith's 'suggested speech'. Politically, however, the industry knew

Sir Cyril Smith invites TBA's input prior to a parliamentary debate on asbestos

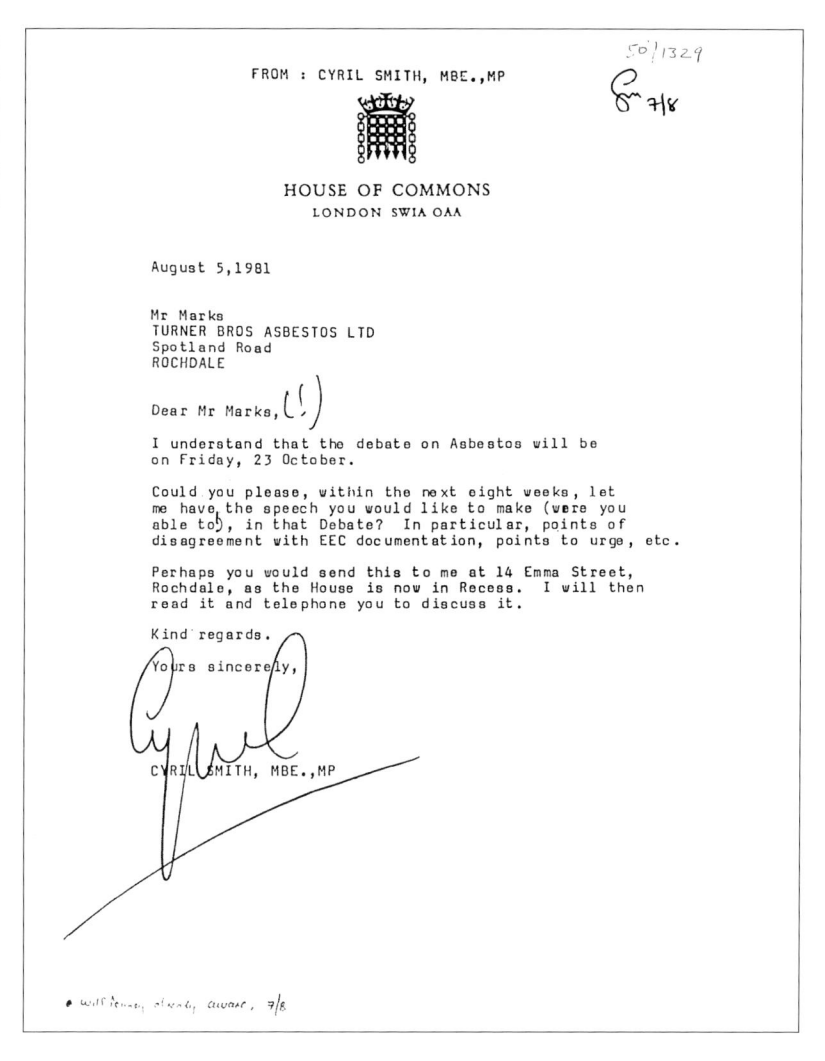

> FROM : CYRIL SMITH, MBE.,MP
>
> HOUSE OF COMMONS
> LONDON SW1A 0AA
>
> August 5, 1981
>
> Mr Marks
> TURNER BROS ASBESTOS LTD
> Spotland Road
> ROCHDALE
>
> Dear Mr Marks,
>
> I understand that the debate on Asbestos will be on Friday, 23 October.
>
> Could you please, within the next eight weeks, let me have the speech you would like to make (were you able to), in that Debate? In particular, points of disagreement with EEC documentation, points to urge, etc.
>
> Perhaps you would send this to me at 14 Emma Street, Rochdale, as the House is now in Recess. I will then read it and telephone you to discuss it.
>
> Kind regards.
>
> Yours sincerely,
>
> CYRIL SMITH, MBE., MP

that tighter regulation would come. So T&N did not totally oppose the need for more controls: instead, they argued for 'harmonisation'. In other words, they wanted no action until the UK and EEC regulations were in step. This achieved two objects: harmonization took time and delayed UK regulation (in the shape of Simpson); and it ensured that no foreign rival could gain an unfair advantage.

T&N's lobbying was extended to Barbara Castle, who was MEP for Manchester North; and to other members of the European Labour Party group. In May 1981, Castle and her colleagues toured the TBA factory. In the following month, TBA's directors flew to Strasbourg to present their views to a cross-section of MEPs. The trip was organized through Castle's office, which provided TBA with a list of prospective MEPs, with the Rochdale company paying the costs of the buffet lunch at the Holiday Inn.[30] Meanwhile, attempts were made to persuade trade unions that their cause was best served by supporting the industry. A wide range of Conservative MPs and ministers were also contacted and with some success. Waddington, after his visit to Rochdale, was quick to reassure the industry's public relations body that the government would be seeking a 'harmonised' approach.[31]

In particular, TBA relied on Cyril Smith. On 17 August, another draft of the speech was sent to Smith, with updated sections on 'harmonisation'. Plans were made for Smith and TBA to meet and work on a final version of the speech. Meanwhile, TBA believed it had found another sympathetic MP in a neighbouring constituency. Smith helpfully suggested to TBA that:

> you send him your tabular version of the two [EEC] directives which outline your views on the proposals, telling him that you understand that there is to be a debate on this matter in October and that if he would like any information etc, you would be happy to supply it. The key thing, of course, is that you *do not* send him *my speech*.[32]

A letter was duly despatched, which proclaimed that TBA hoped for a 'balanced debate'. But that MP showed no sympathy for TBA's predicament and took no part in the parliamentary debate for which Smith was preparing so carefully. With the debate impending, Smith was arranging for the company's directors to have reserved seats in the gallery of the House of Commons. TBA planned to send to London its top directors: chairman David Hills, Brian Heron, Norman Rhodes, and Reg Sykes. Smith instructed them to meet him in the lobby of the Commons for dinner. Representatives from the trade unions at TBA would attend the debate, too, but this was not at Smith's invitation. Smith never met them and the trade unionists instead sought out Labour MPs at the House.

The debate took place on Thursday 22 October 1981.[33] The speeches revolved around the EEC directives, but the opposition (Labour Party) had tabled a key amendment that sought to eliminate the use of all forms of asbestos. Waddington spoke first, stressing the need for 'harmonisation', and making it clear that the government had no taste for a statutory ban on blue asbestos. He stressed that asbestos was indispensable and warned about the potential dangers of asbestos substitutes. The next speaker was Barry Jones, Labour MP for Flint, who called for a statutory ban on blue asbestos and eventually on all forms of asbestos.

Smith then rose to speak. He first dismissed Jones's views as 'highly inflammatory and somewhat of an exaggeration of the dangers'. He then praised TBA's 'proud history' and its record in industrial hygiene. Smith ran the gamut of reasons why the industry should continue to thrive. Government and EEC regulation would lead to the loss of 'thousands of jobs'; substitute materials might be dangerous; EEC regulations could lead to unfair competition. He told his audience that he found it difficult to imagine a world without asbestos: 'Let no one underestimate its importance, or fail to understand that, properly used, asbestos protects and saves lives. That is a point that its critics always fail to make'. Above all, the public were not at risk. 'It is necessary to say that time and time again, because the manner in which the subject was dealt with by the Opposition spokesman could cause a great deal of scare and alarm among members of the public'. At the heart of the speech, was an acceptance of workers' risk, because 'every time someone crosses the road he is in danger of being knocked down by a bus. One cannot imagine reaching a point at which all risks in industry will be eliminated'. Smith placed the onus for health and safety on the worker: 'Anti-smoking campaigns among employees would probably do more than any other single factor to reduce the incidence of asbestos-related lung cancer. I hope that everything possible will be done to publicise that fact'.

It is important to note what Smith did not say. He never told the House that he had been briefed by TBA. He made no mention of mesothelioma or any other type of cancer. He never referred to the sufferings of those with ARDs or any compensation issues, with which he was so well acquainted. He never discussed the ancillary trades, such as lagging and shipbuilding, where T&N and other companies had used asbestos so widely and without adequate dust controls. What Smith did in a matter of a few minutes was repeat every mantra that the industry had honed over several years to defend its product. The statements followed closely the text that Smith had been given by TBA. Of course, asbestos and its health impact are often opaque and technical subjects and Smith's reliance on advice from TBA is hardly surprising. What is disappointing is the failure to consider other independent sources that gave a different view. Published evidence had been available for over a decade that showed that the public *were* at risk from mesothelioma; that asbestos was not indispensable; and that working conditions even inside TBA remained hazardous. Indeed, that was why government regulations were being debated.

The speech, however, had served its immediate purpose. To Smith's and TBA's satisfaction, the opposition amendment to ban asbestos was defeated. UK government regulation, including any ban on blue asbestos, was to be postponed in the cause of EEC harmony. The industry's lobby group, the Asbestos Information Committee (AIC), soon issued a press release on the House of Commons debate. The leaflet recorded a triumph in public relations. The material that

TBA had prepared in Rochdale, which had then been relied upon so heavily by Smith in the debate, was now recycled in the AIC leaflet as a set of independent facts. The AIC could have not done better if it had written those views itself. In Rochdale, the press reaction was also favourable. The local newspaper reported its MP's exploits under the heading: 'Cyril Blocks a Job-Buster'.[34] Once back on home ground, Smith was able to score some easy points off the TBA trade unions by accusing them of 'playing politics' by snubbing him at the debate and instead meeting Labour MPs. The trade unionists denied this and complained that when they had tried to meet Smith both before and after the debate they had been turned away. As one trade unionist put it: 'we did not pursue the matter as we knew that Mr Smith had been supplied with all the relevant details by TBA management'.[35] It was an accurate view of the situation.

**The Yorkshire TV ogre**

The debate over asbestos, however, was about to move outside the lobbies of the House of Commons. In 1982, over 500 people died in Britain from mesothelioma. These deaths hardly registered nationally, partly for the reasons that have been detailed above. But in that year, one person became the public face of asbestos suffering in Britain. Her name was Alice Jefferson, a former worker at the Cape Asbestos Company factory in Hebden Bridge, who had developed mesothelioma. She featured in a Yorkshire TV documentary – *Alice: a fight for life* – that was screened on 20 July 1982. As a documentary, it had some unusual features. Not only did it hit a mainstream evening audience, but it was ninety minutes long, and was probably the first documentary to focus so closely on a terminal occupational illness. Never had the public been shown so graphically the horror behind that stock coroner's phrase: 'death due to industrial disease'.

Viewers followed Alice Jefferson through the misery of what was left of her daily life to the final scenes in a hospice. With Alice supplying the human angle, the documentary ripped through the myths surrounding asbestos and emphasized the dangers of environmental exposure and the toxicity of white asbestos (besides blue and brown). Its heaviest punches were reserved for the asbestos companies. Although Alice was a Cape Asbestos worker, the industry leader T&N (which had declined to take part in the programme) and its Rochdale factory were taken to task. *Alice* highlighted not only the appalling levels of compensation for asbestos diseases, but also the collusion of physicians and the government in covering up the extent of these mortal illnesses, so that even the most miserable pittances were never paid.

The documentary's impact was far reaching.[36] As Wilf Penney, the asbestos industry's PR man, put it: 'Until the *Alice* film the various programmes on asbestos made since 1975 had little lasting impact on either the public or the industry ... [but *Alice*] was a different kettle of fish. It was a highly personalised, very emotional, tragic record of one person's suffering. It was two years in the making and was, to put it mildly, a blockbuster'.[37] It hit Turner & Newall's share price and triggered public outrage around the country.

Rochdale families, who had lost relatives to ARDs, watched aghast at the descriptions of lung cancer and mesothelioma. Suddenly, facts began to fall into place. The son of Jack Myers wrote to the PMP about his father's death and was enraged to discover that they and TBA had held lung specimens that proved that asbestos was a factor in the death: information that had never been sent to the widow and thus denied her the information for a legal claim.[38] The widow of Frank Brooks also began to suspect the true cause of her husband's death. Her daughter, Joyce Stott, wrote to TBA immediately after *Alice*, reminding the company that further investigations had been promised, but: 'Neither myself nor my mother, who also worked for Turner Bros for over fifty years ... have ever been told if the investigation took place'.[39] TBA's new personnel manager, Mr I. Waters, reviewed TBA's files. In those files, of course, was Dr Hilton Lewinsohn's letter from the PMP stating that the cause of death was a 'mesothelioma of the right pleura ... [and] the deceased's occupation was an aetiological factor in the death'. This was useful to have, as the Department of Health and Security told TBA that it had already destroyed its files relating to Brooks.[40] Waters was far from disconcerted by a situation in which TBA had clearly failed to fulfil its obligations. He explained the whole matter away with the argument that 'mesothelioma deaths were very rare in 1964 and the link between the disease and asbestos had just emerged'. He hoped to smooth things over with the traditional TBA panacea – a chat over a cup of tea. He wrote to TBA chief executive Brian Heron, that this would be 'a useful PR exercise for Mrs Stott probably still believes that we may have covered up some of the facts relating to her father's death'.[41] Dora Brooks, however, was not mollified. In 1983, a writ was issued against TBA by Mrs Brooks, claiming common law damages for her husband's death.[42] No record of the outcome of this claim is contained in TBA's Brooks's file. The claim appears to have been abandoned (probably because of legal time constraints).

Cyril Smith had watched *Alice*, too. He had not featured in the documentary, but *Alice* had indirectly raised questions about Smith's wisdom in supporting the company so wholeheartedly. Smith immediately told TBA chief Heron that he had been 'deeply moved and disturbed' by the documentary, particularly by the charges of cover-up and injustices over compensation.[43] He requested a meeting. But Heron simply refuted the allegations and dismissed the programme as biased and inaccurate.[44] Smith's concerns apparently evaporated. He was soon reported as saying that the company should sue Yorkshire TV for libel. He reiterated his belief that the Rochdale plant was no more dangerous than any other factory. He lamented the fall in T&N's share price, 'so much so', he told reporters, 'that although in my life I have never owned shares in the company, I have instructed my bankers to purchase some for me'.[45]

TBA made an official complaint to the Independent Broadcasting Authority (IBA). A leading epidemiologist, Sir Richard Doll – who regarded the documentary as 'harmful' – was invited to Rochdale to reassure TBA workers that the risks of asbestos were negligible. Private detectives were hired to rake into the character and background of anyone associated with the film. The programme-makers were smeared as 'subversives' and the industry made attempts to get the film censored. But attempts to undermine the integrity of the programme failed. TBA realized that they would never succeed in ridding themselves of what they termed the 'Yorkshire TV ogre'.[46] *Alice* was shown in the US and in Europe, where the documentary won prizes. It was recognized as a path-breaking work that had put Britain (and other countries) on notice that asbestos was a major hazard.

For several years, the government had been able to sideline the Simpson Committee's recommendations for lower dust levels in the factories, but within days of *Alice* these were suddenly implemented. Smith's reaction to increased dust control was ambiguous. He professed delight that UK asbestos workers were better protected and issued a press release stating that he welcomed the new regulations, 'which, of course, have nothing to do with the television programme'.[47] But he soon returned to his (and T&N's) familiar refrain that more stringent dust controls in the UK would give other European companies a competitive advantage. In the House of Commons, his support for the industry and T&N remained undiminished. Smith accused Yorkshire Television of telling 'blatant lies'.[48] But the company never sued for libel and its complaint to the IBA was rejected. Smith's contacts with TBA lessened and after 1983 his interventions in parliamentary asbestos debates dwindled.

## Straws become haystacks

Asbestos remains controversial in Rochdale. TBA shut down its asbestos production plant in Rochdale in the early 1990s. By 1998, plans were underway for T&N to be sold to an American engineering company, Federal Mogul. Within only two years, however, Federal Mogul had filed for bankruptcy in the US. In effect, T&N's asbestos liabilities had been taken 'offshore' and presently the rump of the company pays only a few pence in the pound for claims for mesothelioma or any other ARD. The rolling demolition of the huge TBA factory began in 2001, which marked the start of another round of controversy. In 2004, a private company began in earnest the final demolition of the factory and total clearance of the site (including the felling of local woodland). This immediately triggered the formation of an action group – Save Spodden Valley – organized by local residents. The group was led by Jason Addy, whose grandfather Ivan Addy was a former worker at TBA and had died in 1974 from mesothelioma. The campaigners demanded safe development and proper decontamination of the site.

In 2008, the *New Statesman* published Smith's 'the speech you would like to make' letter, thereby publicizing his unreserved support for the company.[49] When questioned by journalists about that letter, an irate Smith refuted any suggestion that he had read the speech out verbatim and argued that he had used his own words. He stated that TBA workers did not have to work at the factory, so it was essentially their choice.[50]

These events need to be set in context. The backdrop is provided by the rising national mortality for mesothelioma. The Brooks's case did indeed prove to be – as TBA's physician Dr Knox forecast – a straw in the wind. Brooks's death occurred in 1964, in the same year that a New York conference gave international publicity to mesothelioma and warned of the dangers of asbestos exposure even to those individuals who worked outside the asbestos industry. That knowledge should have signalled a rapid retreat worldwide from the use of asbestos. Instead, asbestos use continued after the 1960s. Not only did it continue, but global use of asbestos actually increased. 80 per cent of global asbestos production in the twentieth century occurred *after* 1960, when mesothelioma and asbestos were irrevocably linked.

The reasons why asbestos use continued are complex. But as this article has shown, local and regional events played a key part in shaping national agendas on asbestos in the 1970s and 1980s. These events ensured that the most dangerous types of asbestos (such as crocidolite) were only banned with the greatest reluctance; that amosite use continued through the 1970s, particularly in construction materials; and that the use of white asbestos remained a commercial product into the 1980s (and was not banned until the millennium). The current mesothelioma epidemic is therefore far from 'incomprehensible': it was the inevitable outcome of actions and policies that were forged in localities such as Rochdale, where powerful industrial interests, local officials, and politicians proved so expert at defending asbestos and slowing regulation.

**Notes**

1. HSE statistics, http://www.hse.gov.uk/statistics/causdis/asbestos.htm, accessed 26 Nov. 2009.
2. 'One in 10 Doomed', *Daily Mirror*, 4 Mar. 2009.
3. J. Peto, C. Rake, J. C. Gilham, and J. Hatch, *Occupational, domestic and environmental mesothelioma risks in Britain: a case-control study* (HSE Report RR 696, 2009), http://www.hse.gov.uk/research/rrpdf/rr696.pdf, accessed 26 Nov. 2009.
4. Professor Julian Peto, quoted in *Daily Mail*, 20 Feb. 2007.
5. G. Tweedale, *Magic mineral to killer dust: Turner & Newall and the asbestos hazard* (Oxford, 2nd edn., 2001).
6. Bruce W. S. Robinson, Arthur W. Musk, and Richard A. Lake, 'Malignant mesothelioma?', *Lancet*, 366 (30 July 2005), pp. 397–408.
7. J. C. Wagner, C. A. Sleggs and P. Marchand, 'Diffuse pleural mesotheliomas and asbestos exposure in the north-western Cape Province', *British Journal of Industrial Medicine*, 17 (1960), pp. 260–71.
8. B. I. Castleman, *Asbestos: medical and legal aspects* (Englewood Cliffs, NJ; 5th edn., 2005), p. 108.
9. PM Report on Frank Brooks by Dr A. S. Coupe, 4 Dec. 1964.
10. J. Arnold to TBA board, 11 Dec. 1964.
11. Tweedale, *Magic mineral*, p. 194.
12. J. F. Knox to J. Waddell, 21 Jan. 1965.
13. Knox to R. A. Wells, 18 Jan. 1967.
14. Brian Whittle and Jean Ritchie, *Prescription for murder: the story of Harold Shipman* (London, 2004).
15. S. Marks to R. D. N. Somerville, 30 Nov. 1982.
16. Death certificate, 26 Jan. 1977.
17. Dr S. Jegarajah to Rochdale Health Authority, 30 Mar. 1977.
18. I. Waters to S. Marks, 26 Feb. 1979.
19. TBA Memo on R. Maitland, 13 June 1978.
20. *RAP*, 112, Oct. 1982.
21. S. Marks to J. B. Heron, 6 Oct. 1982.
22. For example, Norman Fowler (1914–1972), a worker at T&N's Newalls Insulation subsidiary in Tyne & Wear, died from 'abdominal carcinomatosis'. That was the cause of death (without an inquest) certified by the coroner on the death certificate. The autopsy showed peritoneal mesothelioma/asbestosis.
23. James Cutler, 'Cover-up on asbestos victims', *New Statesman*, 104 (15 Oct. 1982), p. 4.

24. D. Waddington to S. Marks, 22 July 1918.
25. Miss Sandra Newton (HSE) to S. Marks, TBA, 21 July 1981.
26. C. Smith, 'Letters from Westminster', *Rochdale Observer*, 25 July 1981.
27. Smith to Marks, 5 Aug. 1981.
28. 'Suggested speech by Mr Cyril Smith in forthcoming debate in the House of Commons on EEC Directives on asbestos-containing materials', forwarded with covering letter from Marks to Smith, 11 Aug. 1981.
29. J. McCulloch and G. Tweedale, *Defending the indefensible: the global asbestos industry and its fight for survival* (Oxford, 2008), pp. 109–18.
30. Marks to B. Castle, 22 Dec. 1980; S. Marks to B. Castle, 25 May 1981.
31. D. Waddington to Wilf Penney, 10 July 1981.
32. Smith to Marks, 24 Aug. 1918.
33. Hansard, Commons Debates, 22 Oct. 1981, vol. 10: cc 450–99, http://hansard.millbanksystems.com/commons/1981/oct/22/asbestos, accessed 26 Nov. 2009.
34. *Rochdale Observer*, 24 Oct. 1981.
35. 'TBA men deny "political snub" over asbestos', *Rochdale Observer*, 27 Feb. 1982.
36. Alfredo Menéndez-Navarro, 'Alice – A fight for life (1982) and the public perception of the occupational health risks of asbestos', *Journal of Medicine and the Movies,* 3 (2007), pp. 47–56.
37. Penney, AIC, 'Asbestos ... fair hearing', memo, 30 June 1983.
38. James Cutler, 'Rochdale widow kept in dark', *New Statesman*, 12 Nov. 1982.
39. Mrs Joyce Stott to TBA, 2 Aug. 1982.
40. DHHS to I. Waters, 21 Sep. 1982.
41. I. Waters to J. B. Heron, 22 Oct. 1982.
42. Dora Brooks (plaintiff) and TBA Industrial Products (defendants), 'Statement of claim', 10 Oct. 1983. Served by Field Fisher & Martineau.
43. Smith to Heron, 23 July 1982.
44. Heron to Smith, 27 July 1982.
45. 'Sue 'em, Cyril tells TBA', *Rochdale Observer*, 14 Aug. 1982. Smith later declared that he held 1,300 shares in T&N.
46. Heron to Smith, 17 Feb. 1983.
47. Liberal Party press release, 25 Aug. 1982.
48. Asbestos debate, Hansard, Commons Debates, 8 Nov. 1983, vol. 48: cc 243–74, http://hansard.millbanksystems.com/commons/1983/nov/08/asbestos#S6CV0048P0_19831108_HOC_455, accessed 26 Nov. 2009.
49. Ed Howker, 'The lies that killed', *New Statesman*, 1 Sep. 2008, pp. 22–6.
50. Mike Keegan, 'Sir Cyril Smith faces fury for backing asbestos firm', *Manchester Evening News*, 2 Sep. 2008.

# ARCHIVES
# 'From the cradle to the grave': the National Co-operative Archive

*Gillian Lonergan*

If this were solely a narrowly defined labour organisation this would itself be sufficient to signal the uniqueness and international significance of the collection. But, unlike many organisations / institutions, the Co-operative represented much more than a single focus in terms of organisational attributes or functional practices. It penetrated whole areas, often literally in geographic terms, of British life. It served as insurer, undertaker, film-maker, chronicler, political party, educational provider, farmer, bootmaker and much else as well, of course, as retailer. In the last role its historical significance is immeasurable, for some fifty years it was by far the largest retail organisation in Britain. Whilst Marks and Spencer were operating out of single fronted shops in a handful of northern cities the Co-op was building dedicated, modern (and modernist) department stores and pioneering new forms of retail organisation, including self-service supermarkets.[1]

In 1995, the International Co-operative Alliance's *Statement on the Co-operative identity* included the definition: 'A co-operative is an autonomous association of persons united voluntarily to meet their common economic, social, and cultural needs and aspirations through a jointly-owned and democratically-controlled enterprise.'[2] This definition is reflected in the breadth of the co-operative movement, which involves approaching a trillion members in just under 100 countries across the world.

The modern UK co-operative movement has its origins in the north-west of England, with the Rochdale Pioneers in 1844, and nearly all the national organizations have their head offices in Manchester. The National Co-operative Archive is based in Manchester and enables researchers to understand this breadth. This article will give an outline of the development of the Archive and some of its collections, giving some examples of how the collections can be used.

## Development of an archive

The origins of the National Co-operative Archive can be traced to the deposit of the Robert Owen Correspondence Collection with the Co-operative Union in 1903. In 1911, the Co-operative Union moved into new headquarters, Holyoake House, built as a memorial to George Jacob Holyoake whose talks and writings had inspired generations of co-operators. The design for the building included a library, recognizing the importance of research and knowledge exchange to the co-operative movement.

The Co-operative College, which provides learning, consultancy and research for the co-operative and mutual sectors, was founded in 1919 in Holyoake House, moving away in the 1940s to a residential facility, and moving back to Holyoake House in 2001 when the needs of co-operative societies changed to a more responsive and flexible provision of learning, with activities taking place in all parts of the UK and internationally.

During the twentieth century, the archive collection of the Co-operative Union (now Co-operatives UK) developed as more material was deposited and a major collection also grew with the Co-operative College. At the end of 1999 the decision was taken to merge the two collections, giving researchers for the first time a single centre where they could consult the original records of the national co-operative organizations and a range of local co-operative societies and correspondence collections along with secondary material and films. The merged archive was called the National Co-operative Archive and based at the Co-operative College.

The Archive and the Rochdale Pioneers Museum are owned by

Thirteen of the twenty-eight founders of the Rochdale Equitable Pioneers Society, 1865

the Co-operative Heritage Trust, a charitable trust set up in 2007 to preserve the museum building and the archive and museum collections and to make them accessible as widely as possible, and managed by the Co-operative College. The Rochdale Pioneers Museum is unusual in that the building, which is where the UK co-operative movement began in 1844, is the most important artefact; it became a museum in 1931.

In 2007, the Museums, Libraries and Archives Council awarded Designated Collections status to the National Co-operative Archive, recognizing the collections as being of national and international importance. The archive is one of 131 collections held in non-national museums, libraries and archives recognized in this way, demonstrating the value of the co-operative collections to the heritage of England. Researchers who use the archive include co-operative societies and their members, academic researchers, schools, subject researchers, local historians, family historians, biographers and the media.

**The collections**

The National Co-operative Archive's collections cover a period of 200 years, and can be used by researchers on nearly every aspect of human life, demonstrating the co-operative movement's proud claim to look after its members 'from the cradle to the grave'. As membership-based organizations, the members of each co-operative society democratically control the organization, deciding on activities undertaken in what is often called 'a different kind of business'. The involvement of members in their co-operatives covers much more than shopping in the co-operative store, living in a housing co-operative or working in a worker co-operative.

While the modern movement started with the Rochdale Equitable Pioneers Society, this was not the first co-operative. The Pioneers learned from the experiences of earlier co-operators to develop a robust model of co-operation that spread rapidly. The archive has collections from those early co-operators to the present day and a broad collecting policy, covering materials from the UK co-operative movement, the International Co-operative Alliance and international co-operative movements. Collections on the co-operative movements in other countries include material given to the Co-operative Union by visiting delegations of co-operators or to the Co-operative College by international students. International students in the 1950s to 1970s sometimes wrote dissertations on the situations of co-operative societies in their home countries.

### Correspondence collections

The correspondence collection of Robert Owen (1771–1858) contains approximately 3,000 letters written by and to Robert Owen between 1821 and 1858. The papers were cared for by George Jacob Holyoake (1817–1906), who appears to have been the first to study them, writing four articles that appeared in the *Co-operative News* between April and June 1904. Owen was known as the 'Father of Co-operation' and was a founder of British socialism. The correspondence is between those involved in the various labour movements of the early nineteenth century, for example co-operative, trades union and socialist, in the UK and abroad, and includes his involvement with communities in America. With the exception of a few letters in French, the correspondence is in English. There is an associated collection of books, pamphlets and journals written by and about Owen, which includes modern biographies as well as nineteenth-century material.

Following the death of George Jacob Holyoake, his own collection, numbering around 4,000 items, was deposited by his daughter, Emilie Holyoake Marsh. The collection comprises letters, notes for speeches and drafts for publications which, along with his published writings, give a vivid feel for the co-operative movement of the nineteenth century. Holyoake was known as the historian of the movement, though he described himself as a journalist and often wrote more to inspire than to document. In the 1830s, Holyoake was one of the 'Owenite Missionaries' who travelled across Britain, talking to groups about Owen's ideas. He spoke in Rochdale and knew many of the Rochdale Pioneers personally. Within a few years of publication, his book *Self-help by the people: the history of the Rochdale Pioneers, 1844–1857* (1858) was translated into languages including German, French and Russian and was widely read, leading to the story of the Rochdale Pioneers inspiring the establishment of co-operative societies in many different places.

Further aspects of the co-operative movement are seen in the third major correspondence collection, that of Edward Owen Greening (1836–1923). Greening was involved in agricultural and horticultural co-operatives, productive co-operatives, the establishment of the International Co-operative Alliance and even the arrangement of co-operative concert parties, providing social events for co-operatives that included a talk on co-operative topics. The collection includes items received by Greening, letter books in which he kept copies of his own letters and manuscripts of some of his published books. Greening kept a scrapbook on events he attended, including the invitations or menus along with the notes for speeches that he gave.

His son compiled a scrapbook of letters of condolence received by the family on Greening's death, from a wide range of co-operative organizations.

**Education**

Co-operatives have, throughout their history, been involved in education. Many communities in the UK had their first access to libraries in the mid nineteenth century through their consumer co-operative as societies opened lending libraries and reading rooms for members. Educational activities enabled co-operative members to undertake courses on a wide range of subjects, from reading, writing and arithmetic, through languages, history and economics to sciences. The Rochdale Pioneers had education as one of their first objectives and by 1850 the society had its own classes, and the members agreed to put 2.5 per cent of the profits of the society into education. The Pioneers did not believe that education should be limited to the young, and courses and activities were open to all members. They invited lecturers from universities to teach, and one of the many subjects that caught the imagination of the Rochdale Pioneers Society's members was astronomy. Professor James Stuart gave a series of lectures and the society had part of the roof flattened so that the members could have access to a permanently mounted telescope.[3] The society's library loaned scientific equipment as well as books, including zoetropes, microscopes and telescopes.[4]

In addition to formal classes, co-operative members had access to informal learning through cultural activities and involvement in the Women's Co-operative Guild, or Men's Guild. By the beginning of the twentieth century, vocational classes for co-operative employees included book-keeping and salesmanship.[5] Resources include the records of individual societies, such as the minutes of educational committees, periodicals, course prospectuses, books and pamphlets. The records of the Co-operative College, from its inception in 1919, show courses for both UK and international students including visits to co-operative societies and cultural and social events in addition to the formal curriculum.[6]

**Co-operative society records**

The original records of co-operative societies give an invaluable resource for research. Minute books give detail of the operation of societies, showing the involvement of the elected committees in all levels of decision making. They can be used for business history, local history and genealogy.

Second World War sandbagging of 1 Balloon Street, head office of the Co-operative Wholesale Society

The archive's collections include the records of national co-operative organizations – which are often secondary co-operatives where the members are other co-operative organizations – and of a range of primary co-operatives. At the turn of the twentieth century, there were just over 1,500 consumer co-operatives in the UK, and gradually many of these have come together to form larger organizations.

The Co-operative Union (now called Co-operatives UK) is the national federation of co-operative societies, formed in 1869 as an information and advisory body. In addition to the original records of the society, the collections include the Co-operative Union's reports giving information on its own activities and on its member societies, including *Co-operative Statistics* which, from 1876 to the present day, gives information from the balance sheets of co-operatives enabling research on individual societies or societies in particular geographic areas.

The annual Co-operative Congress, organized by the Co-operative Union, has been the national delegate conference of the co-operative movement since 1869 and the reports to Congress and verbatim reports of discussions provide a valuable record of activity. Throughout its existence, the Union has published pamphlets and books giving information, analysis and advice on different aspects of co-operation, and the collection includes a wide range of these publications.

The UK co-operative movement has the only political party linked to a co-operative movement in the world. The Co-operative Party was established in 1917 to give co-operators a voice in parliament and the collections include minutes, publications and conference proceedings.

The Co-operative Press dates from 1871 with the publication of the first edition of the *Co-operative News*, the weekly newspaper of the co-operative movement (now published bi-weekly). The records of the society include material on the *Co-operative News* and other publications which are included in the archive's periodicals holdings such as *Woman's Outlook* (1919 to 1967), *Millgate Monthly* (1905 to 1953) and *Scottish Co-operator* (1894–1974).

The Co-operative Wholesale Society (CWS) was formed in 1863 as the wholesaler for the co-operative movement. In 1873 it moved into manufacturing with the opening of a biscuit factory at Crumpsall in Manchester, and a boot- and shoe-works in Leicester. Gradually the CWS opened depots in different parts of the world, and in the 1870s started its own shipping fleet. During the first half of the twentieth century, the CWS was involved in manufacturing a wide range of co-operative brand products, from food to furniture. Starting in the 1970s, the CWS became involved in retailing as consumer societies transferred their engagements. The name was changed in 2001 to the Co-operative Group. It is the largest co-operative in the UK, involved in retailing, banking, insurance, pharmacy, travel, funerals and farming. Collections held by the archive include primary and secondary materials relating to the CWS and to many of the consumer co-operatives that have become part of the Co-operative Group, particularly those in the South East, south midlands and northern regions. The archive holds the records of the co-operative societies that have come together to form the Midlands Co-operative Society which trades principally in Derbyshire, Leicestershire and the Greater Midlands.

The range of co-operative society records held enable researchers to compare national activities with local activities and include published histories of co-operative societies and periodicals, some produced for their members. The archive can advise researchers on locating records held in other public archives.

**Women's Co-operative Guild**

While co-operative societies such as the Rochdale Pioneers did not differentiate between male and female members, it was often difficult for female members to have the confidence to speak at meetings. Requests from female co-operators led to a new 'Women's corner' column in the *Co-operative News* at the beginning of 1883, edited by Alice Acland. The development was well received and within a few months, a national organization – which became the Women's Co-operative Guild (and is now called the Co-operative Women's Guild) – had been set up and local branches (including one in Rochdale) were being established. The Guild collection includes the records of some branches, publications, periodicals and, of course, includes the full run of the 'Women's corner' in the *Co-operative News*.

### Periodicals

The archive holds a range of co-operative and labour movement periodicals from the early nineteenth century including Robert Owen's *The Crisis* and the *Co-operative Magazine* (1826–8) and the famous *Co-operator* journal written by Dr William King from 1828 to 1830. The start of Henry Pitman's *Co-operator* in 1860 marks the beginning of an unbroken run of periodicals to the present day, with the *Co-operative News* starting publication as the *Co-operator*, changing to the *Anti-Vaccinator* in 1871.

Specialist journals from the twentieth century include the *Co-operative Official* (1916–1968) for co-operative managers, the *Wheatsheaf* (1899–1945) for members, and the *Producer* (1916–1966) for the CWS and productive societies. Journals aimed at members often include general interest material as well as co-operative material, for example, serial stories, poetry, recipes and household hints.

### Youth

Young people are involved in the co-operative movement in different ways, with youth groups such as the Woodcraft Folk, educational activities, events, and with running their own societies. The journals aimed at members often include pages for young people and their own journals such as *Ourselves* (1907–1960) and those of the British Federation of Co-operative Youth are a particularly useful source of information and entertainment aimed at children. *Ourselves* in the early part of the twentieth century included articles on the co-operative movement in different parts of the world and included lessons in Esperanto to facilitate contact between co-operators without language barriers.

Counter service in a grocery shop of the Manchester & Salford Equitable Co-operative Society, known as M&S

## Photographs and film

The photographic collections include those of the Co-operative Press and show a range of subjects including individuals and business activities, the work of CWS factories and social activities from the early twentieth century onwards. The co-operative movement has been active in making films from the turn of the twentieth century. The films were aimed at promoting co-operative ideas and values to show non-members the benefits of membership of a co-operative society, or to advertise particular societies or products. They range from the serious, such as *Manchester Took it Too*, the record of the Manchester Blitz of 1940, to *Co-operette*, the 1938 musical which includes a Stanley Holloway monologue called *Sam Goes Shopping*. The archive includes both the films and information on how they were used.

## Research

The co-operative movement's archives can be used for a wide variety of research, reflecting the different types of co-operative societies and the different interests of co-operative members. Users of the Archive include schools, academic researchers, those studying local history, subject researchers and family historians. Recent topics include activities during wartime, architecture, biographical research, advertising, fashion, social activities and the development of the travel industry. The National Co-operative Archive welcomes all those who wish to use the collections. Further information appears on the website at www.archive.coop.

**Notes**

1. Dr P. J. Maguire, Head of Historical and Critical Studies, University of Brighton, in [Co-operative College], *Co-operative heritage initiatives: briefing paper* (Manchester, 2006).
2. [International Co-operative Alliance], *Statement on the Co-operative identity* (Geneva, 1995).
3. Phil Barnard, 'Professor James Stuart and the Rochdale Pioneers: astronomy as food for thought became co-op dividend', *Lyra* [the magazine of the Wolverhampton Astronomical Society] (1994).
4. Rochdale Equitable Pioneers Society, *Catalogue of the library* (Rochdale, 1868).
5. Linda Shaw, *Making connections: education for co-operatives* (Manchester, 2009), p. 19.
6. Ibid., p. 23.

complex in the city until overtaken by the neighbouring company of McConnel and Kennedy in the 1820s. Although A & G Murray was in relative decline thereafter it continued to function as a spinning-mill complex and was subsumed into the large combine of the Fine Cotton Spinners' and Doublers' Association in 1898, which for thirty years, with its sixty mill complexes, was the largest and most successful cotton-spinning firm in the world. The decline of the cotton industry after 1930 saw the mill complex close around 1954. Thereafter the buildings had a twilight existence as the home of a variety of garment manufacturers until dereliction set in during the 1980s. The life of the whole complex is thus a good parallel for the rise and fall of Manchester's cotton spinning industry.

The monograph has eight chapters, ranging from the growth of Manchester and its textile industry; the development of Ancoats as a new industrial townscape (which includes important summaries of five other early textile-mill excavations); to the history of A & G Murray; the archaeological survey of the mill structures themselves; a review of the major repair project by the Ancoats Building Preservation Trust; and a concluding overview. There are also several appendices of technical terms and processes, as well a bibliography and an index. The monograph is more than the study of the surviving fabric of one textile mill through detailed elevation drawings, floor plans and reconstructions (excellent though these are). It treats the buildings as archaeological objects in their own right, integrating excavation evidence, with a detailed record of the buildings' fabric and the historical data for the history and machinery of the complex. This methodological approach, whilst far from new in the world of industrial archaeology, is here brought to a very detailed level, and yet the volume also puts this evidence in its local, regional and national context.

The volume is thus an important contribution to the archaeological study of the early steam-powered textile mill. Its detailed archaeological recording, and the context within which this is put, both technical and social, is a model for the study of such large industrial complexes. The publication signals a further maturing in the discipline of industrial archaeology and deserves to be treated as a classic archaeological study of a single production site, as well as an important indication of how archaeology can contribute to the understanding of the emergence of Manchester as the world's first industrial city.

*Michael Nevell*
*University of Manchester*

## A. J. Randall

*Riotous assemblies: popular protest in Hanoverian England* Oxford: Oxford University Press, 2006. 354pp. ISBN 0199259909.

The focus of *Riotous assemblies* is not that of mere economic dislocation – thus creating social tensions that the early historians of riots used as a starting point – but power relations. It concerns the tensions between those who held power and those who outwardly held none, and, as we shall see, nowhere was this felt more harshly than in the North West.

Randall is following in the formidable

footsteps of E. P. Thompson, two of whose concepts are taken here to be the guiding methodology. The first is the idea of the existence of a 'field of force' whereby elites are obliged to face up to their responsibilities by the actions of the crowd. The second is the persistence of a 'moral economy' which again allows for the crowd to act to defend its customary rights. We are offered a useful historiographic survey of how historians of protest have interrogated the Thompson thesis. John Bohstedt, for example, included shopkeepers and employers, often in opposition to the customary rights of plebeians, in with agents of authority attempting to control the conflicting factions. However, the chief danger with such tri-polar models is that they themselves need to be refined lest they be easily confused with an anachronistic view of class. Randall instead reminds us to place into historical context the kind of protest adopted.

This in essence is what *Riotous assemblies* is primarily concerned with, and Randall's answer is to confirm a refined bi-polar model. Historians like David Rollison and Dror Wahrman have also come via their very different research routes to confirm the bi-polar model by noting how the rise of national consumer culture informed attitudes. Conflicts like the shock of the new set against the stability of the tried and trusted, and the local as opposed to national bi-polar trends, can also be found in the work of Norma Landau and Bob Bushaway.

Randall acknowledges the value of all these various approaches in what was a rapidly changing society, but correctly asserts that none of them essentially diminishes the fundamental basis of the original Thompson model. Instead, Randall suggests refinements, firstly to the bi-polar model. Here, all the groupings stand either as sympathetic to the grievances of the crowd, or opposed to them. In the decades immediately preceding 1776 the new market and economic theories encapsulated in Smith's *Wealth of nations* began to have an enormously influential pull, and the effectiveness of the moral economy began to wane. A second deviation Randall is chiefly attempting to develop (which Thompson was not entirely convinced should be done) is to carefully extend the use of the moral economy concept beyond its market relationship into the realm of industrial grievances. Here again it was believed by working people that long-held customary practices, backed by magisterial rulings, were increasingly under assault by newer and damaging industrial modes of production. Without diluting the ideological power of the concept, I would contend Randall largely succeeds in achieving this.

Two distinct types of riot tended to occur throughout the entire duration of the long eighteenth century and these concerned food pricing and distribution, and changes in industrial practices. It was these two areas that were of direct concern to people living and working in the North West. The rising population and the decline in agricultural production in the region meant tectonic changes in the corn market, hitherto relatively unchanged for centuries. Now Lancashire demanded ever more supplies of corn and other necessaries of life and this placed pressure on other parts of the country to meet this demand. Nowhere else in the country underwent the dramatic growth or change in the means of production. The anxieties of violent change were to be raised to a new height in the course of the eighteenth century. The North West also offers the opportunity to note Randall's second refinement of the original Thompson moral-economy model identifying how a market-oriented conflict could escalate into the industrial. Randall identifies the rise of the North West as a major market for food processed outside its boundaries, and how this created problems for the older centres of distribution. In doing so, it gave rise to a whole new species of middlemen – wholesalers and dealers who ran the gauntlet of the wrath of the crowd at the points of production (underselling the producers) and distribution (overcharging, or making a profit out of hunger).

One example was in June 1757, when in Manchester a riot broke out over dwindling supplies of corn. (Curiously, Randall does not refer to this by its adoptive name of the 'Shude Hill Riots'.) These riots soon spread throughout the region and by November the volunteers and the regular army were being attacked by colliers and weavers. Examples such as these placed more strain on the responsibilities of local government, which, in preventing civil disorder, had now to put in place preventative measures to ensure that food supplies could be got through. This again was to have a profound and lasting effect on the system of marketing food and on the degree of involvement and duties of the local state.

Given the reluctance of the mercantilist national state to import anything from outside the empire, it fell on the local state to attempt to organize extra supplies of food, especially grain. Whilst the local powers of Norwich or Bristol scoured Europe for surplus grain, their counterparts in Liverpool simply contacted their agents in Belfast and Dublin. This was fine as long as supplies could be gleaned from Ireland but when these dried up and were combined with a severe trade depression, as in the 1790s and early 1800s, Lancashire and Manchester became the focus of truly national apprehension. However, Randall cites only the 1757 episodes – as food riots in the North West which escalated into disturbances embracing broader grievances – before moving to the period covering the 1790s and early 1800s. For the latter there is now an extensive historiography, and Randall is correct to call for new research to cover the intervening thirty-five years.

Professor Randall's *Riotous assemblies* is a well sourced and researched piece of work, and is a welcome addition to the growing interest in eighteenth-century studies. The writing is articulate, erudite but light in touch. Primary sources used include contemporary publications and the local press. This is an assured book from an author in command of his material and as such should be read by any student interested in the impact of the modern over the traditional, social and economic protest and, of course, power relations during this period of fundamental change.

*David Walsh*
*Manchester Metropolitan University*
*Dr Walsh was the Senior Research Associate for the ESRC-funded project 'Social protest and community change in the west of England, 1740–1830', University of Liverpool, 1991–1993, led by Professor Randall and Andrew Charlesworth*

# Cécilia Lyon
*Adolphe Valette* Stroud: Phillimore, 2006. 160pp. ISBN 978860774263.

Despite everyone's best endeavours, Adolphe Valette – or Mr. Monsieur Valette as he was affectionately known – has once again evaded our scrutiny. Cécila Lyon's book is a labour of love, a homage to this enigmatic and beguiling artist whose reputation is so bound up with the startlingly beautiful images he made of Manchester in the early part of the last century. The book does Valette a great service in reproducing so much of his work; indeed the reproductions are of a high quality and capture something of the artist's subtlety of colour and sensitive handling of paint. However, the text does not add anything substantially new to Sandra Martin's Manchester Art Gallery publication of 1994. Written originally in French, Lyon's substance and style of the writing reveals much about the writer's love for her subject, but little in the way of serious analysis. The biographically centred text, though fulsome in its praise of the artist, does not pretend to offer a serious critical analysis of the artist's work and its relationship to his chosen subject matter.

Valette was born in the industrial city of Saint-Etienne in France in 1876, and after a successful student career, for reasons that are still not entirely clear, he travelled to Manchester via London, enrolling as a student at the School of Art in 1906. Shortly afterwards, his talent being recognized, he was appointed as an 'Art Master' at the school where he taught for the next fifteen years. He seems to have been widely respected and his paintings had a decisive effect upon the development of a fellow student who enrolled in the same year as Valette, L. S. Lowry.

In some ways it is a depressing story – an artist of rich promise who, it seems, turned his back on (or found himself unable to continue) the promise evident in his Manchester paintings of c1906 to 1913, a mere six years. These works are indeed masterly, documents of a city in transition, figures dwarfed by the looming architectural forms and, it seems, stifled in a sea of perpetual fog. Then, in 1928, the year in which Manchester Art Gallery purchased nine of his major works, Valette, for a variety of reasons, retired. He returned to France where he continued to paint until his death in 1942, but with nothing of the power and originality of his Manchester works. They are his legacy and deserve to be better known. Like the man, they are characterized by a certain reserve, reticence even. These large impressive *grands machines* correspond exactly with Whistler's exhortation, aptly quoted by the author, to show the harmony brought to the city by the twin effects of pollution and departing light: 'when the evening mist clothes the riverside with poetry, as with a veil – and the poor buildings lose themselves in the dim sky – the tall chimneys become campanile' (James Abbott McNeill Whistler, *Ten o'clock lecture* [1885]). As Whistler and Monet had done in London, as Atkinson Grimshaw had done in Leeds and Liverpool, so Valette did in Manchester: transforming the grimy labyrinthine city into a thing of order and beauty. And if something of this is caught in Valette's large canvases, then how much more is it the case in his exquisite *pochades*: in these small works we see, as in the work of his pupil Lowry, an artist who could synthesize various strands of art to create his own unique vision. He was never an impressionist, if anything his work evokes the mysterious atmospherics of late-Victorian city photographers or the melancholy soul of the painters of northern European symbolism.

A poignant picture of his family life emerges from these pages, including a number of delightful pictures of his first Argentinian wife Gabriella who died in 1917, and his son Tita who died in 1929, aged only nineteen.

Michael Howard<br>Manchester Metropolitan University

Hilary Fawcett, ed.
*Made in Newcastle: visual culture* Newcastle: University of Northumbria Press, 2007. 200pp. ISBN 9781904794264.

Based in Newcastle, Northumbria University Press creates an outlet for research on lives, livelihoods, landscapes and languages across north-eastern England. This emphasis enables writers to position their work readily within broader debates and terms of reference while uncovering the particularities of local histories, geographies, peoples and places. *Made in Newcastle: visual culture* extends this regional remit by combining voices and topics that collectively clarify and deepen understanding of socio-historical and cultural changes in different contexts. Focusing upon identifiable visual and visible expressions and practices, the eleven single and co-authored chapters offer a fascinating wealth of perspectives and details that explore some of the continuities, contrasts and transformations that have characterized Newcastle, Gateshead and Tyneside in recent decades.

This collection exemplifies the value of in-depth regionally based research that supplements the generalizations and metropolitan perspectives on which national narratives are often based. It acknowledges too the North Sea connections in Newcastle's changing identity, long before BALTIC helped to change the city's skyline and reputation.

The opening chapter, for instance, captures the local flavour of retailing histories, fashion opportunities and individual entrepreneurs and innovators that combined to bring tangible expressions of modernity, affordable fashions and new design motifs to the people of Newcastle. Another chapter uncovers the nuanced variations of modernities' trajactories mapped at regional level and distant from London, the fashion epicentre of supposedly swinging-sixties Britain.

Subsequent chapters chart post-war architectural and planning developments as well as innovative art and design curriculum developments within the North East's higher education sector. The visual impact of the city's attempts at regeneration, re-branding and revitalization of retailing, commercial, historic and quayside areas cannot mask, however, the legacies and continuing consequences of social exclusion, disadvantage and poverty that still affect many people's lives, despite the city's iconic structures, fluttering banners and resin Roman models that also gain scrutiny. Film-making and television provides powerful testimony to lives and struggles in the bleak housing areas far from high streets, prestigious arts developments and chic style-promoters that have helped to construct other contemporary identities.

Fascinating glimpses into the region's diversities, charted through consideration of the Newcastle-based Amber Film Collective, as well as discussion of cinematic provision, behaviour and programming, and the role of television series in mediating messages about identities, ethnicities, and organizations, including the police, explore how contested notions of northernness and the North East have been mediated and circulated both on and off the screen. Somewhat varied in written style and, at times rather hastily proof-read, these carefully discussed case-studies represent an interesting, informative and important contribution to the critical study of changing regional identities.

*Heather Norris Nicholson*
*Manchester Metropolitan University*

**Gary James**
*Manchester: a football history* Halifax: James Ward, 2008. 512pp. ISBN 9780955812705.

Gary James is well known to Manchester football fans, particularly those of a blue-shirted persuasion, for his extensive writing and media work on the local game. His latest work is a highly ambitious undertaking that seeks to provide a history of Football League and leading non-League sides in the Manchester region. Divided into two sections that cover, respectively, the 'chronological story of football within the region' and wider thematic aspects 'such as ground developments, the media and statistical information' (p. 13), the book is the result of ten years of interviewing and patient trawling through a vast body of individual club and player histories and a rich array of primary sources. Weighing in at 512 pages, it is in all senses a substantial tome.

James's narrative begins in 1608 with the Court Leet's decision to ban folk playing football on the grounds that the 'lewd and disordered persons' playing the game were responsible for 'breaking many men's glass windows ... and other great enormities' (p. 16). Although there is some attention paid to the emergence of the modern, codified game from the 1860s, the book really picks up momentum as it moves into an era of professionalism from the 1880s. It is never intended to provide an exhaustive coverage and obviously much has to be ignored or glossed over in the narrative history section. However, James has a good eye for relevance and one of his shrewdest decisions was deciding not to build the central narrative around what are now the two elite clubs. While City and United receive the greatest attention, they have to take their place alongside other clubs whose achievements (or lack of them) might have been lost in a more selective treatment. Bury's Cup Final successes against Southampton in 1900 and Derby in 1903 are properly described – one observer saw Derby County's poor display in their 6–0 destruction as 'like opera bouffe' (p. 101) – but so too is the emergence of Pine Villa/Oldham Athletic; the short-lived attempt to develop Manchester Central FC as a major club at Belle Vue in the inter-war period; Stockport County's 'Go-Go-County' Friday night matches in the late 1960s; the rise of FC Manchester United (an interesting section), and much more.

James keeps his own preferences and prejudices well hidden and prefers to feed football debate with solid historical information rather than any descent into tribal bickering. One of the book's great pleasures is its wealth of illustrations. Photographs, press cuttings, cartoons and facsimiles of a variety of archive sources – my favourite was the letter from Manchester City Manager, Tony Book, taking time to explain to a young fan why Francis Lee had left the club (p.278) – jostle for attention and provide literally hours of enjoyable browsing. Indeed, the book, especially the second section, is well suited for browsing with its rich store of factual information and anecdote. The section on radio coverage is good value in the latter regard, not least in the story of Piccadilly Radio's Tom Tyrell attempting to get score flashes from Stamford Bridge back to the studio on a borrowed mobile phone, following the non-appearance of his press pass. As if constant verbal abuse from a Chelsea fan was not problem enough, he was later evicted by a steward who had identified him as a troublemaker.

The book is clearly intended to reach a wide audience and it deserves to do so. Although the detail-laden text can be hard work at times, it is certainly readable and it provides by some way the most comprehensive synthesis of Manchester's footballing history yet produced. Those approaching the game from an academic perspective will find much useful information here, although they might be slightly disappointed at the complete absence of scholarly work in James's bibliography – popular historians should not assume that academe has nothing to teach them – and at the limited impact that their work has clearly had in some cases. This reviewer was certainly slightly irritated to find albeit qualified support given to the long-exploded myth that William Webb Ellis invented rugby one fine day in 1823 by picking the ball up and running with it. However, the final note should be positive. For relatives and friends of Mancunian football fans, the perfect birthday or Christmas purchase is at a bookshop near you.

*Dave Russell*
*Institute of Northern Studies*
*Leeds Metropolitan University*

### Robert G. Hall

*Voices of the people: democracy and Chartist political identity, 1830–1870* Monmouth: Merlin Press, 2007. ix+218pp. ISBN 9780850365573.

This interesting book focuses upon what Dorothy Thompson, the doyen of Chartist historians, has termed 'the most radical and Chartist of all the factory towns': Ashton-under-Lyne. Along with nearby Stalybridge, Ashton gained a reputation during the 'Chartist decades' of the 1830s and 1840s not only for its political radicalism, but also for its acute industrial conflict, its 'ultra theological' opinions and for being generally a 'turbulent' and 'fanatical' 'frontier' town. In 1842 14,200, 'about 62 per cent' of Ashton's population, signed the Chartist petition calling upon parliament to introduce the vote for all adult males. Three years earlier Ashtonians had drilled on the local moors in preparation for a national insurrection. They were also prominent in the 'general strike' of 1842 and the agitation for the third and final petition in 1848. Having failed to achieve their goals by means of Chartism, from the mid 1840s they increasingly sought to realize them by means such as trade unionism, the co-operative movement, friendly societies, educational 'improvement' and within the confines of the Liberal and Conservative parties. If the years around mid century saw a transition from an open confrontation with the 'system' to a more widespread popular desire to work and achieve reforms within it (the onset of 'reformism'), this transition, as exemplified in the case of Ashton, was never smooth and easy.

Robert Hall, a North American scholar, has already conducted impressive research on Chartism in Ashton and its environs and has worked closely with Stephen Roberts, Owen Ashton and other distinguished Chartist scholars. This book represents the fruits of many years of hard work. While concerned to explain the rise and fall of Chartism in Ashton, Hall is not seeking to write 'a traditional local history'. Rather, he approaches Ashton Chartism 'from the micro-history perspective' and attempts 'to utilize the local to investigate some new perspectives on the movement'. These include 'the politics of place', 'the relationship between the local and the national' and, above all, the question of 'the ways in which democratic practices shaped and defined Chartist political identity'.

Hall thus engages with the 'new' political history in its concerns with political languages and representations. At the same time, however, he does not see political language as either uniform in character or 'free floating'. He is at pains to point to the many-sided and often contested nature of politics languages and messages, and to the fact that they must be firmly situated within their historical contexts, including daily experiences of the world, in order to reveal their meanings. In sum he combines a 'new' concern with identity with the more 'traditional' emphasis upon the importance of linking, rather than separating, politics and the socio-economic and cultural worlds in which it develops and which it both shapes and is shaped by.

Hall maintains that 'the making' of political identities in Ashton took place on 'the factory floor', through the activities of 'a new kind of political entity – the democratic mass movement', and as a result of the influence of 'plebeian intellectuals' such as William Aitken, a mule-spinner-turned-schoolmaster. The core of the book is devoted to a detailed and impressive study of these three influences. His thesis is that technological and other 'dishonourable' changes in the workplace (with special reference to the deteriorating position of the male mule spinner), economic depression, intensified employer oppression and exploitation, declining living standards, the strains imposed by rapid urbanization and industrialization, the hostility displayed by the Whigs and Tories to reform and the growth of an impressive and increasingly independent form of political radicalism, provided the necessary impetus to the development of Chartism. Within this context of 'overlapping' socio-economic, cultural and political crises, working-class autodidacts of the Aitken type (Antonio Gramsci's 'organic intellectuals'), were able, 'by relating the cause of democratic reform to the "bread-and-cheese" questions of everyday life', to 'draw in ordinary men and women who knew "nothing of Political principles" and to make Chartism a mass movement'.

As a description and explanation of the rise of national Chartism, this is all very familiar. Hall, however, enhances our knowledge and understanding in significant ways by highlighting the particularly acute nature of the interlocking crises in 1830s Ashton, the many-sided character of local radicalism and the ways in which local activists played a key role in 'movement' building. He also convincingly demonstrates the profound ways in which the easing of the crises during the 1840s adversely affected Chartism, combined, however, with the impressive ability of local radicals to pursue other means of 'emancipation' rather than passively accepting the *status quo*. Unfortunately, however, the author misses a ready-made opportunity to compare and contrast the experiences of Chartism in Ashton with other urban centres in the North West, for example, Bolton, Stockport, Preston, Oldham and Stalybridge. Why, for example, was Chartism so strong in Ashton as compared with weaker and more class-conciliatory Bolton? Why did the movement persist more strongly in some local communities as opposed to others? These important comparative questions demand urgent attention from historians of the Manchester region and north-west England. Robert Hall is especially well equipped to address them in future. Hopefully he will do so.

In conclusion I enjoyed this book. It is clear, well written and holds the reader's attention throughout. It is reasonably priced and makes a very welcome addition to the Merlin Press's 'Chartist Studies Series'.

*Neville Kirk*
*Department of History*
*Manchester Metropolitan University*

### Robin Daniels
*Cardus: celebrant of beauty* Lancaster: Palatine, 2009. 496pp. ISBN 9781874181583.

Robin Daniels will already be well known to students and admirers of Sir Neville Cardus for his highly successful *Conversations with Cardus* published in 1976 only months after the cricket and music writer's death. With this rather sprawling but intensely affectionate and always thoughtful work, Daniels, himself once a music critic, now a Jungian analyst, returns to the life of his friend and inspiration. He offers us not a biography, but what he terms a 'memoir' in which a broad outline of Cardus's life is married to both pleasurably extensive quotation from his work and Daniels's own discussion of the nature of criticism. The author admits that his 'new energy and interest in writing about the art of criticism' delayed completion of the book and sees his own thoughts on the critical process as a 'tribute' to Cardus and a partial realization of Cardus's unfulfilled desire to write a substantial work on music criticism (p. 149). While always intelligent and rooted in wide-ranging scholarship and learning (albeit not always lightly worn), Daniels's own intellectual excursions are perhaps less successful than those parts of the book that bring us into the closest contact with one of the twentieth century's greatest essayists. Too frequently in these sections, the central character disappears from view.

The book is strong on Cardus's upbringing in Rusholme – he was illegitimate and both his mother and aunt worked at times as prostitutes – his self-education in the libraries, music halls and theatres of Manchester and his early career on the *Manchester Guardian* under C. P. Scott, to whom he served as part-time secretary while also pursuing his remarkably versatile journalistic career. Daniels is also a rich and perceptive guide to his subject's intellectual and stylistic influences, with the lengthy chapter on Walter Pater a particularly fruitful contribution, and to Cardus's own love of the 'scent and savour of words' (p.xxviii). Probably correctly, there is more here on music than cricket, but both of Cardus's loves are well explored and his warmth as an individual and his extraordinary gifts as a writer of lucid, discerning and witty prose are apparent in the coverage of both. Daniels adroitly demonstrates that Cardus's great underpinning skill lay not in technical analysis – he consciously avoided it in his music criticism – but in a remarkable ability to capture an individual performer or player's character, or, at least, his reading of it, and then pass to the reader a rich sense of the aesthetic and emotional experience that flowed from his engagement with it. His humour, arguably the characteristic which has most endeared Cardus to generations of readers, is particularly well captured. Often, especially in the cricketing context, it was essentially affectionate, but elsewhere it could sometimes be laced with a dryly sardonic tone that weighted the skilfully directed barb quite perfectly. Noting that rival music critic Ernest Newman had expressed difficulty in following Wilhelm Furtwängler's beat while conducting the Berlin Philharmonic, Cardus opined 'So long as all the members of the Berlin Philharmonic were able to follow Furtwängler's beat, as they clearly could, then it scarcely matters much if our most learned critic was unable to' (p. 93).

The book is excellently researched with many new pieces of information, often in illuminating footnotes, and some corrective comments on Cardus's own writings. Cardus married Edith King in 1921 during a break from watching a county match at Old Trafford, and Daniels takes some pleasure in pointing out that his record of events in *Autobiography* (1947) incorrectly names the Leicestershire batsmen whose partnership framed the wedding (p. 71). It is not without moments of objective criticism – Cardus's last book *Full score* (1970) is seen as lacking in coherence and novelty – and the author is certainly attuned to the ways in which Cardus's style can disguise more problematic personal notes, observing 'the cheerful and romantic gloss' with which Cardus covered recollections of his childhood (p. 213). Daniels is, nevertheless, too much the loyal devotee to have produced the full critical biography that his subject deserves. Given the range of Cardus's interests and expertise, such a biography might indeed prove beyond the skill of a single author and perhaps collective endeavour will be required to consider his role as creator of cricketing myths and northern regional stereotypes, his place within the history of British music criticism, the significance of his peculiar mixture of formal, informal and workplace education and, not least, a personal life that saw Cardus and Edith live in separate locations (p. 215). However, whatever the future for 'Cardus Studies', all those involved in it will have much cause to thank Robin Daniels for this beautifully produced and richly suggestive book.

*Dave Russell*
*Institute of Northern Studies*
*Leeds Metropolitan University*

Brian Hollingworth, ed.
*The diary of Edwin Waugh, 1847–1851* Lancaster: Carnegie Publishing, 2008. xviii+172 pp. ISBN 9781904244493.

Those people interested in nineteenth-century industrial culture, in British regionalism, and in writing by what is now usually known as the 'labouring classes' have long owed Brian Hollingworth a debt of gratitude for his thoughtful and timely 1977 anthology *Songs of the people: Lancashire dialect poetry of the industrial revolution*. Thirty years on he has edited another text of considerable value and interest, the diaries of the mid Victorian dialect poet and writer Edwin Waugh. The diaries have been edited and abridged from a manuscript in the Manchester Central Reference Library, and produced in a sprightly and attractive edition by Carnegie, along with Hollingworth's succinct introduction, an additional section of Waugh's journal concerning the 1851 Great Exhibition, eight mainly topographical illustrations, and a helpful annotated list of many of the people who appear in the diaries. Hollingworth's editorial practice has been to try to omit repetitious material, most obviously Waugh's constant self-searching re-iterations of his own worthlessness, anxiety, and (to use Patrick Joyce's term) 'sorrows'. The diary describes Waugh's everyday life, caught between his failing marriage, literary ambition, and unsatisfying round of precarious jobs, both artisanal and clerical, in the period before he reached both local celebrity status and national notice as a professional writer in dialect, a process of transition built largely on the publication of his first paid work, the powerfully sentimental 'Come Whoam to thi' Childer an' Me' which was published in the *Manchester Examiner* in 1856.

While it is a pleasure to have Waugh's diary made available in such an accessible form, it is a text that has already had a long virtual life. It was deeply inscribed into Martha Vicinus's eye-opening 1974 survey of the literature of British nineteenth-century industrial society *The industrial muse*. Vicinus had studied and partially transcribed the diary during time spent in Manchester, and chapter five of her study, 'An appropriate voice: dialect literature of the industrial north', was instrumental in posing a series of difficult questions about the status of dialect writing as a potentially 'authentic' expression of region, class, or other form of social affiliation.

But the Waugh diary became more visible, and was given permanent scholarly significance with the publication of Patrick Joyce's *Democratic subjects: the self and the social in nineteenth-century England* (1994), the third of Joyce's brilliant studies of the social dynamics of industrial culture. The first sixty pages of Joyce's book – aptly called 'The sorrows of Edwin Waugh: a study in working-class identity' – are devoted to a close study of Waugh's life using the diary as his primary source along with the later verse. Joyce quotes extensively from the diary in his extended examination of the complex social negotiations that characterized Waugh's experience, and this chapter still remains one of the most subtle and successful readings of working-class writing ever undertaken. Joyce uses a three-part structure for his analysis drawn from the French writer Jacques Rancière which focuses on, first, the relationship between the worker and his work; second, the relationship between the working-class intellectual and other workers; and third, ideas of class consciousness. Within this structure he considers the gendered nature of the metaphysical and spiritual preoccupations of the worker-intellectual, and the extent to which the 'labour' of writing was essentially a quest for moral self-realization rather than for monetary reward or fame. Joyce deals well with some of the obvious repeated refrains of the diary – Waugh's frustrations with his illiterate wife; his continuing sense of physical horror when visiting industrial Manchester, usually rendered in almost hysterically apocalyptic language; and his disillusion with the progress made by the Lancashire Public Schools Association, which employed Waugh from 1847 on. Joyce's work renders any further commentary here redundant and I would recommend anyone interested in reading this edition of the diary to do so alongside a simultaneous reading of Joyce's chapter. Perhaps the only way in which Joyce's account might be usefully augmented is through a more sustained consideration of what Hollingworth notes in his introduction: that Waugh uses his diary 'to practise the writer's craft' (p. x). While much of the diary suggests a relatively unselfconscious authorial persona, some of the set pieces rise towards a much more self-conscious and often anachronistic 'literariness' – the account of an 'unhappy confusion' (in fact a family row in a bookshop) on pp. 44–5 is a characteristic example. The splenetic responses to Manchester, too, are constructed using the conventional denunciatory epithets of broadsides and popular songs, and lose something of their power as a result.

The diary is, despite Waugh's evident failings, endlessly repeated self-recriminations, and sometimes indulgently formulated misery, an intensely moving and unusual piece of writing, and a complex literary achievement. Thus this edition represents an important act of recovery and rediscovery for those interested in industrial culture and regional writing.

It is worth saying a little more about the scholarly 'recovery' of the literature associated with the industrial labouring classes, because recent years have shown an extraordinary and significant augmentation of scholarly resources in this field. Hollingworth's *Songs of the people* was part of the early, ideologically driven move to recover writing by labouring men and women for both the academy and the 'people'. As well as Vicinus's crucial survey, written in the American Midwest, the first wave of textual recovery depended on anthologies of Chartist and radical literature edited in Russia (Kovalev) and East Germany (Ashraf). Hollingworth's anthology alone suggested that British industrial literature might be an apposite site of interest for British schoolchildren, students and researchers, although the likes of Roy Palmer and Jon Raven sought to bring songs, ballads and broadsides back into the educational curriculum, reinforcing the belief that 'history from below' was hugely significant. My own anthology of writing by and about self-taught writers, *The poorhouse fugitives* (1987), came very late in the day, and after the drive to insist on the presence in the curriculum of vernacular, 'working-class' or industrial literature had lost much of its force. Since then, there have been a number of key books on Victorian poetry (those by Anne Janowitz, Isabel Armstrong and Linda Hughes, for example) that have assimilated such writing into broad discussions of the range of nineteenth-century poetry, and, of course, Joyce's work has brought the literary production of Lancashire forcefully to the attention of social historians.

Until recently, then, both research and pedagogy in these areas seemed to have fallen silent. But the last few years have seen a remarkable revival of interest in both the recovery and the pedagogic deployment of what might be broadly called 'industrial literature'. John Goodridge's mighty Pickering & Chatto set of volumes, *Nineteenth-century English labouring-class poets, 1800–1900* (2006) has brought a new comprehensiveness and objectivity to the field. Florence Boos has been a key champion of work on working-class writers, producing, in addition to an important overview chapter in Blackwell's 2002 *A companion to Victorian poetry* and an issue of the periodical *Victorian Poetry* on the poetics of working-class writing, a wonderfully rich anthology of writing by Scottish working-class women writers – an important challenge to Joyce's complex account of what he sees as the necessarily conservative gender-politics to be found in Waugh's diary. Such anthologies and overviews have key significance for the university curriculum, and I gather that the Modern Language Association is about to issue a book on the pedagogy of teaching Victorian working-class writing. It was indeed heartening to find two full panels on working-class writing (with several papers by graduate students on Lancashire dialect writing) at the North American Victorian Studies Association conference in New Haven last November, and to find both Martha Vicinus and Florence Boos approvingly present on both occasions. But still, apart from Mike Sanders's extended study of *Chartist Poetry* recently published by Cambridge University Press, British scholarship still seems reluctant to engage with such topics. Given the vastly increased and immediately accessible resources now available, of which this edition of the Waugh diaries is a significant part, there is little excuse for such neglect.

*Brian Maidment*
*Salford University*

# SHORT REVIEWS

I. Haynes *History of the cotton industry in Droylsden with Audenshaw and Denton* Ashton-under-Lyne[: the author], 2004. 63pp. Illus. £4.75. ISBN 9781852160807.

I. Haynes *Hyde cotton mills* Ashton-under-Lyne[: the author], 2nd. ed., 2005. 66pp. Illus. Map. £4.75. ISBN 9780954217129.

I. Haynes *The cotton industry in Hollingworth and Mottram-in-Longdendale* Ashton-under-Lyne[: the author], 2008. 36pp. Illus. Map. £4.25. ISBN 9780954217136.

In the nineteenth and early twentieth centuries, Tameside was an important centre for the south-east Lancashire and north-east Cheshire cotton industry, with towns such as Hyde, Dukinfield and Ashton-under-Lyne dominated by the mills and their chimneys that have now disappeared. The history of these mills and the textile industry in these towns has never been fully documented, but these three books go some way to doing this. Ian Haynes has already written several other books on the mills and cotton industry in specific towns in Tameside and these three are a welcome addition to the series. They follow the same pattern as the previous books in that they all begin with an account of the development of the textile industry in the town concerned, followed by chapters on working and social conditions, and concluding with histories of individual mills. There are illustrations of many of the mills as well as brief biographies of some of the leading mill owners in the area. Taken with his earlier works on Ashton-under-Lyne, Stalybridge and Dukinfield, these three create a comprehensive history of the cotton industry in Tameside.

D. O'Connor *A history of the motor trade in Bolton* Stoneclough: Richardson, 2009. 80pp. Illus. £6. ISBN 9781852161668.

When people buy cars, they tend to purchase them from a dealer or garage. Until now there has been very little published on the motor trade of the area, although there are a few histories of individual companies. This new book examines the development of the motor trade in Bolton from the late nineteenth century to 1945. According to the introduction, the book 'chronicles the use of the motor vehicle and garage development in Bolton and district'. It is not only a history of those companies which dealt in cars, but also a history of motoring in Bolton. The book is well illustrated with photographs of many different types of cars that were sold by the various garages in the town as well as copies of a few advertisements for cars. It will be of interest not only to those interested in the history of Bolton, but also in the history of the car, motoring in general and those who set up businesses to sell cars to the public.

A. Searle *A celebration of Kersal Moor* Salford: Unity Publishing Project, 2009. 39pp. Illus. Bibliog. £3. ISBN 9780956169112.

On the boundaries of Salford and Prestwich lies an area of higher ground known as Kersal Moor. In the Middle Ages there was a Cluniac monastic cell, later known as Kersal Cell, located there, whilst in the eighteenth century, the moor itself was the venue for some of the earliest race meetings in Manchester, and in the nineteenth century, the location of

Chartist meetings. This well illustrated little booklet does not claim to be a comprehensive history of the area, but it provides a valuable and fascinating insight, in an entertaining and readable style, into the history of this part of Salford from the earliest times to the present day.

S. Goods and D. Leitch *Didsbury's heritage: a self-guided family walking trail around some of 'old' Didsbury's historic places of interest* Didsbury: Didsbury Civic Society, 2009. 15pp. Illus. £1.

As the title suggests, this book seeks to point out to its readers some of the more interesting places in this important Manchester suburb. Each page is dedicated to a particular building where there is a photograph of it and a brief history. For each building there is at least one question that seeks to encourage the reader to use their eyes to look for details that might otherwise be missed. This is an excellent guide to the most important buildings of the area and one that should be an encouragement to other groups to produce similar publications for their own areas.

I. Carroll, D. Leitch and J. Smith *The Towers: a short history of the estate and its occupants, 1830–2009* Didsbury: D & D Leitch, 2009. 17pp. Illus. Map. £1.

Using a visit in 1965 by Paul Hamlyn as its basis, this booklet describes the interior of the house and outlines the histories of the families who lived there after its construction. It includes its role as the research centre for the cotton industry when it was known as the Shirley Institute, named after the daughter of William Greenwood who contributed towards its purchase in 1920. This is a fascinating booklet and hopefully will provide the residents of Didsbury, the former employees of the Shirley Institute and those interested in the Taylor and Adamson families with an insight into what is one of Didsbury's most impressive buildings.

R. Taylor *Pioneers of calico printing on the Cheshire-Derbyshire border* New Mills: New Mills Historical Society, 2009. Illus. Maps. Diags. £5.

Calico printing was an important part of the textile industry once the cloth had been woven. To be successful, the printing industry required large amounts of clean water, as 'effluent from one works may contaminate the supply of another works downstream'. In order to reduce the risk of contamination, many print works had large reservoirs where the water was allowed to stand before being used. This important well written and well illustrated book traces the history of calico printing, the power sources used by the print works, those involved – both entrepreneurs and the workers themselves – taxation, and the transport infrastructure required by the industry, along the north Cheshire and Derbyshire borders. Over half the book is taken up with the histories of fourteen print works stretching along the Goyt and Sett valleys, from Chadkirk to Kinder, bringing together information from a variety of sources, resulting in a reference work of great importance. It is a book that should be of interest to all those involved in studying the history of the textile industry, especially the ancillary businesses that were essential for its success, as it provides valuable background information on this particular branch of the industry as well as for local historians

of Marple, Disley, New Mills, Birch Vale and Hayfield.
*Available from the Hon. Editor, New Mills Historical Society, c/o 'The Thorns', Laneside Road, New Mills, High Peak SK22 4LU.*

*History alive: Tameside* Tameside Local History Forum, iss. 4, 2009. 70pp. Illus. Free.

This annual publication seeks to publicize the history of those parts of south-east Lancashire and north-east Cheshire that were formed in the metropolitan borough of Tameside in 1974. As with the previous issues, the articles cover a wide range of subjects, such as the rectory at St Mary's, Haughton Green, the Gorse Hill Murder Mystery, extracts from The National Archives relating to Ashton Poor Law Union, railways of the area and the history of Stalybridge and district Sunday School Billiard, Snooker and Whist League. This series enables researchers to publish short articles that would not otherwise have been published and which might be of interest to a wider readership. In addition there are reports of work undertaken by various local historians and societies in Tameside and reviews of local books, many published by Tameside Libraries service. The Tameside Local History Forum is to be congratulated on maintaining a high standard and making available much important research on the area.

N. Mundy, ed. *Diary of Rachel Leech, 1846–48* Manchester: Chethams Library, 2009. 24pp. £2. ISBN 9781899430048.

E. Collins, ed. *Memorandums of Sarah Leech, 1844–46* Manchester: Chethams Library, 2009. 24pp. £2. ISBN 9781899430031.

R. Woodward, ed. *Memorandums of Ellis Leech, 1852–53* Manchester: Chethams Library, 2009. 24pp. £2. ISBN 9781899430055.

M. McBride, ed. *Diary and memorandums of Thomas Leech, 1839–1840* Manchester: Chethams Library, 2009. 24pp. £2. ISBN 9781899430024.

Some of the most interesting and informative documents that local historians can use are private journals and diaries. Chetham's Library is fortunate in that it has been donated a large number of these relating to one particular family, the Leech family. These four transcripts have been prepared by students from the Department of History and Economic History at the Manchester Metropolitan University. They all follow a similar pattern in that there is an introduction about the person who compiled the diary or memorandum, which puts the contents in their historical setting, and drawing attention, where applicable, to a theme that runs through the diary. They shed a fascinating light on the ordinary lives of some of the middle class living and working in and around Manchester and provide much useful material for local historians. It is to be hoped that more of these diaries and memoranda will be published over the years allowing an insight into a family whose best known member was Bosden Leech, who wrote the first history of the Manchester Ship Canal.

H. Fancy *Stockport's first park and museum, 1858–2008* Stockport: Friends of Woodbank and Vernon Park[, 2008]. 28pp. Illus. No price given.

In this book, Harry Fancy traces the history of both Vernon Park and the building that was to become Stockport Museum and its first library. It is an interesting account of the way a public park has developed over the first hundred years of its history and the initial fight to get such a facility in the town in the face of what appears to have been reluctance by the borough council to provide recreational facilities for its residents. The book is well illustrated with photographs of the park and the various structures that were to be found there. This publication is an important addition to the literature available not only on Stockport, but also on parks generally.

S. F. Barnes *Manchester Board Schools, 1870–1902* London: Victorian Society, 2009. 165pp. Bibliog., illus., diags. £9.50. ISBN 9780901657381.

With the passing of the Forster Education Act in 1870, education was made compulsory in England for the first time. In order to achieve this, it was necessary to establish a framework to implement the act and ensure that there were adequate school buildings. To this end, school boards were established with responsibility for ensuring that universal education was provided throughout the country. This new publication from the Victorian Society briefly traces the background behind the passing of the 1870 Education Act before giving a brief but succinct history of the work of the Manchester School Board. The main part of the book consists of details about the schools that the board built, including the name of the architect, the contractor and cost, together with a photograph and many other details such as size, layout, architectural features and subsequent history. Great lengths appear to have been gone to in order that there is an illustration of each of the board schools described. This very readable and informative publication is an important contribution to the history of not only the Manchester School Board, but in the provision of details on specific schools, of which many have now disappeared. It will provide not only the architectural historian with valuable information about this type of building, but also those interested in Manchester's history and the history of education in general.

Singleton History Group *Singleton's story: the Fylde's model village* Blackpool: Landy Publishing, 2009. 72pp. Map. Illus. £8. ISBN 9781872895802.

This collection of photographs with informative captions traces the history of the village of Singleton from its purchase by Alderman Miller of Preston in 1853 to the present day. It also includes a little of the earlier history of the village before its rebuilding by Miller. The book is the work of dedicated group of local historians whose aim was, and still is, to collect and preserve the history of this small community on the Fylde. It should be an inspiration to others to do likewise for their own villages.

K. Warrender *Below Manchester: going deeper under the city* Timperley: Willow Publishing. 272pp. Illus. Diags. Maps. £17.95. ISBN 9780946361427.

*Below Manchester* is a sequel to Warrender's first book on the subject, *Underground Manchester*. In this new book, he introduces us to some new tunnels and underground areas that were not covered or known about when the earlier book was researched and published. In addition, there is a large section on the air-raid shelters that were used during the Second World War, including the ones under Victoria Street, and that created in the tunnel originally carrying the Manchester and Salford Junction Canal between Watson Street and the River Irwell. In addition it has details of those warehouses whose basements, it was suggested, would make suitable air-raid shelters. There is also an interesting chapter on the so-called 'secret' Guardian tunnel running from Ardwick to Dial House by way of Piccadilly and intended to be used in case of nuclear attack during the Cold War. The final chapter, by Sandra Hayton, examines the cellar dwellings that existed in Manchester during the nineteenth century. This is very important as it brings together not only the existing information published on Manchester's cellar dwellings, but also the results of research into the occupiers of such dwellings. The book is the result of much detailed research and includes claims made as to the existence of tunnels that may or may not have existed and, therefore, should be treated with caution. The book is well illustrated, not only with black and white photographs, but also with coloured illustrations, many of which are of recent origin. It is an important addition to the literature available on underground Manchester both in terms of the research that has been done and that which might be done in the future to substantiate some of the claims made by members of the public as to the existence of tunnels and underground storage areas.

R. S. Sephton *S. P. Grundy (1880–1942): a life of social service in Manchester and North Berkshire* Oxford[: the author], 2009. 38pp. Illus.

Although S. P. Grundy was born in Prestwich, much of his life after 1918 was spent in Oxfordshire and Berkshire. He was trained for the legal profession, but in 1907 he became Resident Warden of the University Settlement before becoming the secretary to the Manchester City League of Help, which was part of an organization seeking to help the less fortunate in Manchester. This small booklet throws an interesting light on a little described aspect of the provision of help for those in difficult circumstances and will, hopefully, lead to further research on the League of Help in Manchester and Salford.
*Available from the author, 33 Colley Wood, Kennington, Oxford OX1 5NF.*

P. B. Pixton *Wrenbury wills and inventories, 1542–1661* Record Society of Lancashire and Cheshire, 2009. 562pp. ISBN 9780902593794.

Wills and inventories can be a very useful source of information on the lives of those who lived at a time when written records were less common than today. This volume of wills and inventories covers those relating to Wrenbury for a period of just over 100 years. After a lengthy and an informative introduction, Pixton has transcribed over 150 wills and inventories for the period of those connected with this south-west Cheshire village. Not only do the wills provide information on how the deceased estate was to be divided amongst heirs, but the inventories also provide a fascinating insight into the possessions that they owned – both personal and also farm stock and equipment – and debts owed. Although specific to one district, this publication provides much for historians of the Tudor and Stuart periods to consider when it comes to the lives of farmers and landowners at the time.

E. L. Jones *The quest for public health in Manchester: the industrial city, the NHS and the recent history* Manchester: Manchester NHS Primary Care Trust, 2008. 156pp. Bibliog. Diags. Illus. £15. ISBN 9780955897115.

In recent years, the NHS appears to have been the subject of many reports, yet little has been written about the changes that have taken place in public health provision since the mid nineteenth century when cholera and other diseases were endemic and pollution was regarded by many as the norm. The first chapter of the book sets the scene, outlining what the provision was like in Manchester prior to the creation of the NHS in 1948, before going on to examine the effects of the creation of the NHS and its role in public health up to 1974 when it was re-organized with the creation of Regional Health Authorities. Three of the remaining four chapters examine the effect of this re-organization on public health and its provision within Manchester before the final chapter picks up on a comment made by Professor Madhok in his foreword, that 'those who do not learn from history are doomed to repeat the mistakes'. This excellent book is one that will appeal not only to those interested in many aspects of Manchester's history, as it puts recent developments in their historical setting, but also to those who are involved in shaping the future of public health in Manchester.

H. K. Valier and J. V. Pickstone *Community, professions and business: a history of the Central Manchester teaching hospitals and the National Heath Service* Manchester: Central Manchester & Manchester Children's University Hospital NHS Trust, 2008. 117pp. Illus, bibliog. £12. ISBN 9780955897122.

Since the foundation of the Manchester Royal Infirmary (then known simply as the Manchester Infirmary) in 1752, there have been a number of hospitals founded in various parts of Manchester. Beginning in the late nineteenth century and continuing into the twentieth, several of them moved to sites along Oxford Road, within close proximity to each other and to Manchester University. As the authors point out, in 1948 these standalone hospitals became part of the NHS and formed the United Manchester Hospitals until further re-organization in 1974. This book, written to mark the 250th anniversary of the foundation of the Infirmary, traces its history from the point where Brockbank left off his history in 1948, to the present day, with the important addition of the two children's hospitals that were added to the trust in 2001 running the University Hospitals of Central Manchester. The book outlines the early histories of the hospitals in the group before tracing the changes that have taken place not only in medical services at MRI, but also in administration and its relationship with the NHS and other hospitals in the group. This informative and interesting publication will be an invaluable addition to the literature available on the history of MRI for many years to come.

Mourholme Local History Society Book Club *Warton parish, 1850–1900: Borwick, Carnforth, Priest Hutton, Silverdale, Warton, Yealands* Mourholme Local History Society, 2009. 281pp. Illus. Maps. Bibliog. ISBN 9780953429847.

This book covers a small area of north Lancashire on the edge of Morecambe Bay. Possibly the best known of the areas covered by the book is Carnforth, made famous by a scene on the railway station in the film *Brief Encounter* of the 1940s, and by the existence of a preserved railway, Steamtown. The book is full of facts and is written in an entertaining and readable manner so that the reader is able to build up a picture of life in these communities during the period. Extensive use has been made of census enumerators' returns as well as other surviving archives and the local newspapers, the latter providing an important human element to the history of the communities. The authors have thoughtfully included a number of tables, bar charts and graphs that provide information otherwise difficult to convey in written textual form, such as a breakdown of deaths of under- and over-five-year olds from various diseases; prices; wages and the cost of living; and the population of the various townships. There is also a number of illustrations of activities or places in the area that add to its interest. Mourholme Local History Society is to be congratulated on this publication which will be of great interest to those who live there as well as to those who are interested in the history of the somewhat rural part of Lancashire.

E. A. Rose *The heritage of the Red Hall Methodist church, Audenshaw, 1782–2006* Audenshaw: Audenshaw Local History Society, new ed., 2006. Illus. 25pp.

The original version of this local history work was published in 1982 to mark the bicentary of the establishment of this Methodist chapel. This new edition was prepared to mark the merger of the chapel with several others in the area and the imminent demolition of the chapel buildings for a new multi-purpose place of worship. Alan Rose's original text traces the history of the chapel from its beginnings in 1782 to 1982 whilst a short section at the end, compiled by Mrs Lena Slack, brings the story up to date. This well illustrated book provides an interesting account of the formation of the chapel and its work in the Audenshaw area. It is pleasing that a publication that would only have had a limited circulation is now more generally available for those interested in the history of Audenshaw and the development of Methodism in the area more generally.

P. McKeiver *Peterloo Massacre, 1819* Manchester: Advance Press, 2009. 218pp. Illus. Bibliog. £11.95. ISBN 9780955466311.

Of all the events in Manchester's history, probably the one that has been written about the most and which sparks the most controversy is that of Peterloo. This new publication challenges some of the accepted beliefs about the event and its aftermath, claiming that 'many of the myths associated with this event are of questionable historical validity or, that at least there are other more plausible well documented interpretations and eyewitness accounts that warrant equal consideration'. Apart from the chapters dealing with the background and the event itself, one of the more interesting chapters is that dealing with Radical and Loyalist poetry where the various poems from both sides are reproduced with a short introduction on each. Whether you agree with the views expressed by the author or not will depend on you own reading of the facts as they are known. This book is one which no doubt will find favour with some, but for others will be a distortion of the facts. It will be up to the reader to decide.

*A report on a survey on the Artisans House, 33 Thomas Street, Manchester* Manchester: Manchester Region Industrial Archaeology Society, 2007.

*A report on a survey of the 'hives', Trafford Park* Manchester: Manchester Region Industrial Archaeology Society, 2007.

*Salt works: Some notes on salt extraction in the Bollin Valley and Dunham Woodhouses* Manchester: Manchester Region Industrial Archaeology Society, 2006.

*A survey of the Bridgewater Canal near Altrincham* Manchester: Manchester Region Industrial Archaeology Society, 2007.

*A report on a survey of Mark Massie, Crompton Road dye works, Macclesfield* Manchester: Manchester Region Industrial Archaeology Society, 2006.

*A report on a photographic survey of the Carborundum Works, Trafford Park* Manchester: Manchester Region Industrial Archaeology Society, 2006.

*Some notes and observations on the Black Bear Canal inn and warehouse* Manchester: Manchester Region Industrial Archaeology Society, 2008.

*Agden Bridge* Manchester: Manchester Region Industrial Archaeology Society [n.d.].

These well illustrated reports have been published by the Manchester Region Industrial Archaeology Society and have been compiled by those members of the Society involved in their survey. The basic format of these reports consists of a history of the site or building concerned with diagrams and photographs of the buildings when the survey was made. The historical element of each report brings together information that is often scattered amongst many sources whilst the illustrations draw attention to the important features of each building or structure. They are important additions to the history of the buildings and structures surveyed and will be of interest not only to industrial archaeologists, but also to those interested in the history of the areas where they are located.

*Available from Manchester Region Industrial Archaeology Society, c/o Mr R. Thwaite, 261 Grove Lane, Hale, Altrincham WA15 8PP. Prices available on application, to which postage and packing should be added.*

# ARTICLE ABSTRACTS AND KEYWORDS

## D. M. Higgins and J. S. Toms
*Capital ownership, capital structure, and capital markets: financial constraints and the decline of the Lancashire cotton textile industry, c1880–c1965*

The objective of this analysis is to provide a reinterpretation of the decline of the Lancashire cotton textile industry during the twentieth century. Its principal concerns are with the governance structure of the industry, the resultant capital structures of firms and the constraints thereby imposed on the activities of entrepreneurs. Its central thesis is that ownership of the industry, and the redistribution of ownership claims during booms and slumps, imposed pressures and constraints on decision-makers. These financial constraints dominated the strategic questions of re-equipment and modernization.

**Keywords:** *Lancashire cotton textiles, excess capacity, dividends, debt, capital markets*

## John Singleton
*Lancashire and the New Zealand market in the mid twentieth century: cotton, glass and locomotives*

Lancashire businesses had markets all over the world in the mid twentieth century, not least in the countries of the British empire and commonwealth. New Zealand was a more important market than its size might suggest, partly because of similarities of taste, and the influence of discriminatory international arrangements such as the sterling area and imperial preference. This article looks at how firms in the cotton, glass and locomotive industries sought to make the most of the New Zealand market, albeit with varying degrees of success. Pilkington Brothers were the most successful of the businesses we examine, setting up a local operation in order to take advantage of efforts to protect and develop a domestic manufacturing base.

**Keywords:** *Lancashire, New Zealand, Pilkingtons, cotton, engineering*

## David Martín López and John K. Walton
*Freemasonry and civic identity: municipal politics, business and the rise of Blackpool from the 1850s to the First World War*

The relationship between business and local government in Blackpool's late-Victorian and Edwardian development into the world's first working-class seaside resort is well documented. This article brings an important additional item into the mix by demonstrating the importance of freemasonry in this process. Not only did membership of the craft pull together Blackpool's municipal, business and professional elites, including the Church of England; the symbolism of freemasonry also infiltrated the town's civic and public architecture, including the Town Hall itself. This is the first serious analysis of the relationships between freemasonry, business and municipal politics in an English town, and it is hoped that it will set an agenda for comparative studies elsewhere.

**Keywords:** *Business, local politics, religion, freemasonry, leisure, tourism, resort, Victorian*

**Alistair Mutch**
*Brewing in the North West, 1840–1914: sowing the seeds of service-sector management?*
This paper explores the contours of brewing in the north-west of England in the period 1840 to 1914. While accounts of the region have been dominated by considerations of cotton and engineering, it is argued that there was considerable innovation in the brewing industry in the region, notably in the development of the direct management of public houses in Liverpool. However, such success failed to ensure the expansion of companies outside the region and the paper considers the factors which may have led to this. It concludes that the heterogeneity of practice in the region, in particular the tension between Liverpool and Manchester, meant that the baton of innovation was passed to the Birmingham brewers, whose further development of retailing lay at the heart of their eventual importance at national level.
**Keywords:** *Brewing, public-house management, Liverpool, Manchester*

**Ken Brown**
*'An absorbing epic'? The development of toy-manufacturing in the North West, c1851–1931*
Received wisdom has it that the First World War was responsible for the emergence of an indigenous toy-manufacturing sector in Britain as imports from traditional suppliers in Germany were cut off. Taking Liverpool and Manchester as its focus, this essay shows that contrary to received opinion, an indigenous industry was present well before 1914, that its higher profile during the war was generally short-lived, and that the firms which survived the post-war depression were generally those whose existence predated the advent of the First World War.

**Keywords:** *Toy-manufacture, Liverpool, Manchester*

**Robin Pearson**
*Working on the frontiers of risk: the insurance industry in north-west England since 1700*
This paper surveys the development of the insurance industry in the north-west of England from its earliest days (the late seventeenth century) to the present. In several quite separate fields of insurance – marine, fire, industrial and life – and at different times, the business that developed in the North West played a prominent role in national markets. Moreover, in property insurance some of the companies that emerged in Liverpool during the middle of the nineteenth century became the largest multinational insurers in the world, out-competing not only their London- and Edinburgh-based rivals, but also the leading companies of other nations in the race for market share. This paper examines the reasons for the long-run success of the region's insurance industry and searches for answers both in the nature of local markets, and in the networks and accumulated experience of the local business community.
**Keywords:** *Insurance, Liverpool, industrial revolution, business networks, multinationals*

**Rosine Hart and Geoff Timmins**
*Lancashire's highway men: the business community and road improvements during the industrial revolution*
Recent research has analyzed the fundamental improvements that were made to Lancashire's road network during the industrial revolution period, not only through greatly extending road mileage, but also through easing gradients and laying paved surfaces. This article examines the contribution that local businessmen made

to these improvements, from providing finance for road construction to involving themselves in the formation and running of turnpike trusts.

**Keywords:** *Road construction, management, toll-letting, businessmen, loans*

## Geoffrey Tweedale

*Straws in the wind: the local and regional roots of an occupational disease epidemic*

Asbestos-related deaths in the UK are currently about 4,000 each year, with that total still rising. Most cases involve asbestos-related cancers (particularly mesothelioma). This national epidemic had local roots in the Manchester region, where Turner Brothers Asbestos (the largest asbestos factory in the UK) was located. The paper explores the recognition of asbestos cancers in the 1960s and shows how much of the evidence was either effaced or diluted by industrial interests or local officialdom. The use of asbestos was perpetuated beyond the 1970s with the support of local politicians, such as Sir Cyril Smith MP, who assisted Turner Brothers in fending off government regulation.

**Keywords:** *Asbestos, mesothelioma, Rochdale, Sir Cyril Smith, Turner Brothers, Turner & Newall*